fushigi yûgi™

The Mysterious Play
VOL. 10: ENEMY

Story & Art By
YÛ WATASE

FUSHIGI YÛGI
THE MYSTERIOUS PLAY
VOL. 10: ENEMY
SHÔJO EDITION

This volume contains the FUSHIGI YÛGI installments from Animerica Extra
Vol. 6, No. 9 through Vol. 7, No. 1, in their entirety.

STORY AND ART BY YÛ WATASE

English Adaptation/Yuji Oniki
Touch-up & Lettering/Bill Spicer
Cover, Graphics & Design/Hidemi Sahara
Editor/William Flanagan

Managing Editor/Annette Roman
Editor-in-Chief/William Flanagan
Production Manager/Noboru Watanabe
Sr. Director of Licensing & Acquisitions/Rika Inouye
V.P. of Marketing/Liza Coppola
Sr. V.P. of Editorial/Hyoe Narita
Publisher/Seiji Horibuchi

Printed in Canada.

Published by VIZ, LLC
P.O. Box 77010
San Francisco, CA 94107

Shôjo Edition
10 9 8 7 6 5 4 3 2 1
First printing, February 2004

www.viz.com

store.viz.com

CONTENTS

STORY THUS FAR

Chipper junior-high-school girl Miaka is physically drawn into the world of a strange book—*THE UNIVERSE OF THE FOUR GODS*. Miaka is offered the role of the lead character, the Priestess of the god Suzaku, and is charged with a mission to save the nation of Hong-Nan, and in the process have three wishes granted.

While Miaka makes a short trip back to the real world, her best friend Yui is sucked into the book only to suffer rape and manipulation, which drives her to attempt suicide. Now, Yui has become the Priestess of the god Seiryu, the bitter enemy of Suzaku and Miaka.

The only way for Miaka to gain back the trust of her former friend is to summon the god Suzaku and wish to be reconciled with Yui, so Miaka reenters the world of *THE UNIVERSE OF THE FOUR GODS*. The Seiryu warriors ruin Miaka's first attempt to summon Suzaku, but the oracle, Tai Yi-Jun, has a new quest for Miaka and her Celestial Warriors of Suzaku—to obtain Shentso-Pao, treasures from the countries of the other two gods, Genbu and Byakko. Success will allow them to summon Suzaku. Only seconds after obtaining the first treasure, it is stolen from Miaka's hand by the Seiryu Warriors, leaving her wracked with guilt. Miaka, falling for a Seiryu trick, tries to get the treasure back, but instead is trapped by Nakago, who is intent on forcing sex on her. She is fully in his power as she falls unconscious. Later, Tamahome arrives to save her, inflicting a terrible wound on Nakago, but Tamahome's assurances aren't enough to calm Miaka's heart. She runs away from Tamahome, trips and sprains her ankle, and is immediately found by a Seiryu warrior wielding a deadly weapon!

THE UNIVERSE OF THE FOUR GODS is based on ancient China, but Japanese pronunciation of Chinese names differs slightly from their Chinese equivalents. Here is a short glossary of the Japanese pronunciation of the Chinese names in this graphic novel:

CHINESE	JAPANESE	PERSON OR PLACE	MEANING
Xong Gui-Siu	Sô kishuku	Tamahome's Name	Demon Constellation
Hong-Nan	Konan	Southern Kingdom	Crimson South
Qu-Dong	Kutô	Eastern Kingdom	Gathered East
Bei-Jia	Hokkan	Northern Kingdom	Armored North
Xi-Lang	Sairô	Western Kingdom	West Tower
Shentso-Pao	Shinzahô	A Treasure	God's Seat Jewel
Tai Yi-Jun	Tai Itsukun	An Oracle	Preeminent Person

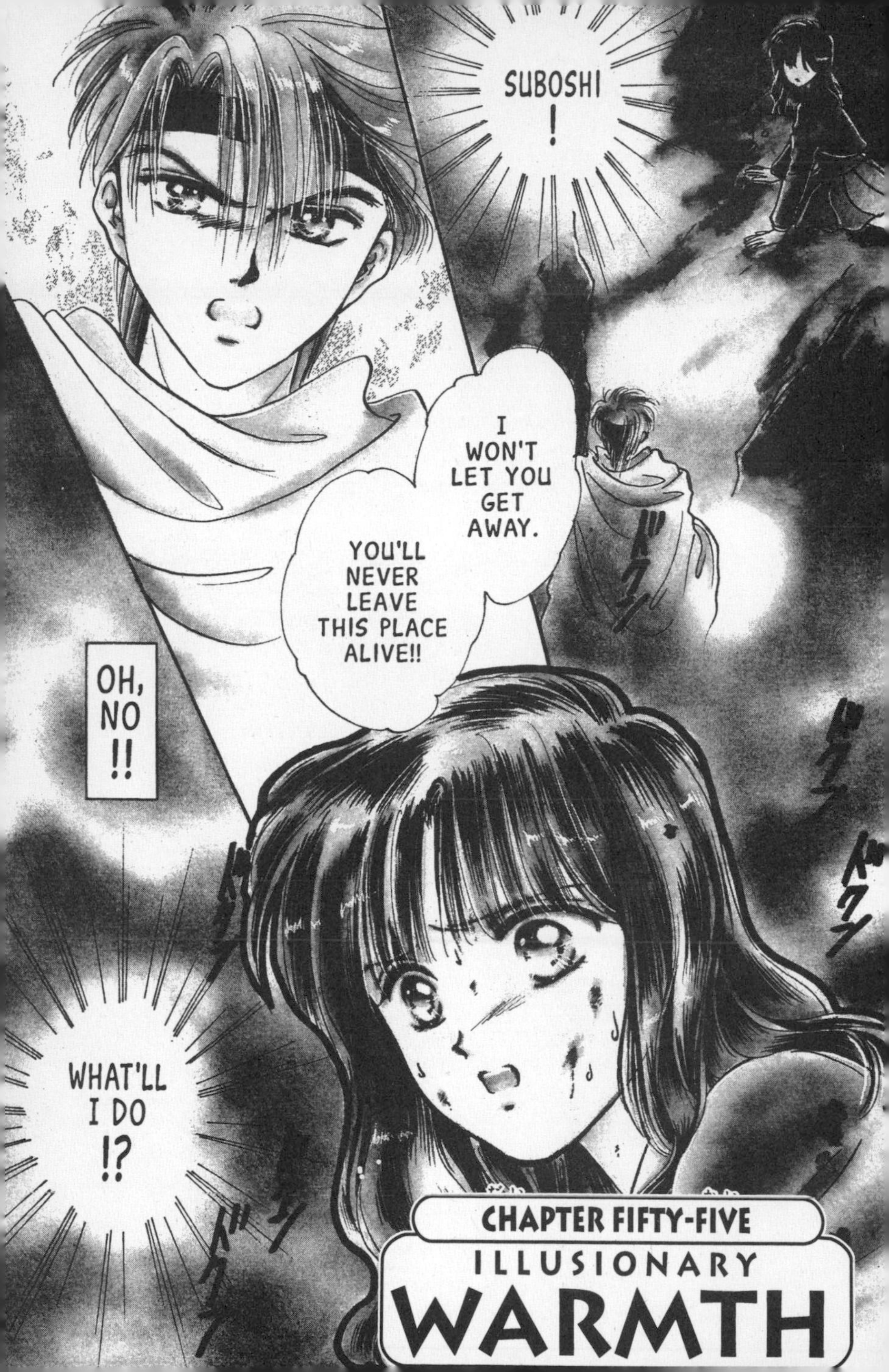
SUBOSHI!
I WON'T LET YOU GET AWAY.
YOU'LL NEVER LEAVE THIS PLACE ALIVE!!
OH, NO!!
WHAT'LL I DO!?
CHAPTER FIFTY-FIVE
ILLUSIONARY WARMTH

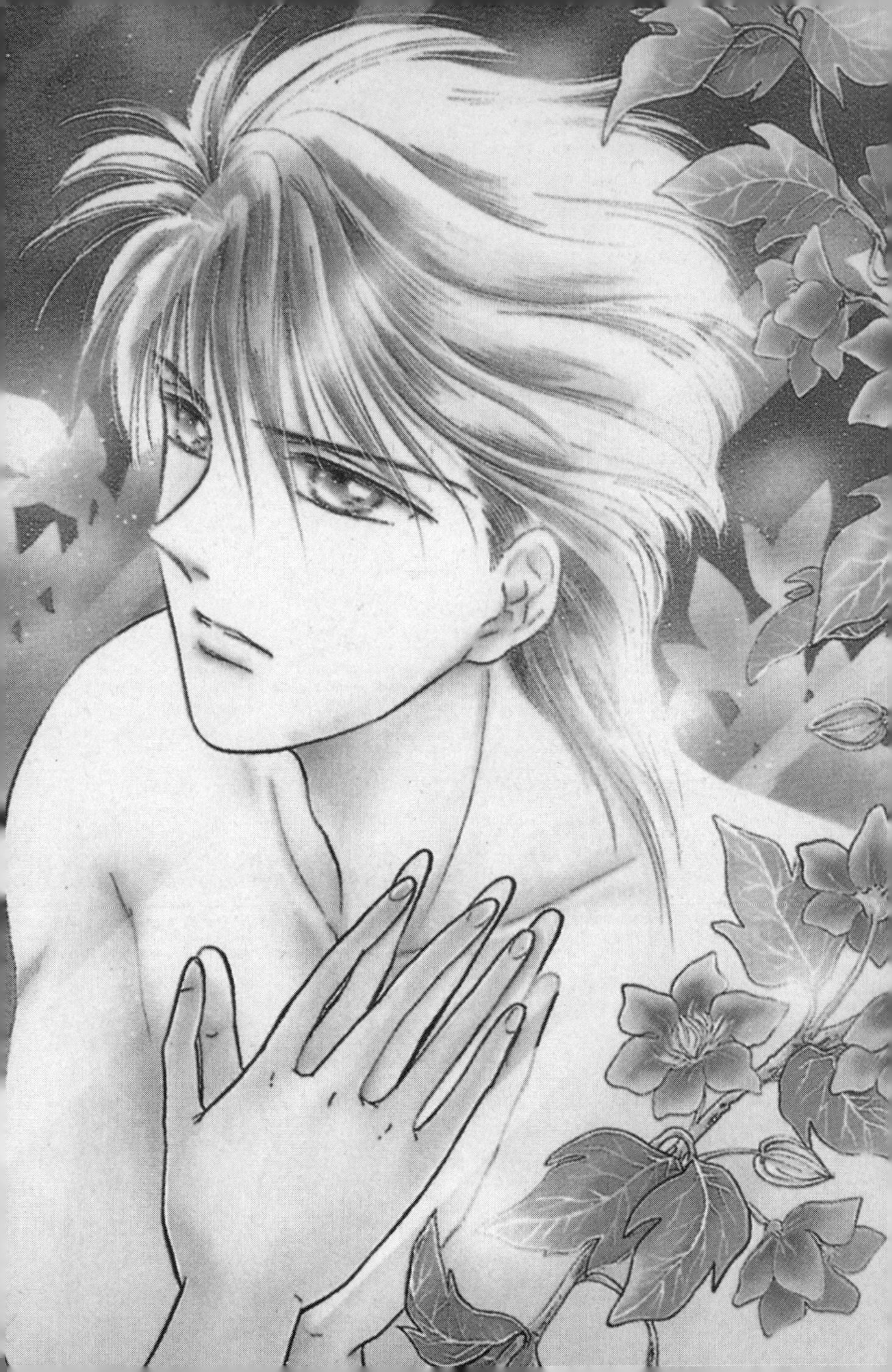

CHAPTER FIFTY-FIVE
ILLUSIONARY WARMTH

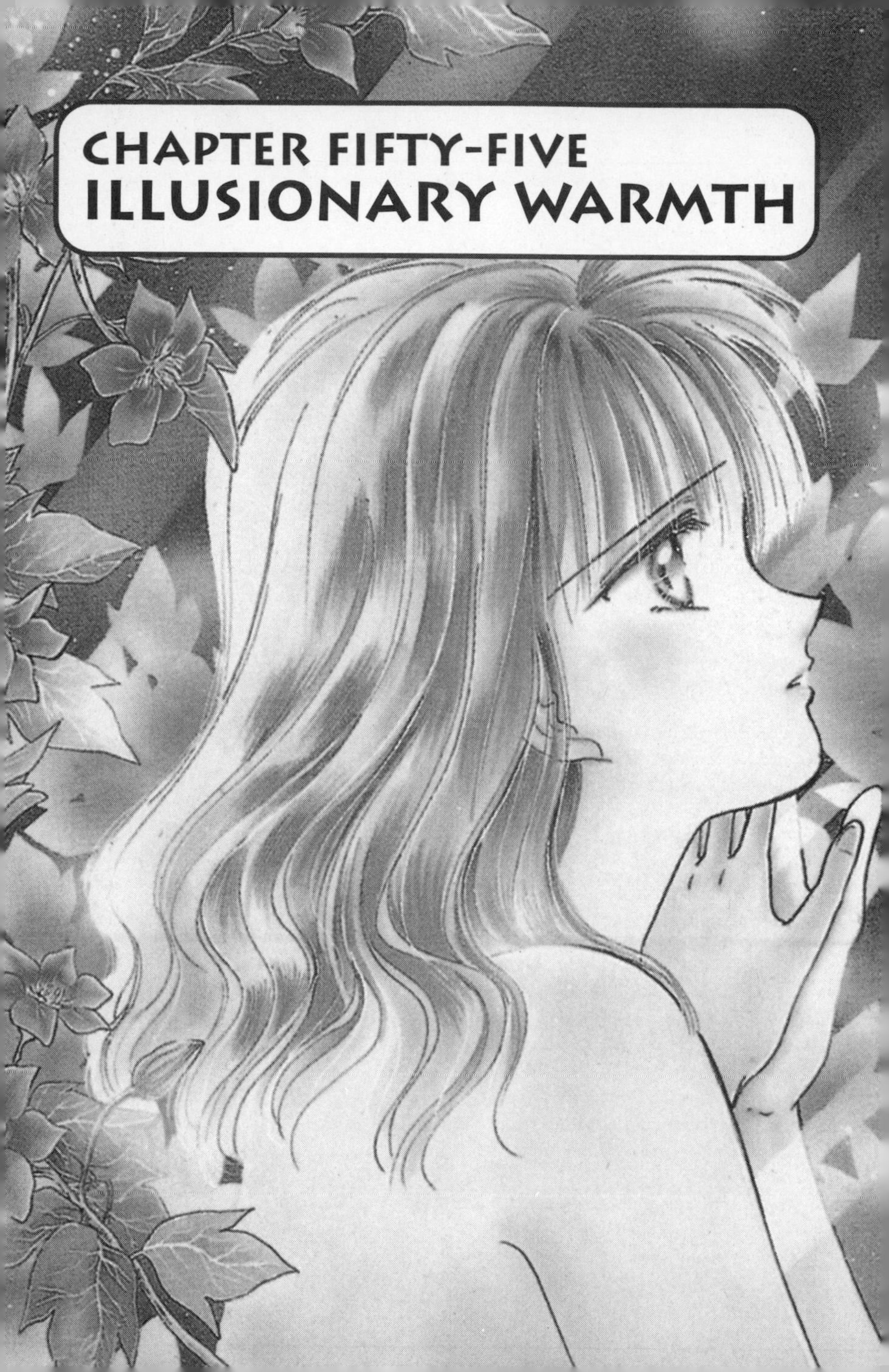

?

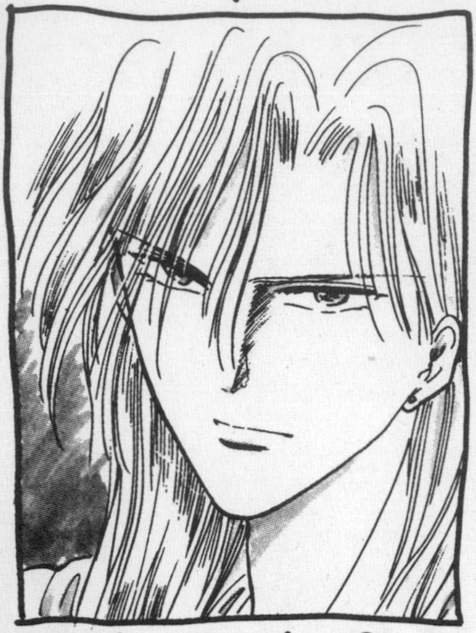

NAKAGO

• He comes from an immigrant tribe of the far west.
• Commander of 2/3 of Qu-Dong's armed forces.
• No living family or friends.
• 25 years old.
• Height: 6' 4" (193 cm.)
• Ability: Chi attack techniques.
• Hobbies: Making Tamahome miserable (ha ha!).
• Personality: Beyond cold, he's Arctic ice! His name is a misnomer (a dwelling for the heart); his plans and actions show a complete lack of mercy. He allows for no emotional distraction nor wasted action. Once someone's usefulness is exhausted, the person is eliminated. On the other hand, he has an undeniable charisma which allows him to skillfully manipulate people. But what goes on in his mind remains a mystery.

HON GŌ YUI
本 郷 唯

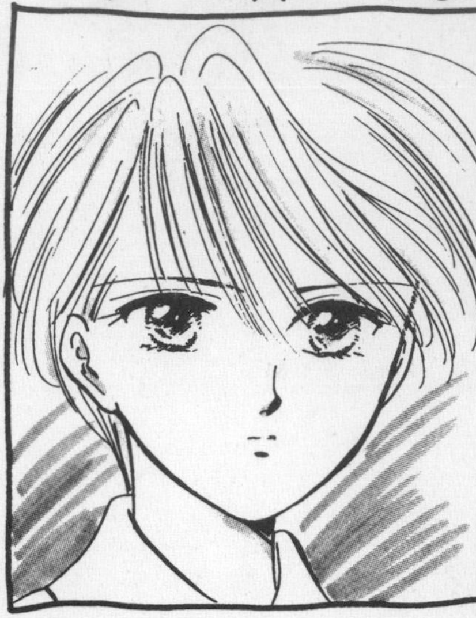

YUI

• Birth Place: Tokyo. Miaka's classmate, 15 years old.
• An only child. Latchkey kid -- both parents work.
• Height: 5' 3" (162 cm.)
• Weight: 108 lbs. (49 kg.)
• Vision: Right 20/18, Left 20/15
• Blood type: AB
• Hobbies: Reading (mysteries), music.
• Personality: In keeping with her looks, she is more mature than an average 15-year-old. Bold and confident in everything she does. Tends to see the world in black and white. Passionate, but passion turns to fury with betrayal. On the outside, she's supremely self-confident, but underneath, she longs for someone to take care of her.

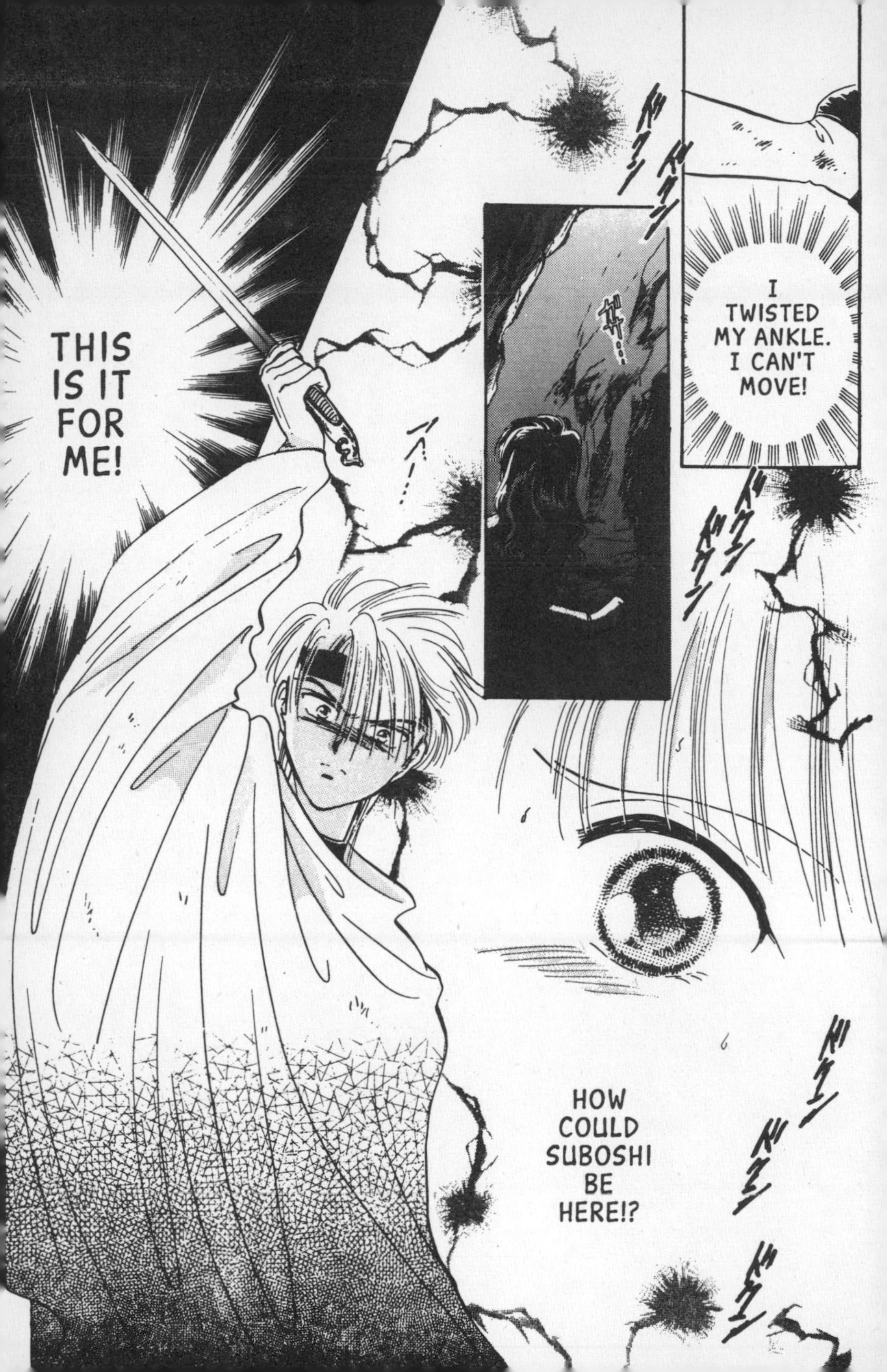
I TWISTED MY ANKLE. I CAN'T MOVE!
HOW COULD SUBOSHI BE HERE!?
THIS IS IT FOR ME!

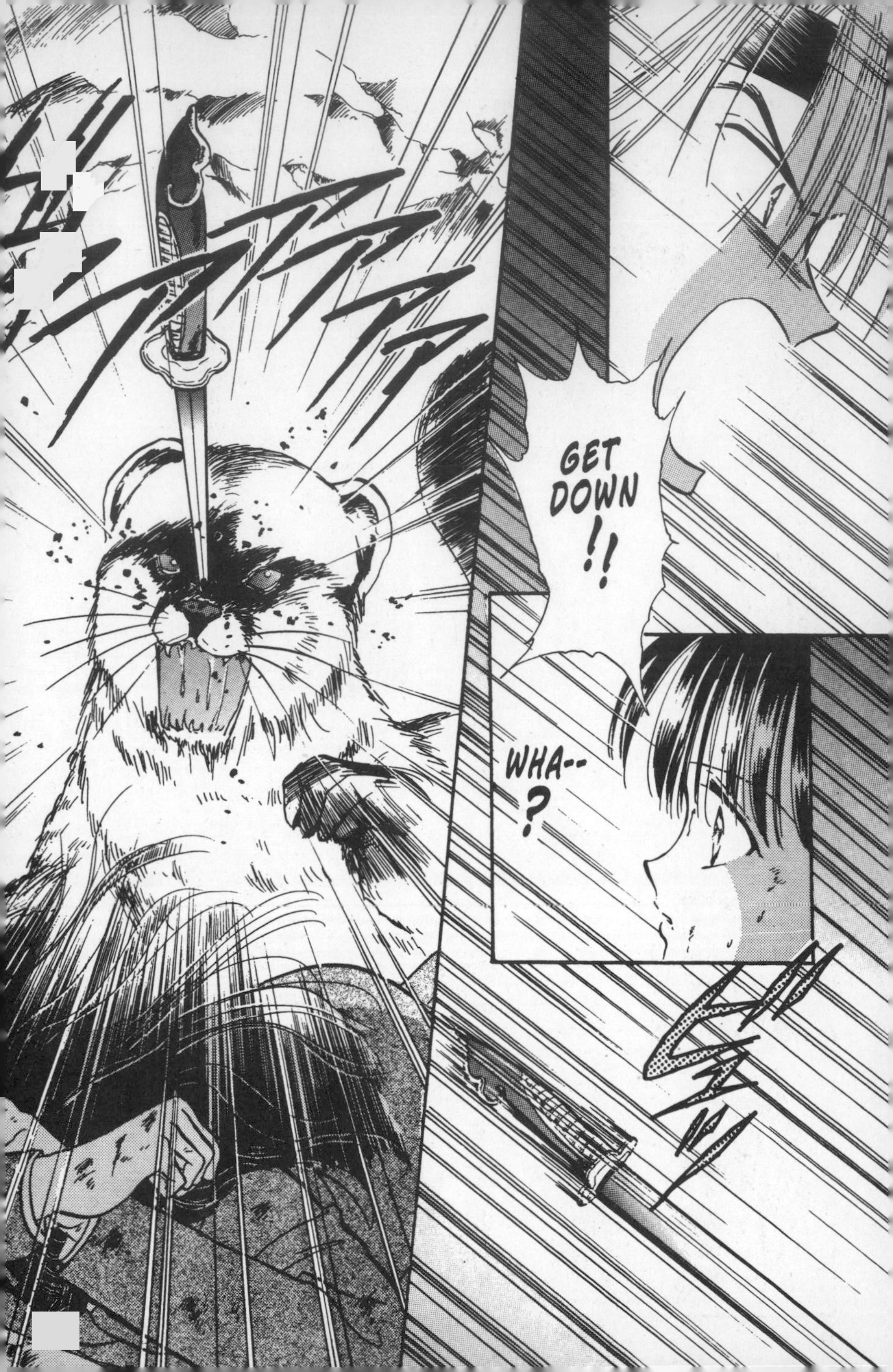
GET DOWN !!
WHA-- ?

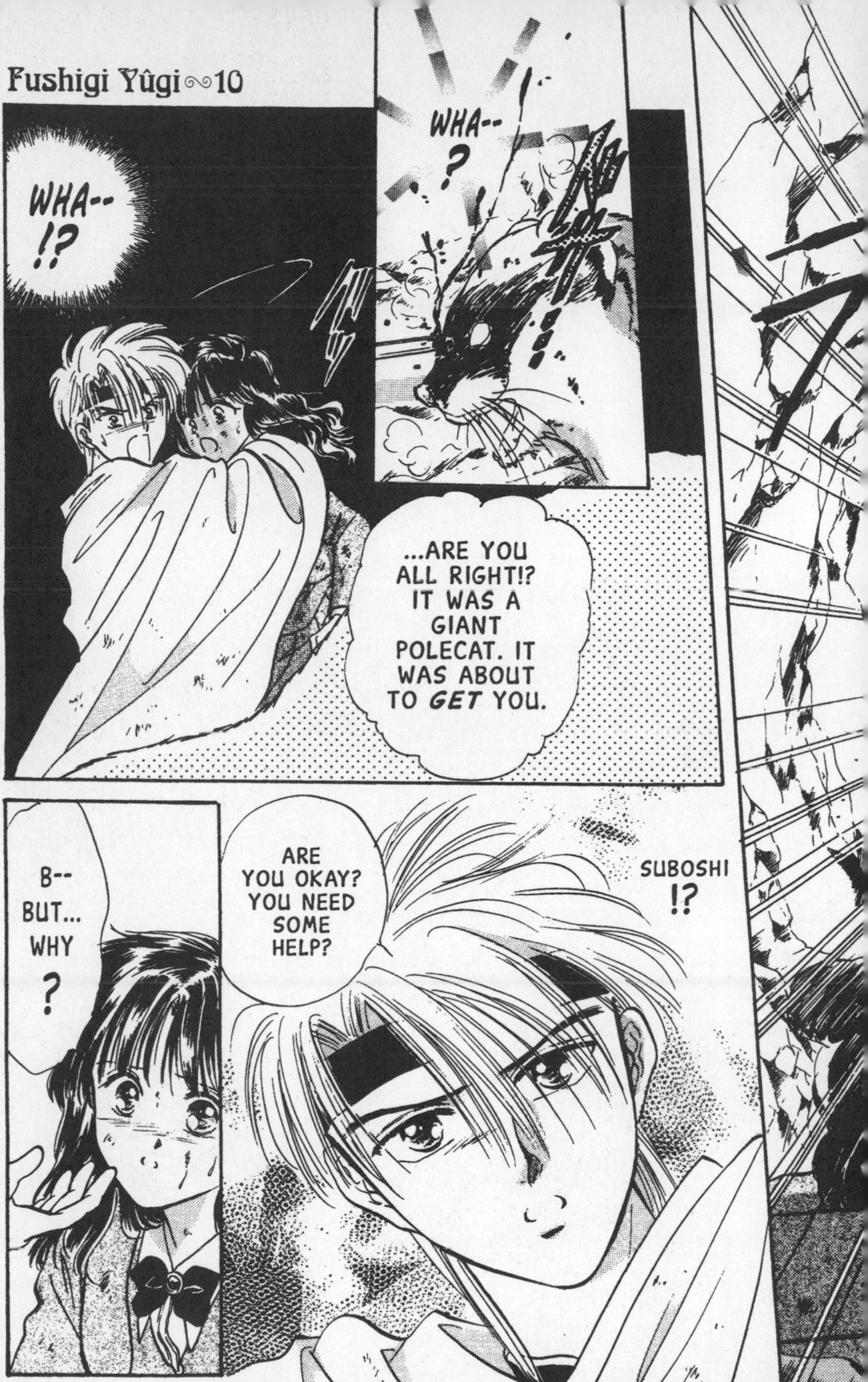
WHA-- ?
WHA-- !?
...ARE YOU ALL RIGHT!? IT WAS A GIANT POLECAT. IT WAS ABOUT TO *GET* YOU.
SUBOSHI !?
ARE YOU OKAY? YOU NEED SOME HELP?
B-- BUT... WHY ?

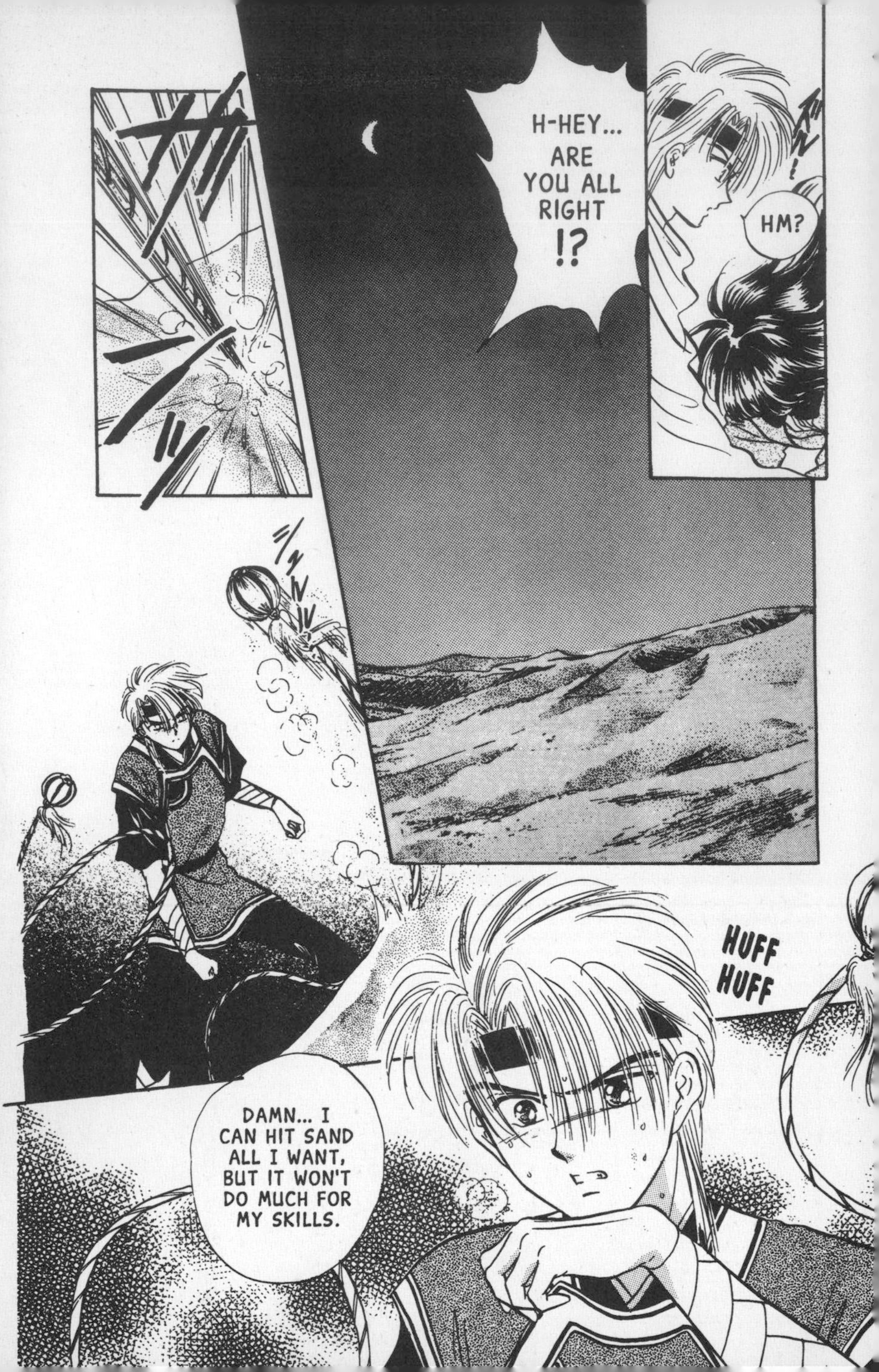
HM?
H-HEY... ARE YOU ALL RIGHT !?
HUFF HUFF
DAMN... I CAN HIT SAND ALL I WANT, BUT IT WON'T DO MUCH FOR MY SKILLS.

Enemy

Hello, it's me, Watase. I just pulled my first all-nighter in quite a while, so I'm totally zoning out... ZZZZ... Hey, wake up! No sleep for me!

I don't really have a theme for this column (how much of a theme can you have in a 1/3-page column like this?)... so I'll just write down whatever comes to my numb mind.

In this story, there's a concept called the 28 constellations. For those who haven't read FY serialized in Shōjo Comic, it had an issue with a supplementary chart of astrological fortunes based on the 28 constellations. Apparently, that was the first time a chart like that has ever appeared in Japan! I tried it, and it was really fun! According to the editor who wrote the text, it was from an Indian 27-constellation astrology system that made its way as far as China! The characters (y'know, my characters) like Chichiri and Tamahome had their own personalities and attributes which ended up corresponding to the historical charts! It really surprised me.

I think my star sign was one of the constellations in Byakko. *I forgot which one.* I read the astrologer's notes and it was so similar to my story. That was another surprise!

The "Eastern Seiryu" was the sea god representing the waters from which life springs. The "Northern Genbu" is the cycle of death and rebirth as represented by the turtle and snake. (As far as death goes, there's Nuriko and Hikitsu. And rebirth means you're reincarnated. Of course, that was just a coincidence.) The "Western Byakko" represents worship of holy mountains. Western China is surrounded by mountains. *And the sea is in the east. See?*

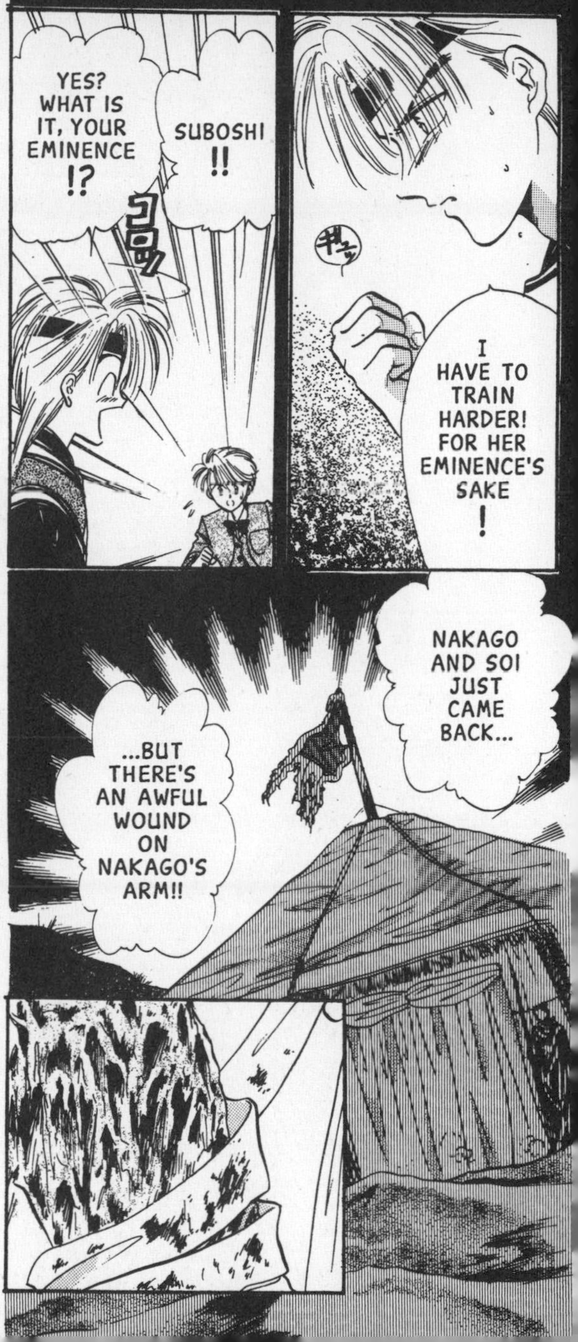
I HAVE TO TRAIN HARDER! FOR HER EMINENCE'S SAKE!
SUBOSHI!!
YES? WHAT IS IT, YOUR EMINENCE!?
NAKAGO AND SOI JUST CAME BACK...
...BUT THERE'S AN AWFUL WOUND ON NAKAGO'S ARM!!

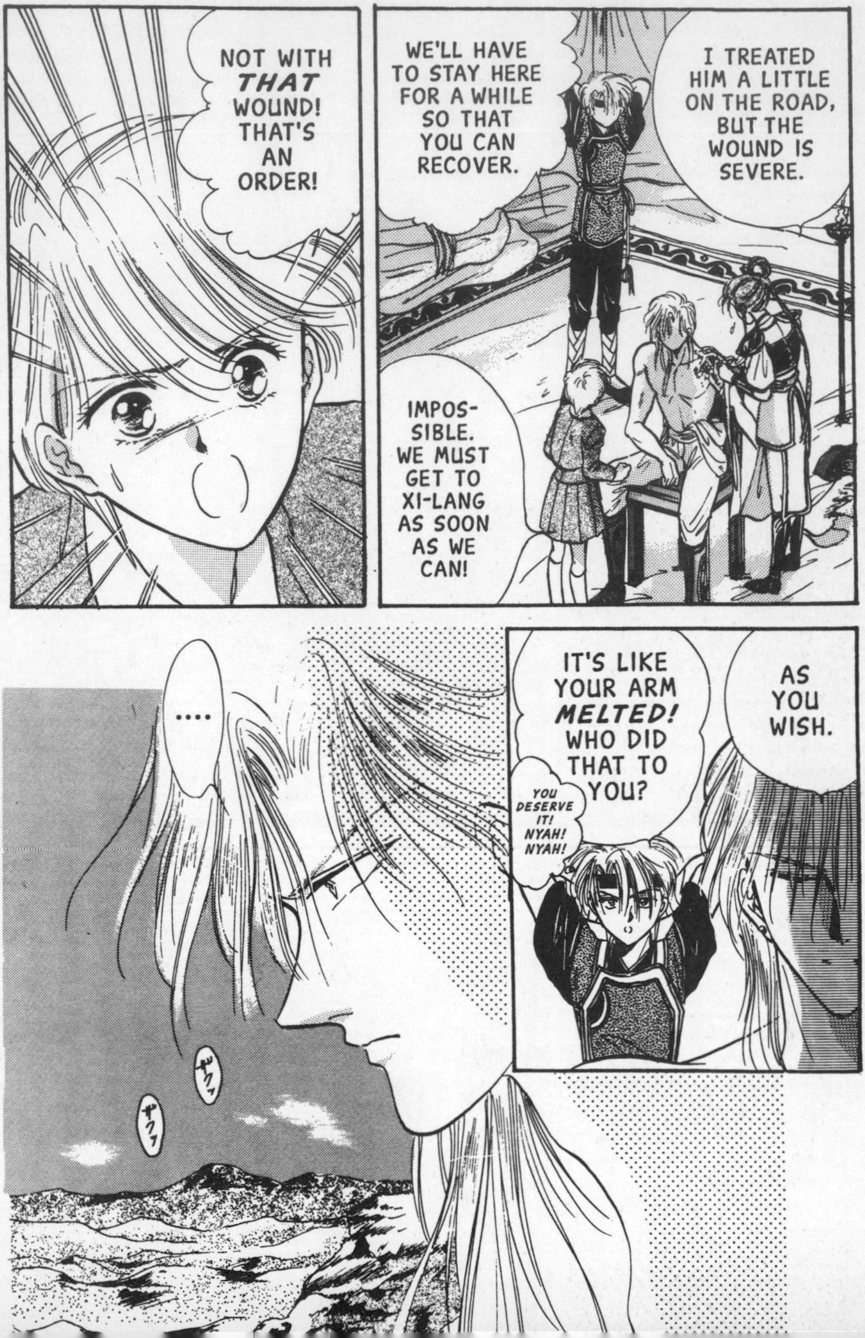
I TREATED HIM A LITTLE ON THE ROAD, BUT THE WOUND IS SEVERE.
WE'LL HAVE TO STAY HERE FOR A WHILE SO THAT YOU CAN RECOVER.
IMPOS-SIBLE. WE MUST GET TO XI-LANG AS SOON AS WE CAN!
NOT WITH *THAT* WOUND! THAT'S AN ORDER!
AS YOU WISH.
IT'S LIKE YOUR ARM *MELTED!* WHO DID THAT TO YOU?
YOU DESERVE IT! NYAH! NYAH!
....

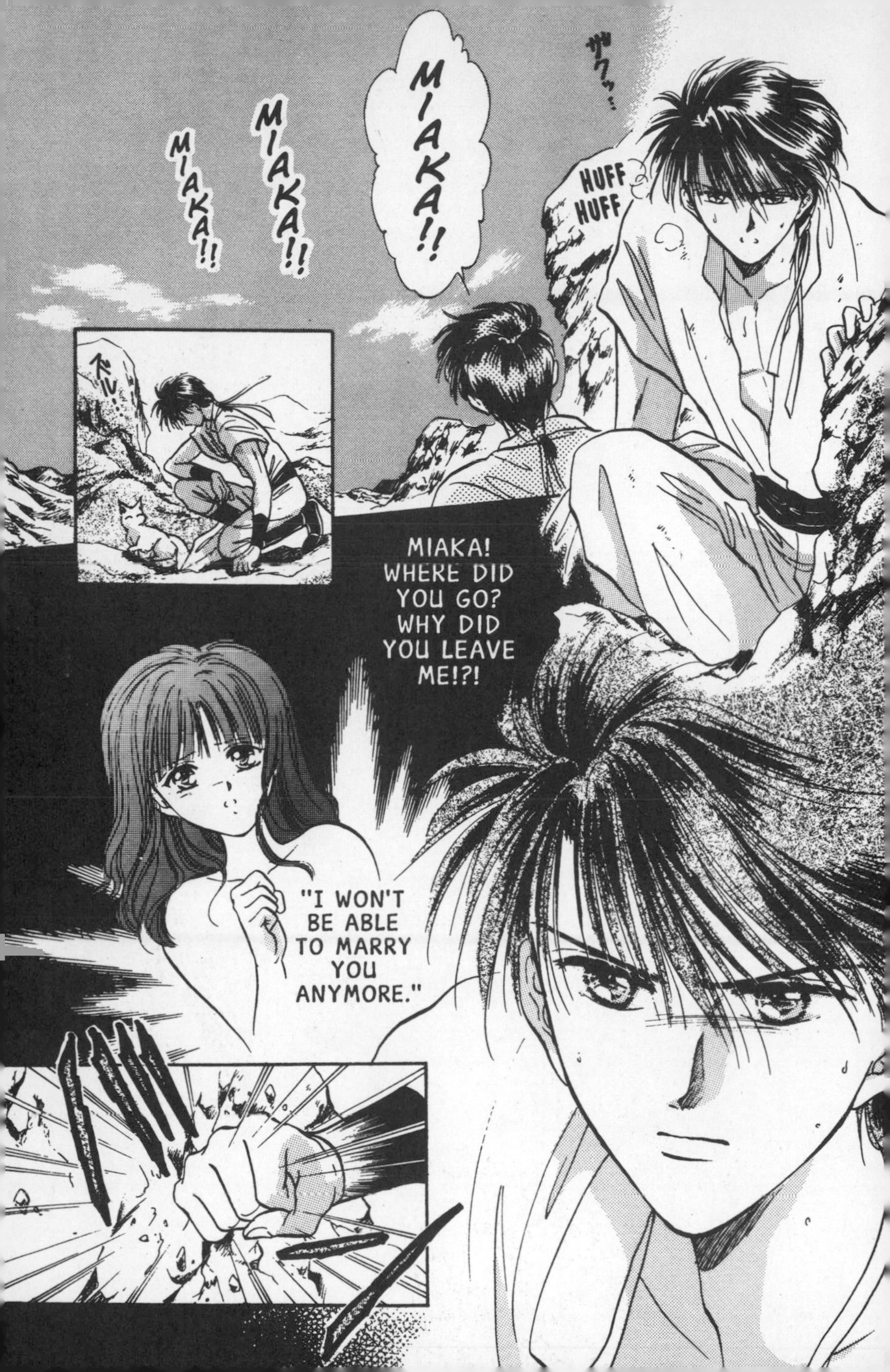
ザクッ
HUFF HUFF
MIAKA!!
MIAKA!!
MIAKA!!
MIAKA! WHERE DID YOU GO? WHY DID YOU LEAVE ME!?!
"I WON'T BE ABLE TO MARRY YOU ANYMORE."

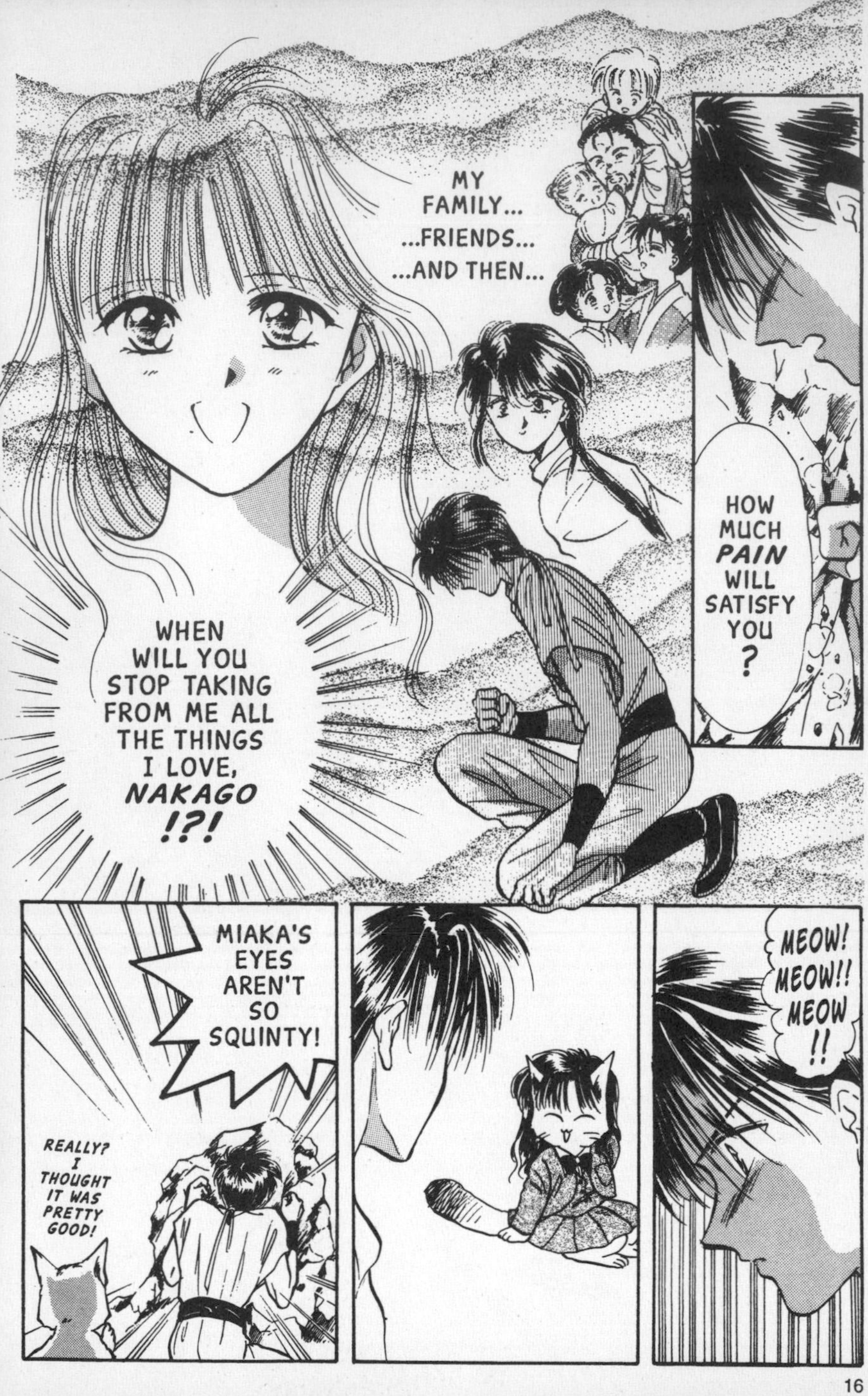
HOW MUCH PAIN WILL SATISFY YOU ?
MY FAMILY...
...FRIENDS...
...AND THEN...
WHEN WILL YOU STOP TAKING FROM ME ALL THE THINGS I LOVE, NAKAGO !?!
MEOW! MEOW!! MEOW !!
MIAKA'S EYES AREN'T SO SQUINTY!
REALLY? I THOUGHT IT WAS PRETTY GOOD!

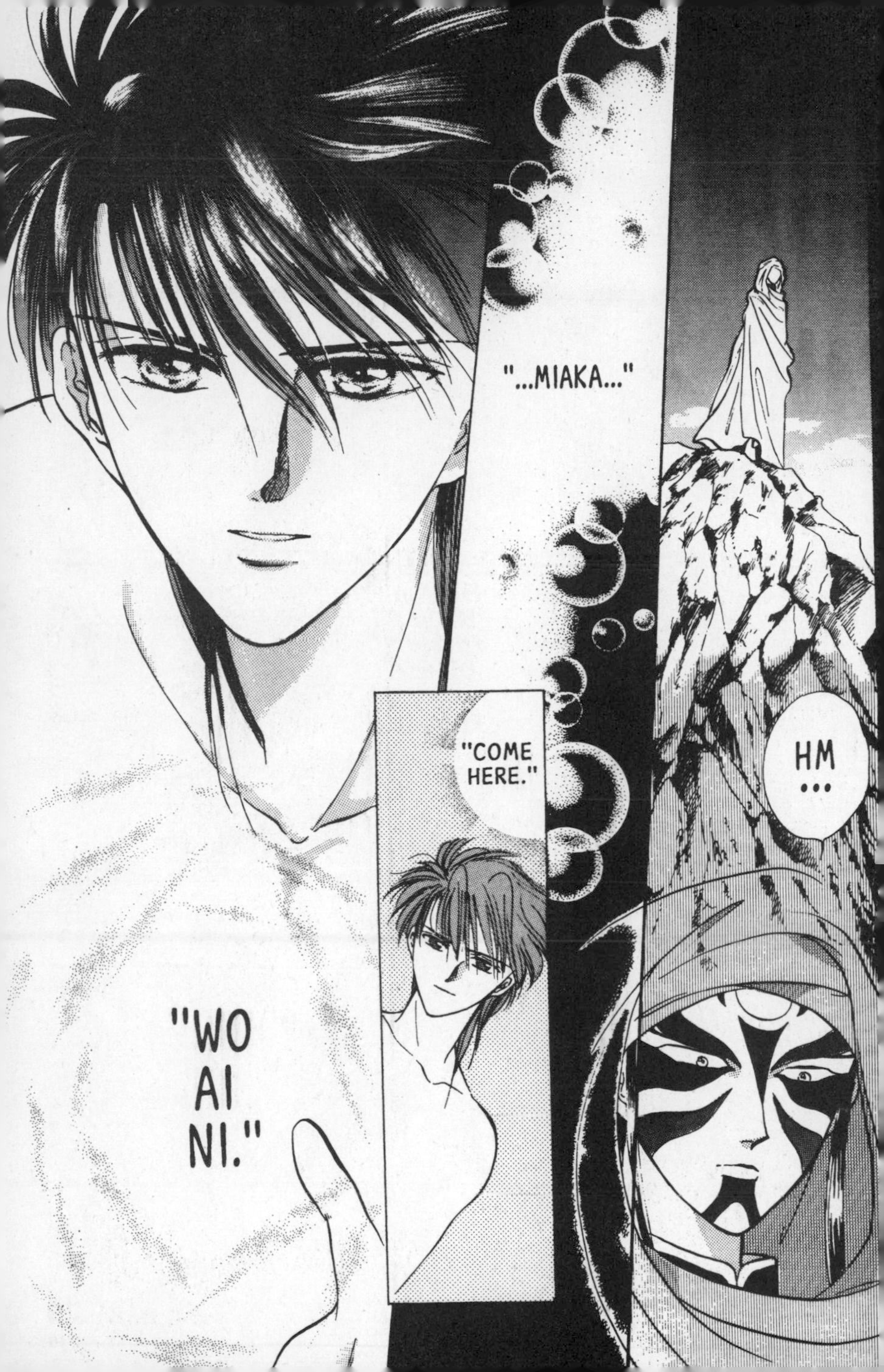
HM ...
"...MIAKA..."
"COME HERE."
"WO AI NI."

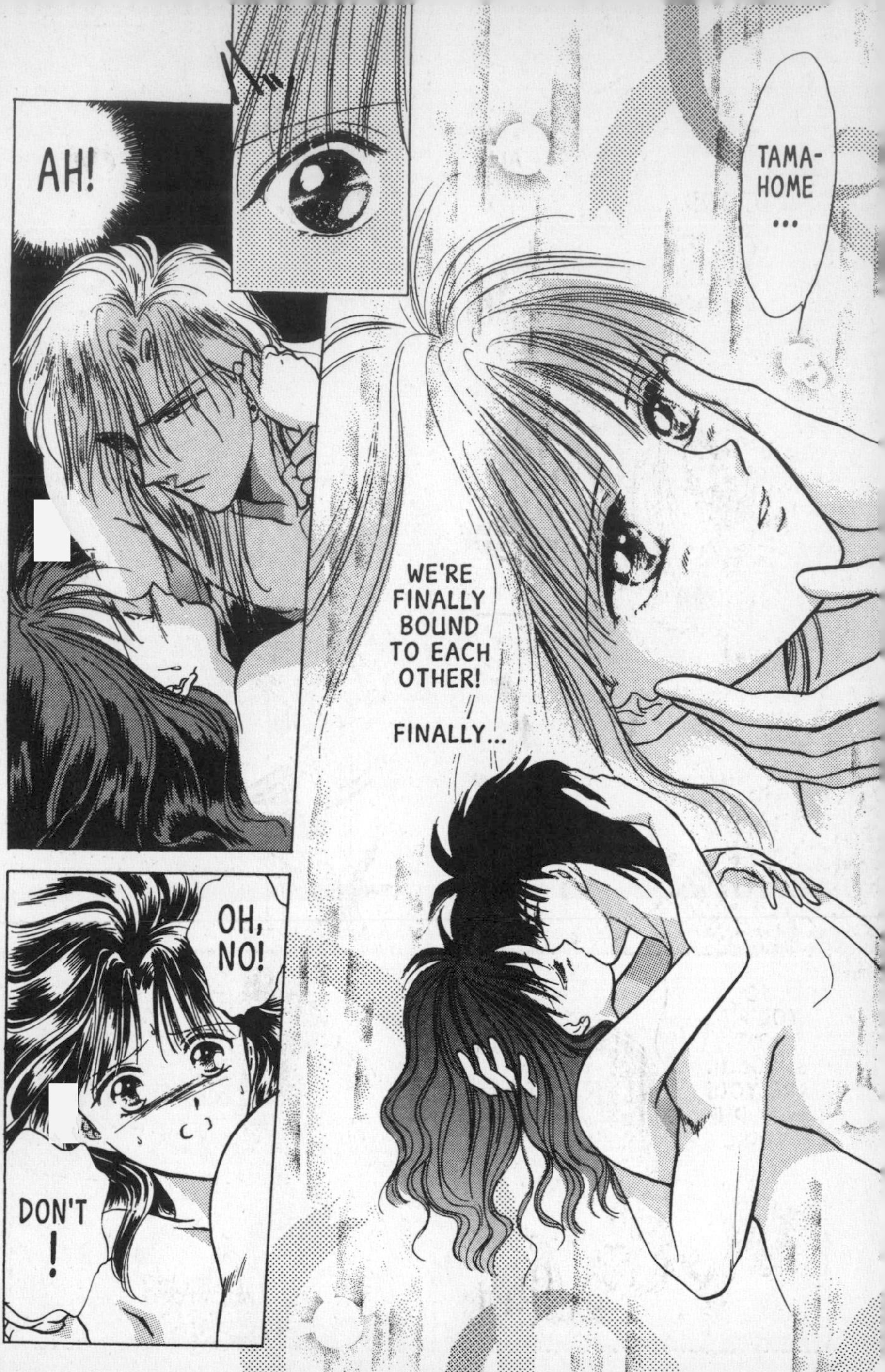
TAMA-HOME...
WE'RE FINALLY BOUND TO EACH OTHER!
FINALLY...
AH!
OH, NO!
DON'T!

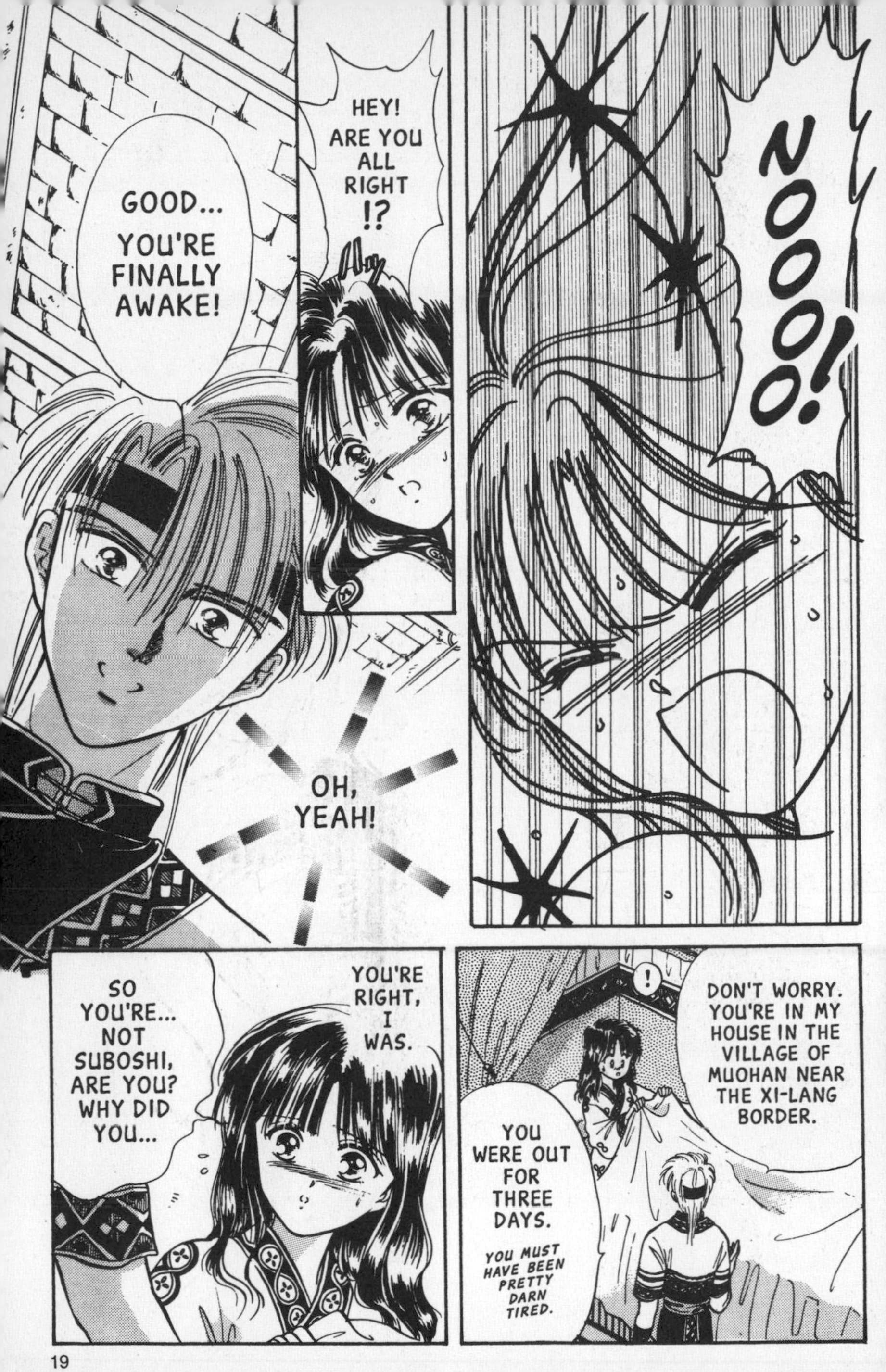
NOOOOO!
HEY! ARE YOU ALL RIGHT !?
GOOD... YOU'RE FINALLY AWAKE!
OH, YEAH!
!
DON'T WORRY. YOU'RE IN MY HOUSE IN THE VILLAGE OF MUOHAN NEAR THE XI-LANG BORDER.
YOU WERE OUT FOR THREE DAYS.
YOU MUST HAVE BEEN PRETTY DARN TIRED.
YOU'RE RIGHT, I WAS.
SO YOU'RE... NOT SUBOSHI, ARE YOU? WHY DID YOU...

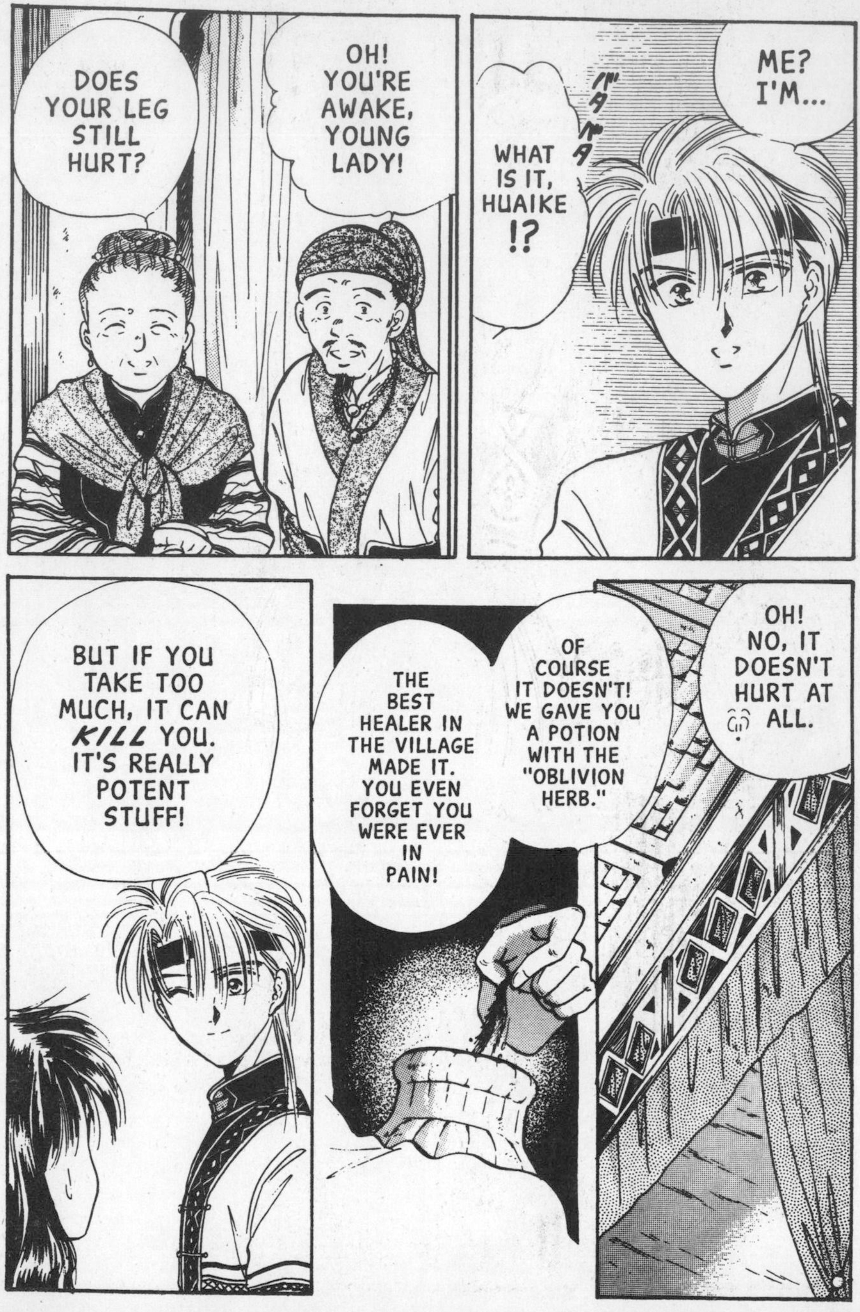
ME? I'M...
バタバタ
WHAT IS IT, HUAIKE!?
OH! YOU'RE AWAKE, YOUNG LADY!
DOES YOUR LEG STILL HURT?
OH! NO, IT DOESN'T HURT AT ALL.
OF COURSE IT DOESN'T! WE GAVE YOU A POTION WITH THE "OBLIVION HERB."
THE BEST HEALER IN THE VILLAGE MADE IT. YOU EVEN FORGET YOU WERE EVER IN PAIN!
BUT IF YOU TAKE TOO MUCH, IT CAN *KILL* YOU. IT'S REALLY POTENT STUFF!

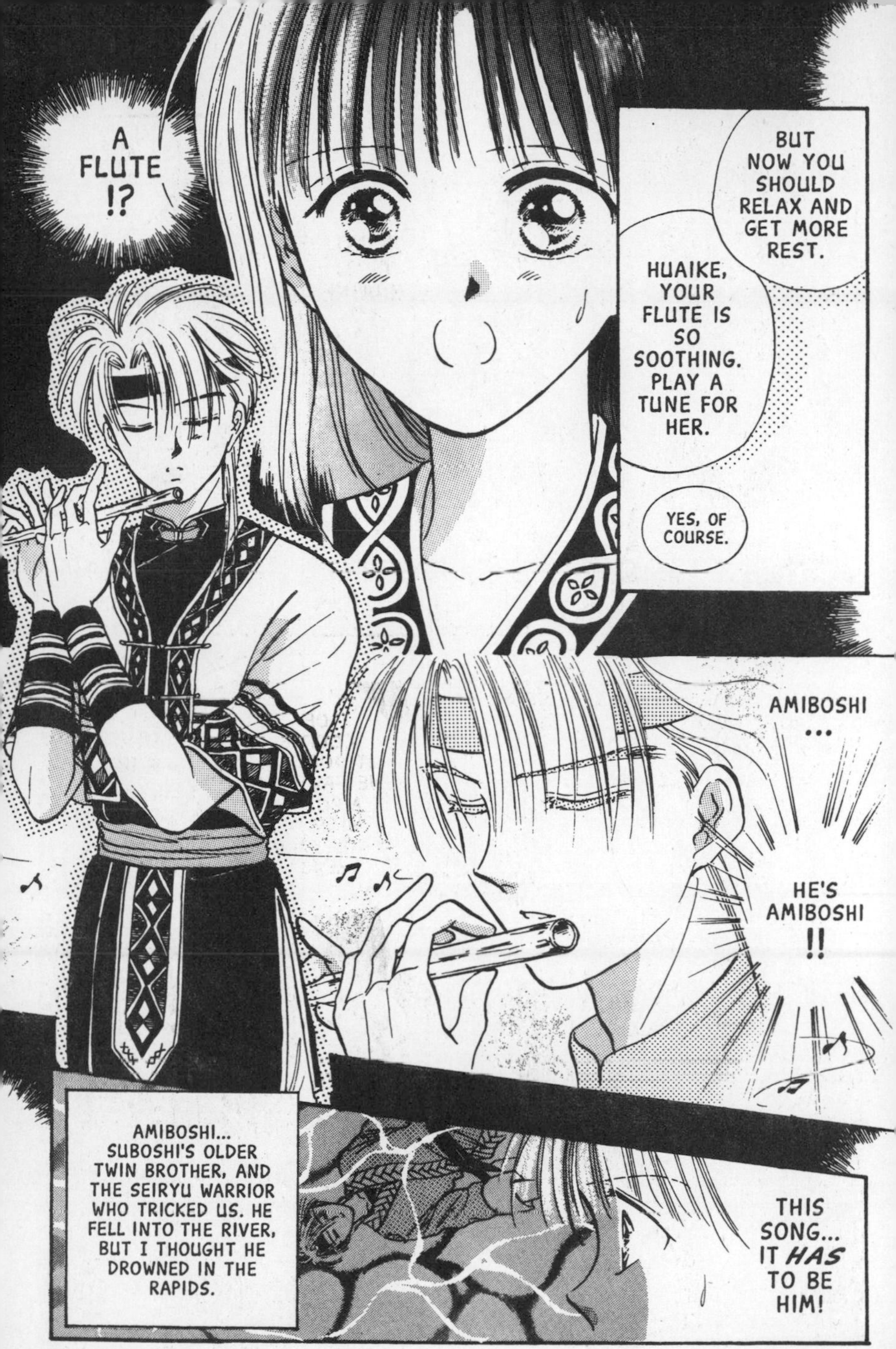
BUT NOW YOU SHOULD RELAX AND GET MORE REST.
HUAIKE, YOUR FLUTE IS SO SOOTHING. PLAY A TUNE FOR HER.
YES, OF COURSE.
A FLUTE !?
AMIBOSHI ...
HE'S AMIBOSHI !!
THIS SONG... IT *HAS* TO BE HIM!
AMIBOSHI... SUBOSHI'S OLDER TWIN BROTHER, AND THE SEIRYU WARRIOR WHO TRICKED US. HE FELL INTO THE RIVER, BUT I THOUGHT HE DROWNED IN THE RAPIDS.

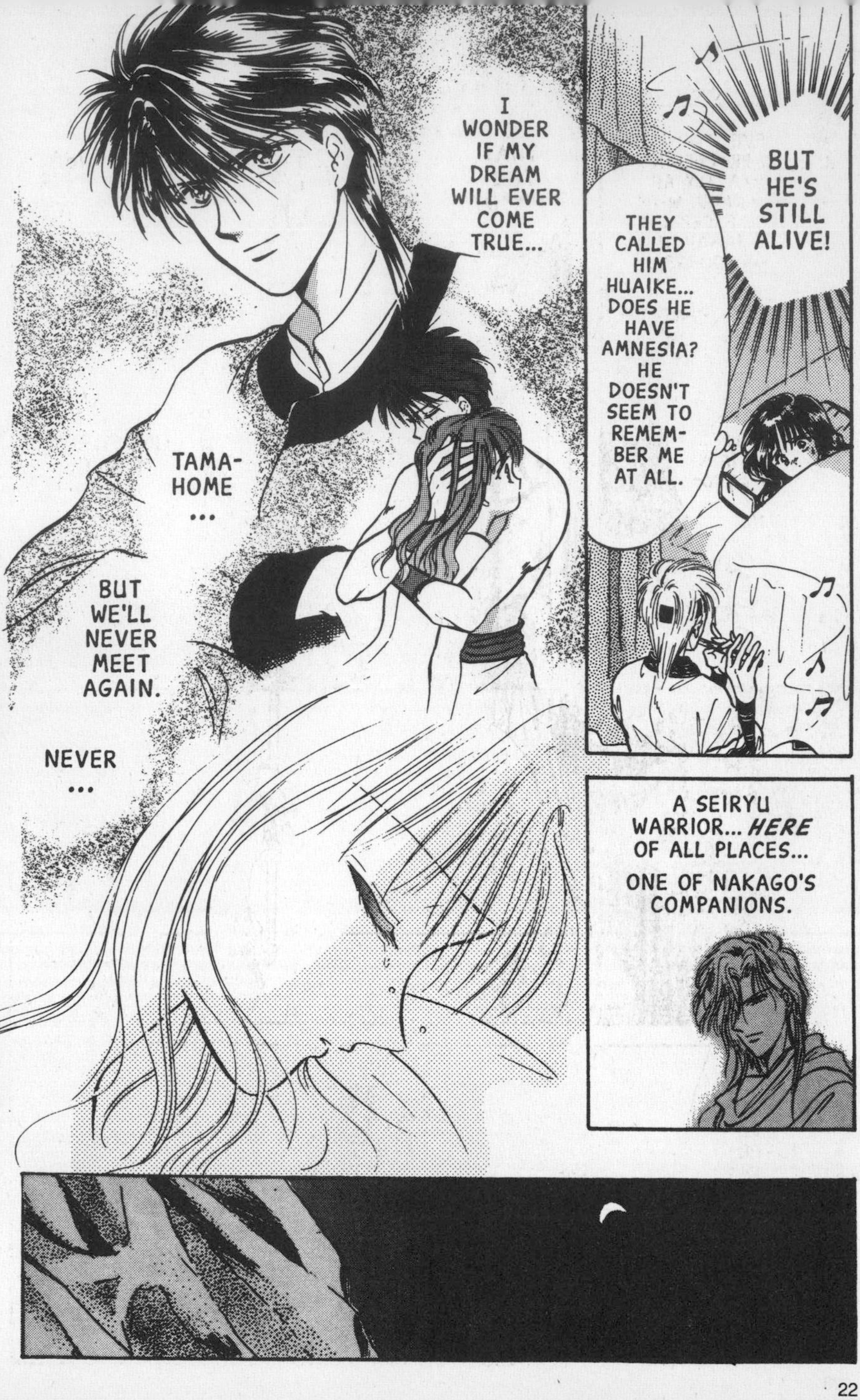
BUT HE'S STILL ALIVE!
THEY CALLED HIM HUAIKE... DOES HE HAVE AMNESIA? HE DOESN'T SEEM TO REMEMBER ME AT ALL.
A SEIRYU WARRIOR... *HERE* OF ALL PLACES...
ONE OF NAKAGO'S COMPANIONS.
I WONDER IF MY DREAM WILL EVER COME TRUE...
TAMA-HOME...
BUT WE'LL NEVER MEET AGAIN.
NEVER...

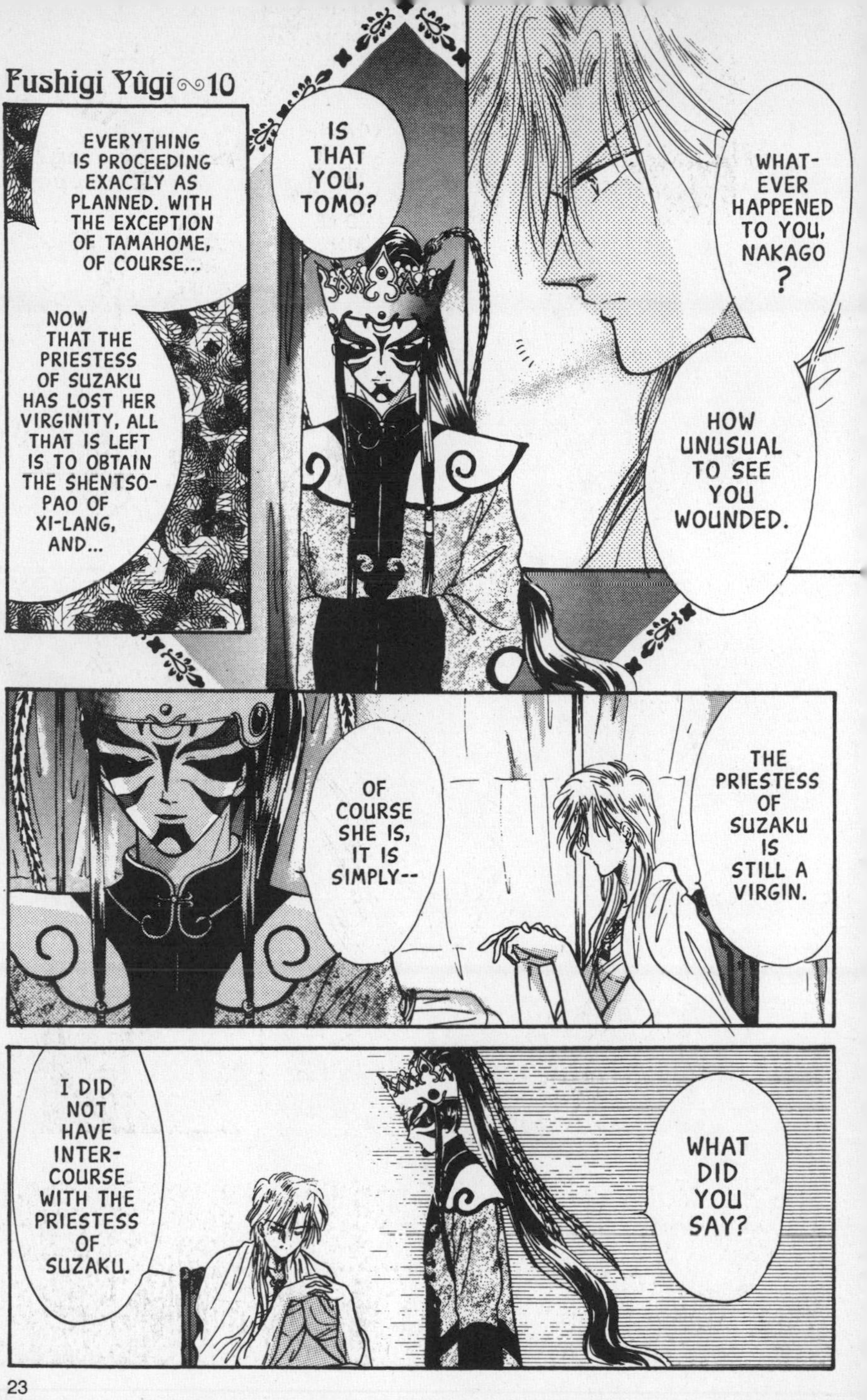
WHAT-EVER HAPPENED TO YOU, NAKAGO?
HOW UNUSUAL TO SEE YOU WOUNDED.
IS THAT YOU, TOMO?
EVERYTHING IS PROCEEDING EXACTLY AS PLANNED. WITH THE EXCEPTION OF TAMAHOME, OF COURSE...
NOW THAT THE PRIESTESS OF SUZAKU HAS LOST HER VIRGINITY, ALL THAT IS LEFT IS TO OBTAIN THE SHENTSO-PAO OF XI-LANG, AND...
THE PRIESTESS OF SUZAKU IS STILL A VIRGIN.
OF COURSE SHE IS, IT IS SIMPLY--
WHAT DID YOU SAY?
I DID NOT HAVE INTER-COURSE WITH THE PRIESTESS OF SUZAKU.

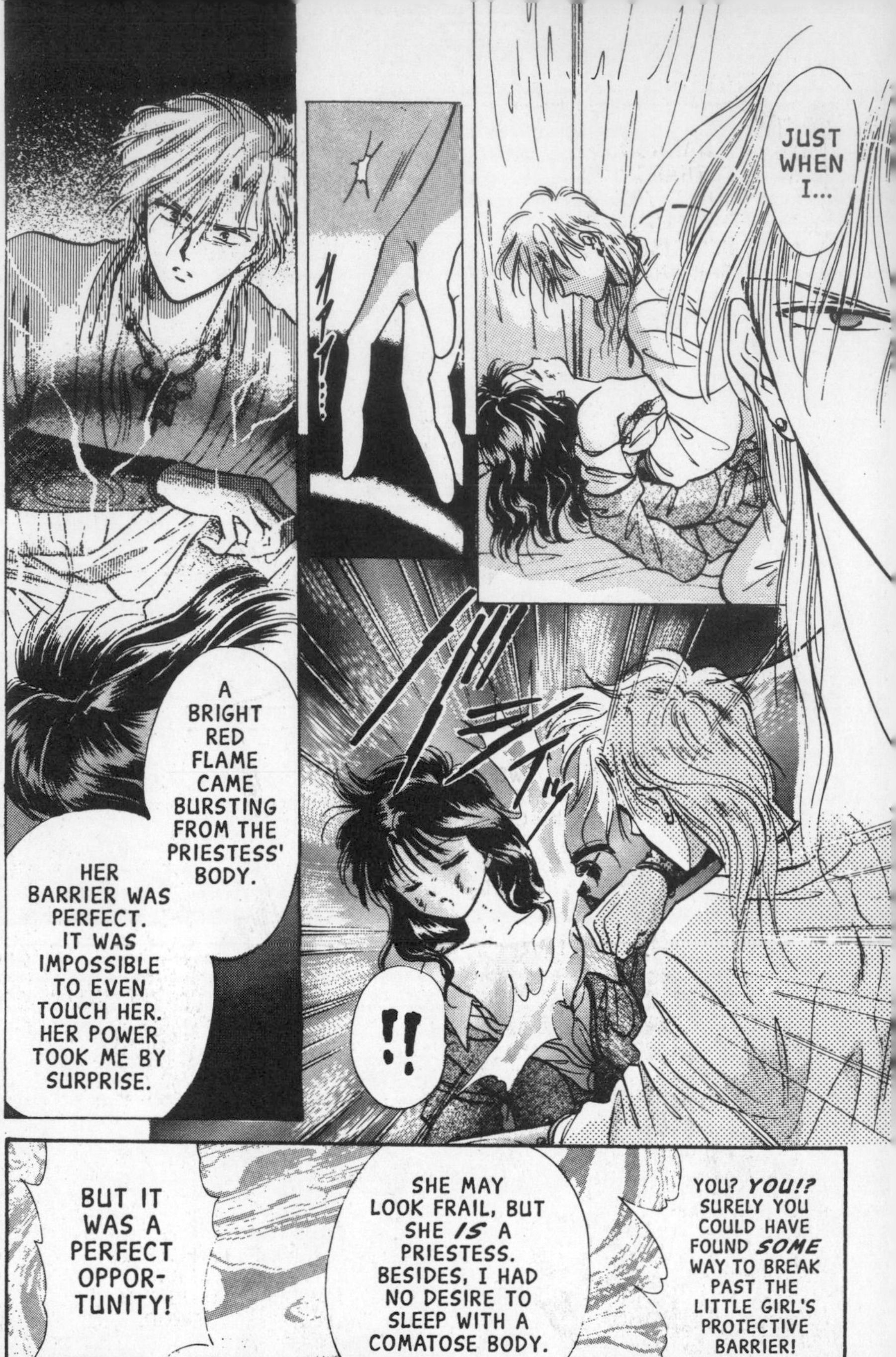
JUST WHEN I...
!!
A BRIGHT RED FLAME CAME BURSTING FROM THE PRIESTESS' BODY.
HER BARRIER WAS PERFECT. IT WAS IMPOSSIBLE TO EVEN TOUCH HER. HER POWER TOOK ME BY SURPRISE.
YOU? *YOU!?* SURELY YOU COULD HAVE FOUND *SOME* WAY TO BREAK PAST THE LITTLE GIRL'S PROTECTIVE BARRIER!
SHE MAY LOOK FRAIL, BUT SHE *IS* A PRIESTESS. BESIDES, I HAD NO DESIRE TO SLEEP WITH A COMATOSE BODY.
BUT IT WAS A PERFECT OPPOR-TUNITY!

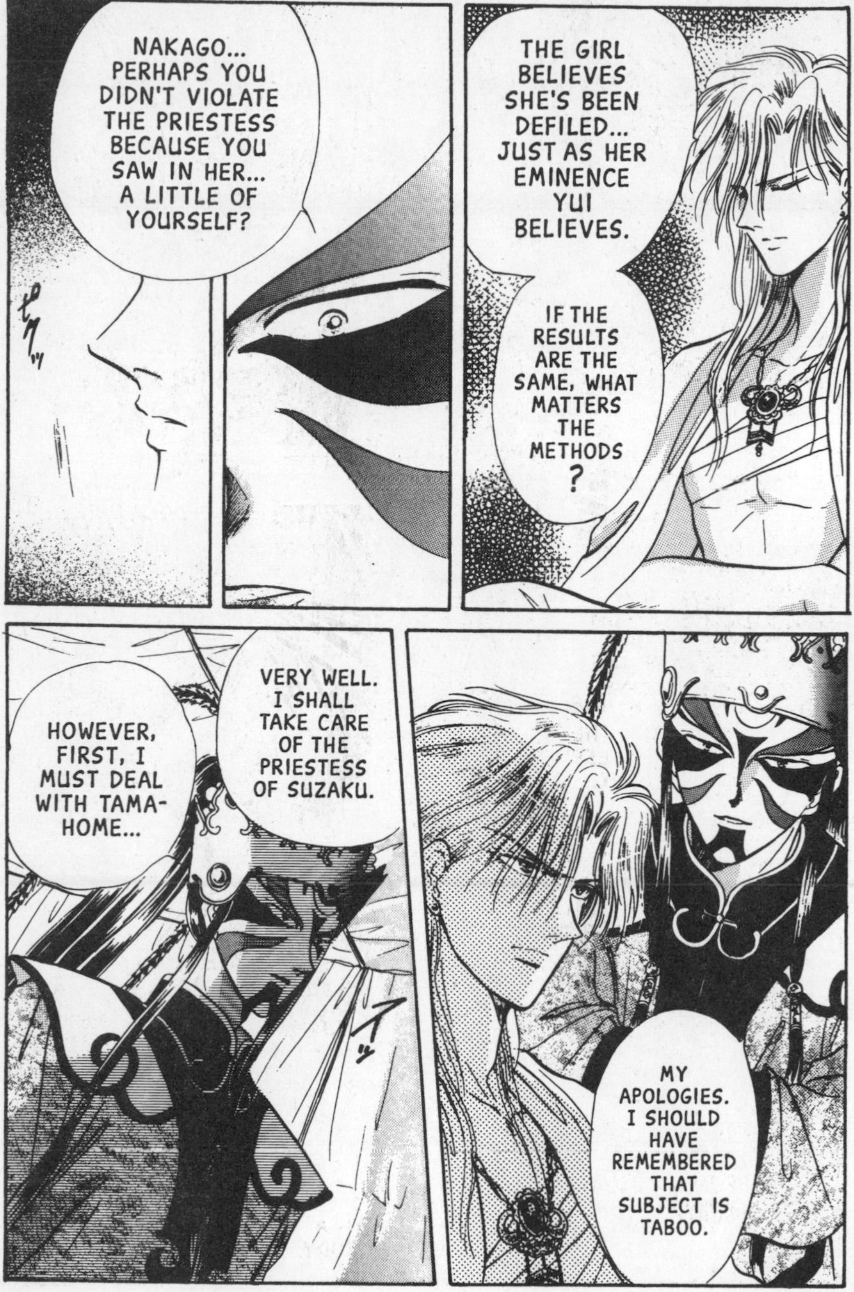
THE GIRL BELIEVES SHE'S BEEN DEFILED... JUST AS HER EMINENCE YUI BELIEVES.
IF THE RESULTS ARE THE SAME, WHAT MATTERS THE METHODS ?
NAKAGO... PERHAPS YOU DIDN'T VIOLATE THE PRIESTESS BECAUSE YOU SAW IN HER... A LITTLE OF YOURSELF?
MY APOLOGIES. I SHOULD HAVE REMEMBERED THAT SUBJECT IS TABOO.
VERY WELL. I SHALL TAKE CARE OF THE PRIESTESS OF SUZAKU.
HOWEVER, FIRST, I MUST DEAL WITH TAMA-HOME...

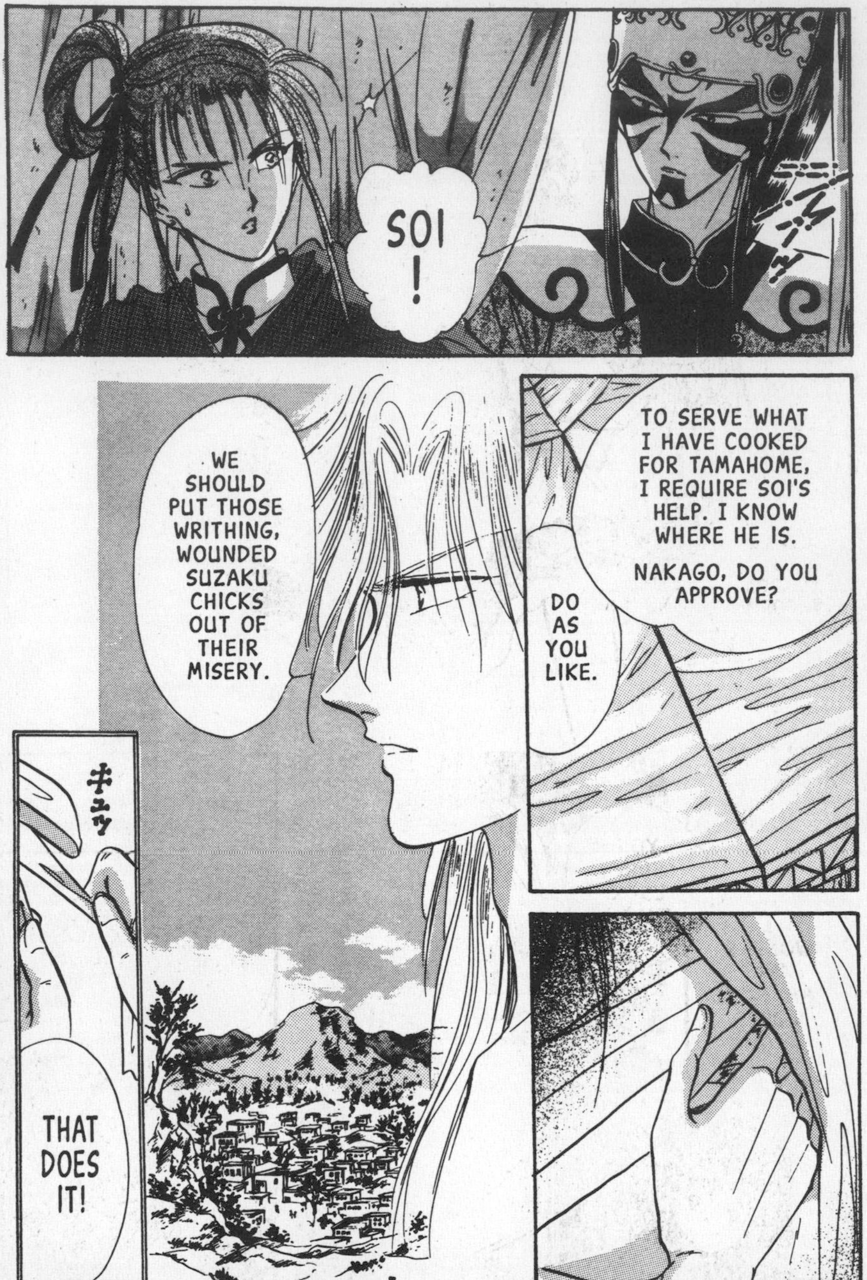
SOI !
TO SERVE WHAT I HAVE COOKED FOR TAMAHOME, I REQUIRE SOI'S HELP. I KNOW WHERE HE IS.
NAKAGO, DO YOU APPROVE?
DO AS YOU LIKE.
WE SHOULD PUT THOSE WRITHING, WOUNDED SUZAKU CHICKS OUT OF THEIR MISERY.
キュッ
THAT DOES IT!

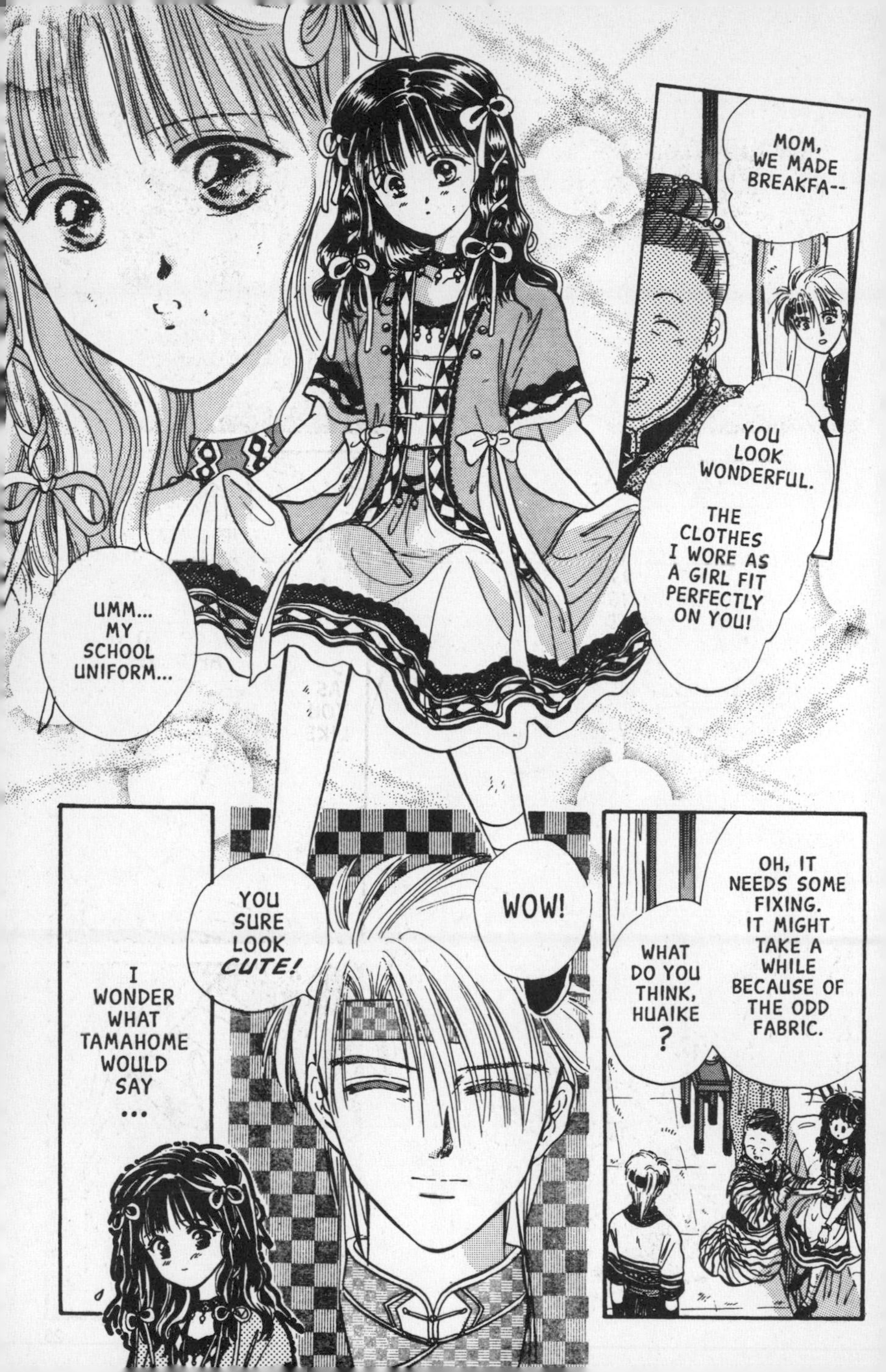
MOM, WE MADE BREAKFA--
YOU LOOK WONDERFUL.
THE CLOTHES I WORE AS A GIRL FIT PERFECTLY ON YOU!
UMM... MY SCHOOL UNIFORM...
OH, IT NEEDS SOME FIXING. IT MIGHT TAKE A WHILE BECAUSE OF THE ODD FABRIC.
WHAT DO YOU THINK, HUAIKE?
WOW!
YOU SURE LOOK *CUTE!*
I WONDER WHAT TAMAHOME WOULD SAY ...

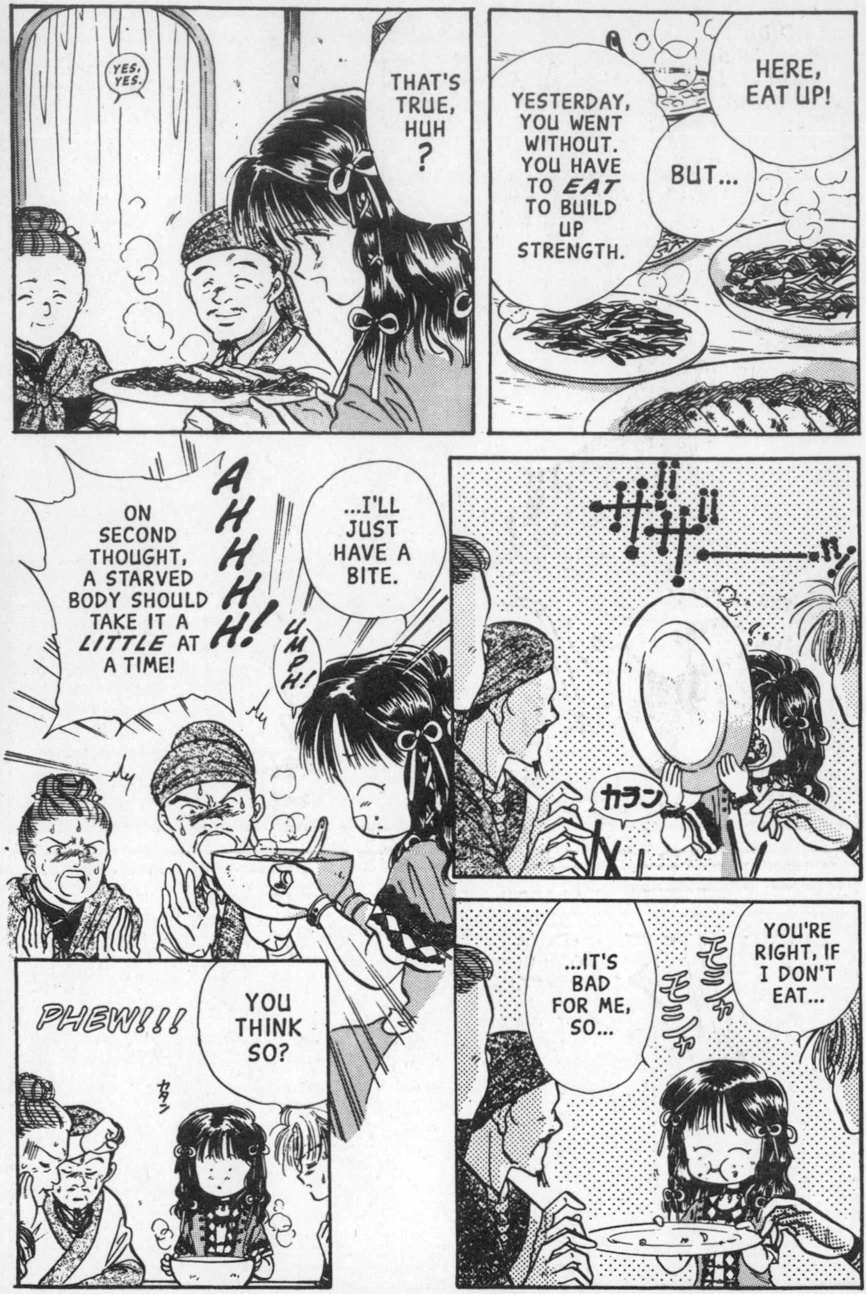
HERE, EAT UP!
BUT...
YESTERDAY, YOU WENT WITHOUT. YOU HAVE TO *EAT* TO BUILD UP STRENGTH.
THAT'S TRUE, HUH?
YES, YES.
カラン
...I'LL JUST HAVE A BITE.
AHHHHH!
UMPH!
ON SECOND THOUGHT, A STARVED BODY SHOULD TAKE IT A *LITTLE* AT A TIME!
YOU'RE RIGHT, IF I DON'T EAT...
モシャ モシャ
...IT'S BAD FOR ME, SO...
YOU THINK SO?
PHEW!!!
カタン

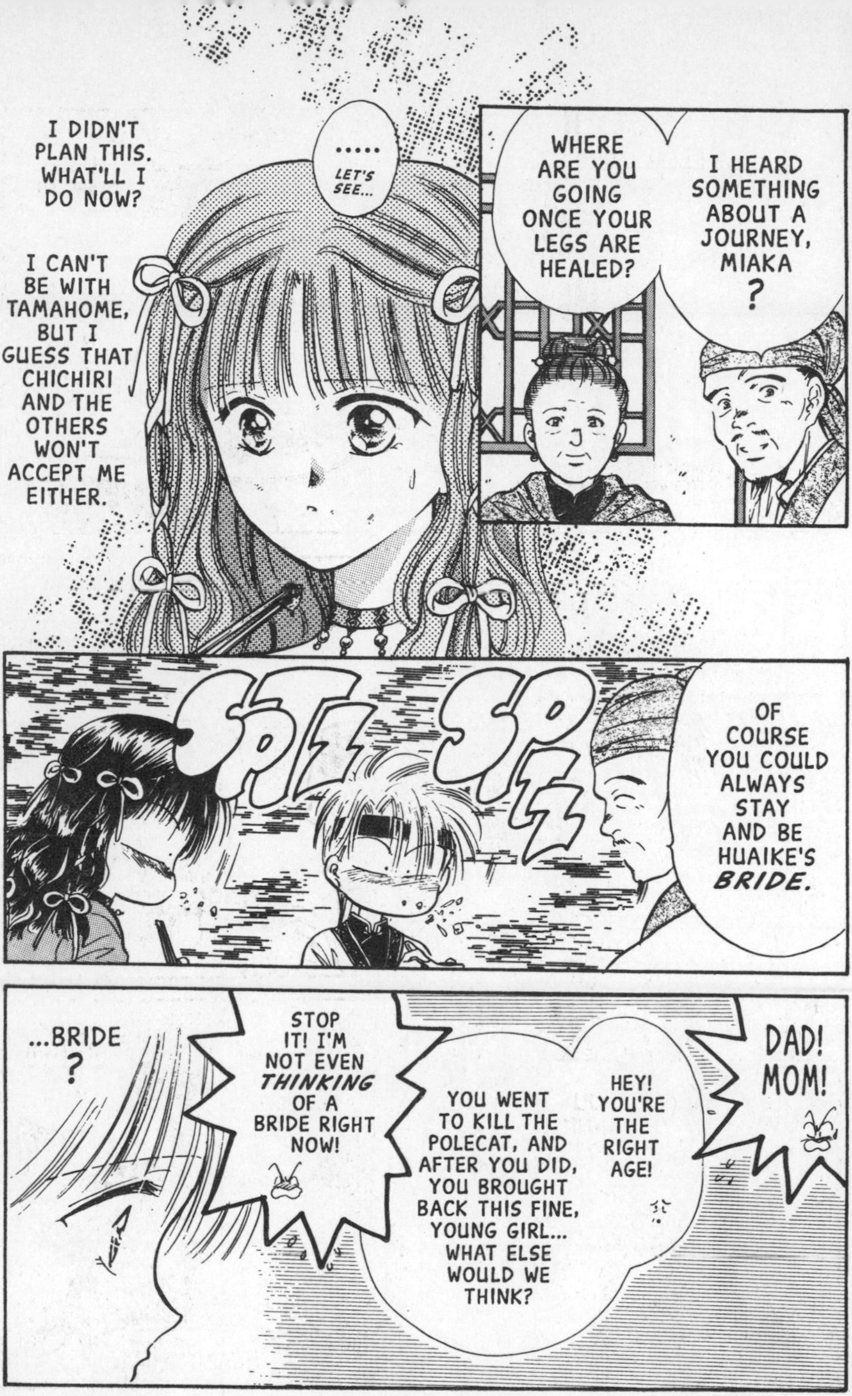
I HEARD SOMETHING ABOUT A JOURNEY, MIAKA ?
WHERE ARE YOU GOING ONCE YOUR LEGS ARE HEALED?
......
LET'S SEE...
I DIDN'T PLAN THIS. WHAT'LL I DO NOW?
I CAN'T BE WITH TAMAHOME, BUT I GUESS THAT CHICHIRI AND THE OTHERS WON'T ACCEPT ME EITHER.
OF COURSE YOU COULD ALWAYS STAY AND BE HUAIKE'S *BRIDE.*
DAD! MOM!
HEY! YOU'RE THE RIGHT AGE!
YOU WENT TO KILL THE POLECAT, AND AFTER YOU DID, YOU BROUGHT BACK THIS FINE, YOUNG GIRL... WHAT ELSE WOULD WE THINK?
STOP IT! I'M NOT EVEN *THINKING* OF A BRIDE RIGHT NOW!
...BRIDE ?

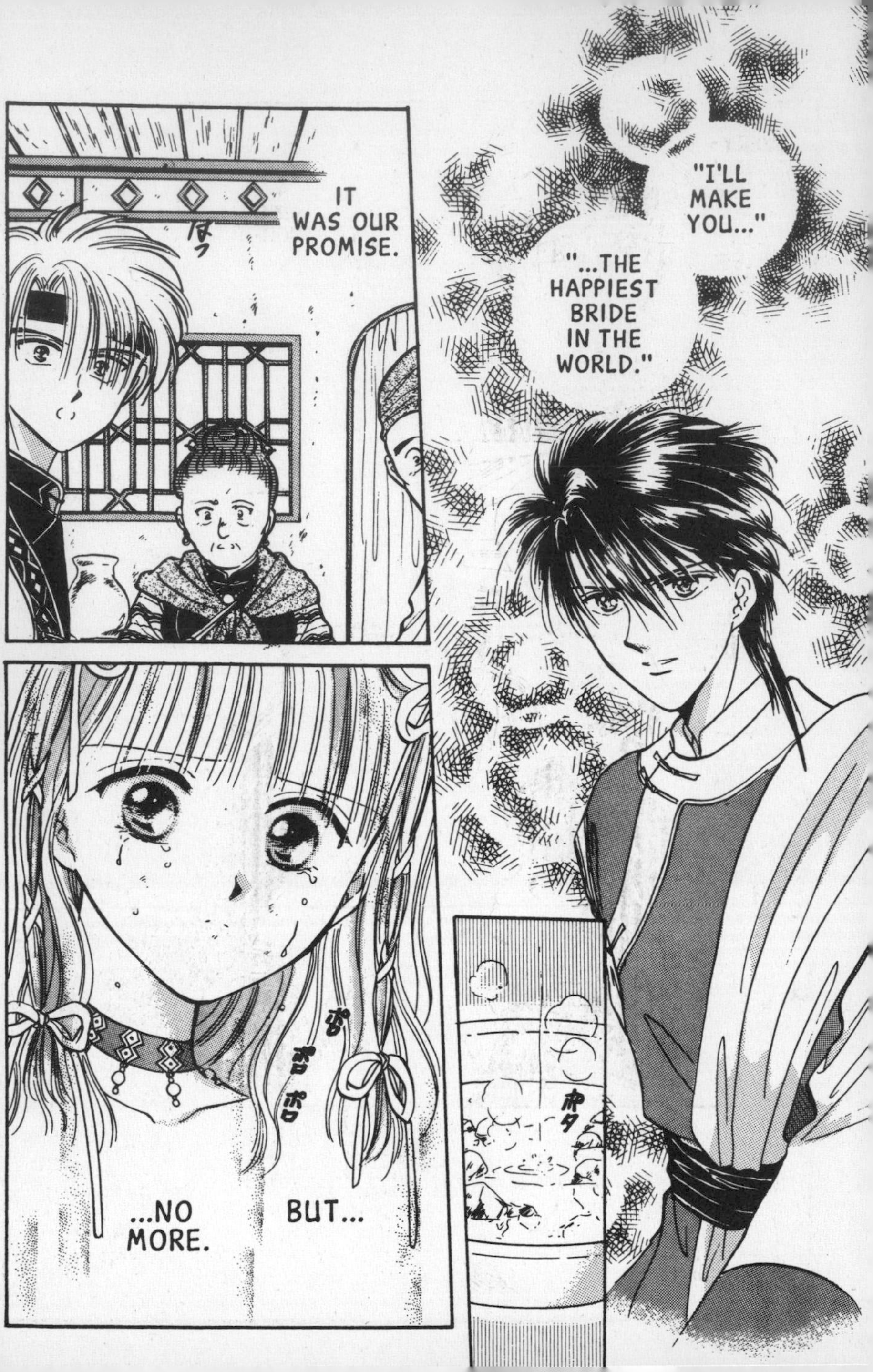
"I'LL MAKE YOU..."
"...THE HAPPIEST BRIDE IN THE WORLD."
IT WAS OUR PROMISE.
BUT...
...NO MORE.

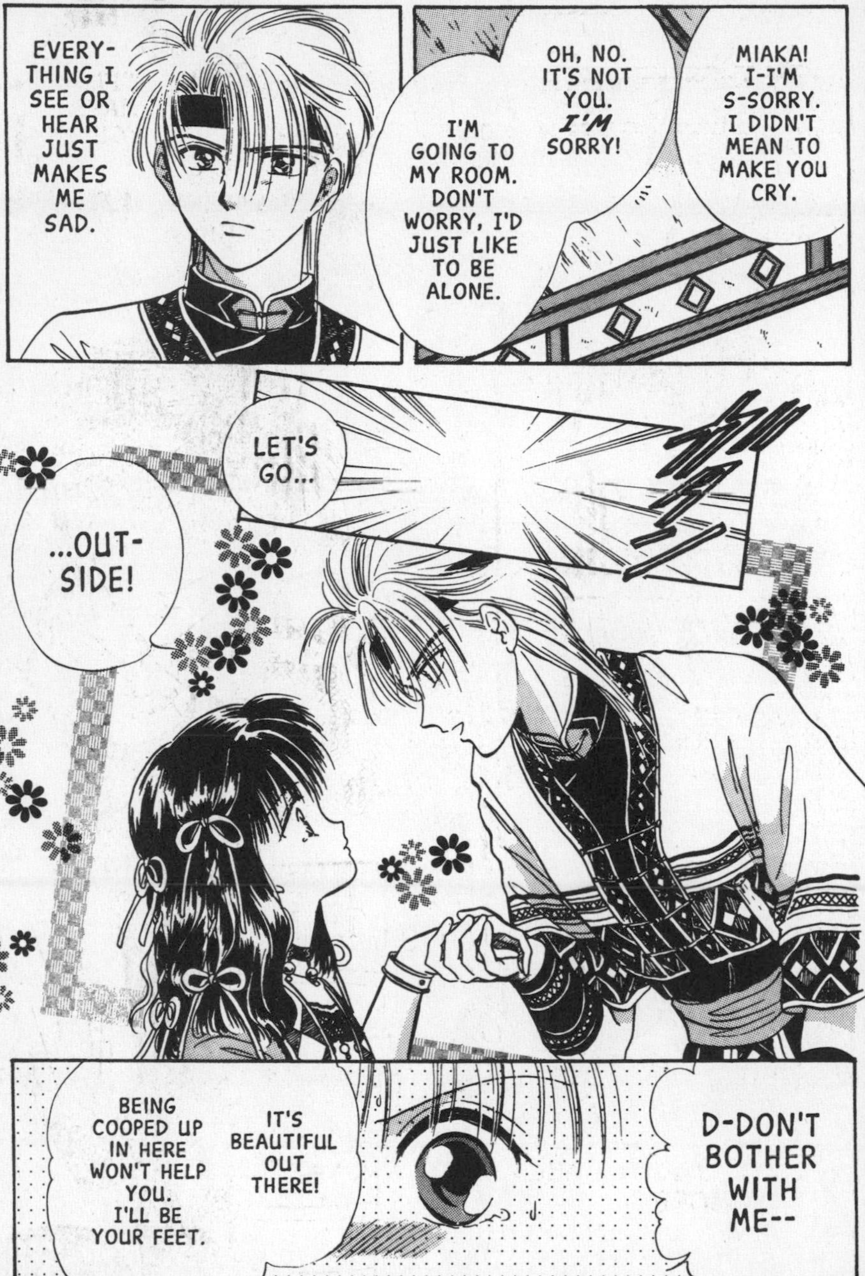
MIAKA! I-I'M S-SORRY. I DIDN'T MEAN TO MAKE YOU CRY.
OH, NO. IT'S NOT YOU. *I'M* SORRY!
I'M GOING TO MY ROOM. DON'T WORRY, I'D JUST LIKE TO BE ALONE.
EVERY-THING I SEE OR HEAR JUST MAKES ME SAD.
LET'S GO...
...OUT-SIDE!
D-DON'T BOTHER WITH ME--
IT'S BEAUTIFUL OUT THERE!
BEING COOPED UP IN HERE WON'T HELP YOU. I'LL BE YOUR FEET.

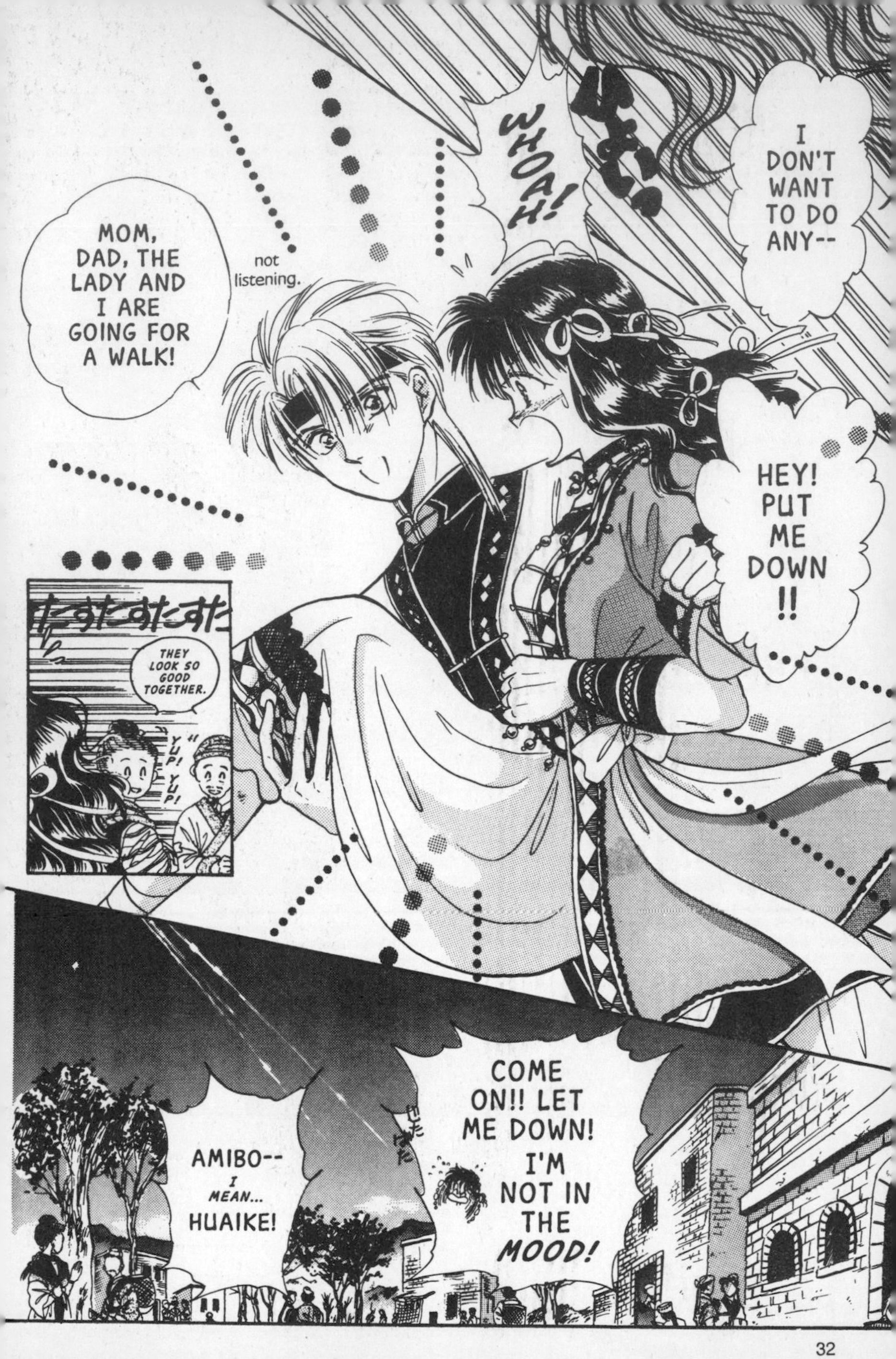
I DON'T WANT TO DO ANY--
WHOAH!
MOM, DAD, THE LADY AND I ARE GOING FOR A WALK!
not listening.
HEY! PUT ME DOWN !!
THEY LOOK SO GOOD TOGETHER.
YUP! YUP!
COME ON!! LET ME DOWN! I'M NOT IN THE MOOD!
AMIBO-- I MEAN... HUAIKE!

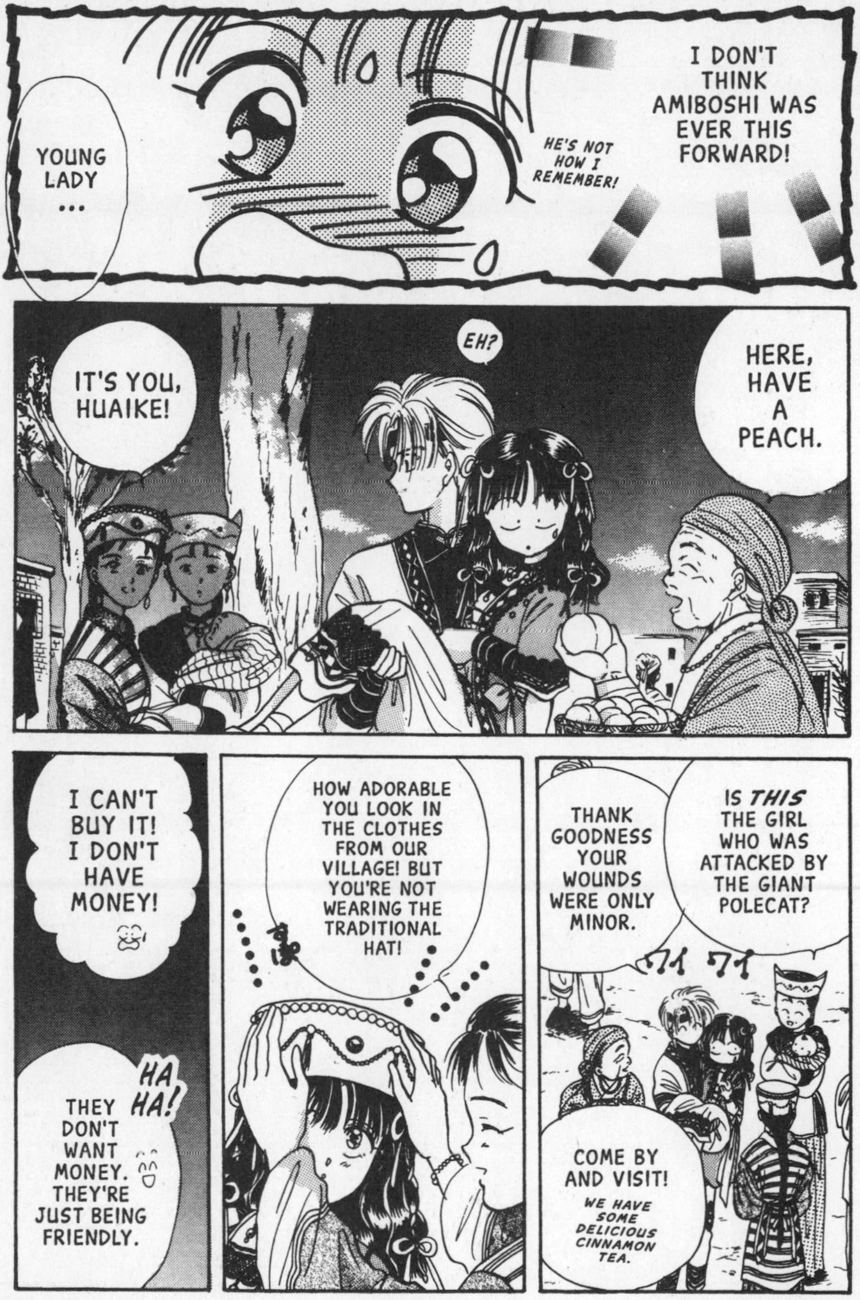
I DON'T THINK AMIBOSHI WAS EVER THIS FORWARD!
HE'S NOT HOW I REMEMBER!
YOUNG LADY ...
HERE, HAVE A PEACH.
EH?
IT'S YOU, HUAIKE!
IS *THIS* THE GIRL WHO WAS ATTACKED BY THE GIANT POLECAT?
THANK GOODNESS YOUR WOUNDS WERE ONLY MINOR.
ワイ ワイ
COME BY AND VISIT!
WE HAVE SOME DELICIOUS CINNAMON TEA.
HOW ADORABLE YOU LOOK IN THE CLOTHES FROM OUR VILLAGE! BUT YOU'RE NOT WEARING THE TRADITIONAL HAT!
I CAN'T BUY IT! I DON'T HAVE MONEY!
HA HA!
THEY DON'T WANT MONEY. THEY'RE JUST BEING FRIENDLY.

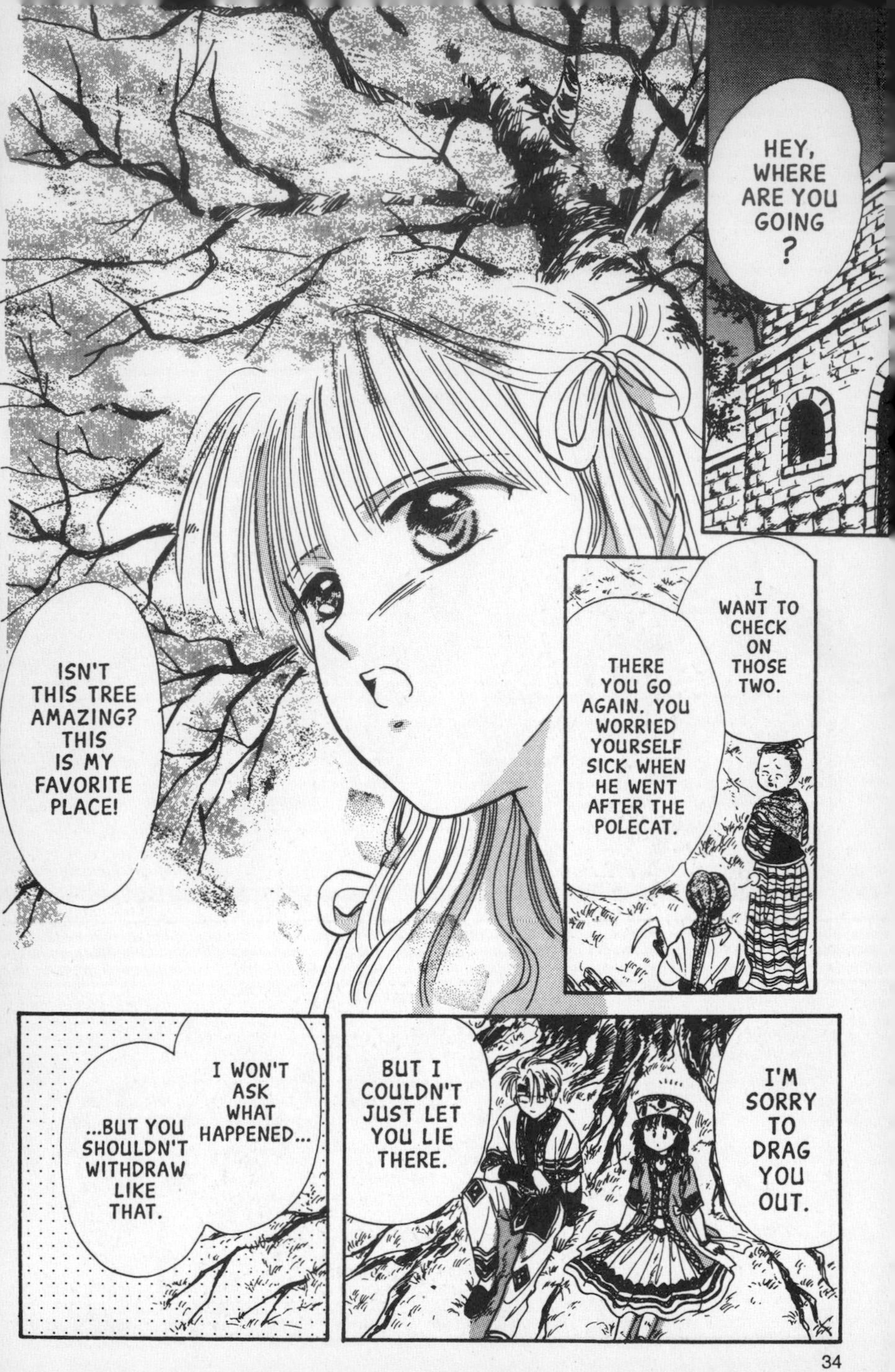
HEY, WHERE ARE YOU GOING?
I WANT TO CHECK ON THOSE TWO.
THERE YOU GO AGAIN. YOU WORRIED YOURSELF SICK WHEN HE WENT AFTER THE POLECAT.
ISN'T THIS TREE AMAZING? THIS IS MY FAVORITE PLACE!
I'M SORRY TO DRAG YOU OUT.
BUT I COULDN'T JUST LET YOU LIE THERE.
I WON'T ASK WHAT HAPPENED...
...BUT YOU SHOULDN'T WITHDRAW LIKE THAT.

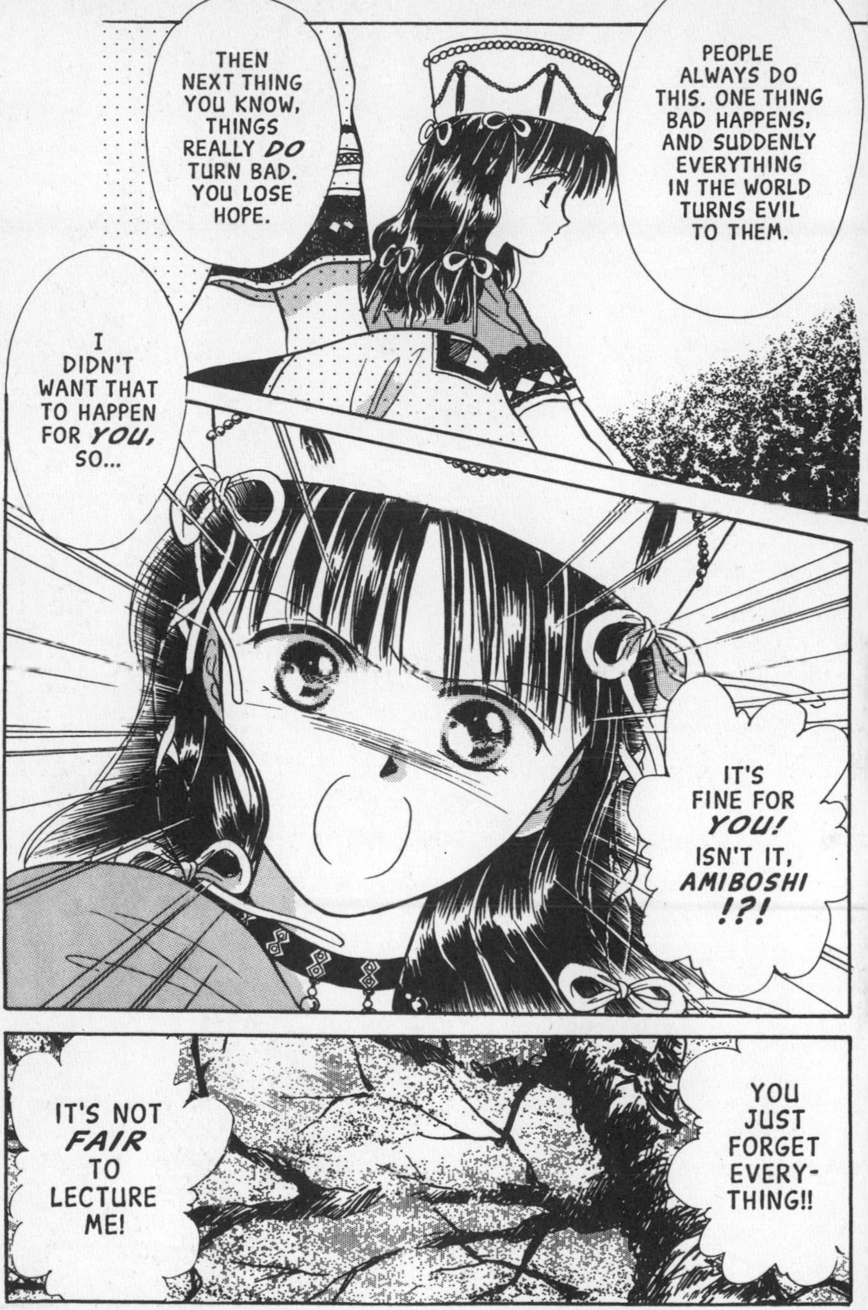
PEOPLE ALWAYS DO THIS. ONE THING BAD HAPPENS, AND SUDDENLY EVERYTHING IN THE WORLD TURNS EVIL TO THEM.
THEN NEXT THING YOU KNOW, THINGS REALLY *DO* TURN BAD. YOU LOSE HOPE.
I DIDN'T WANT THAT TO HAPPEN FOR *YOU,* SO...
IT'S FINE FOR *YOU!* ISN'T IT, *AMIBOSHI !?!*
YOU JUST FORGET EVERY-THING!!
IT'S NOT *FAIR* TO LECTURE ME!

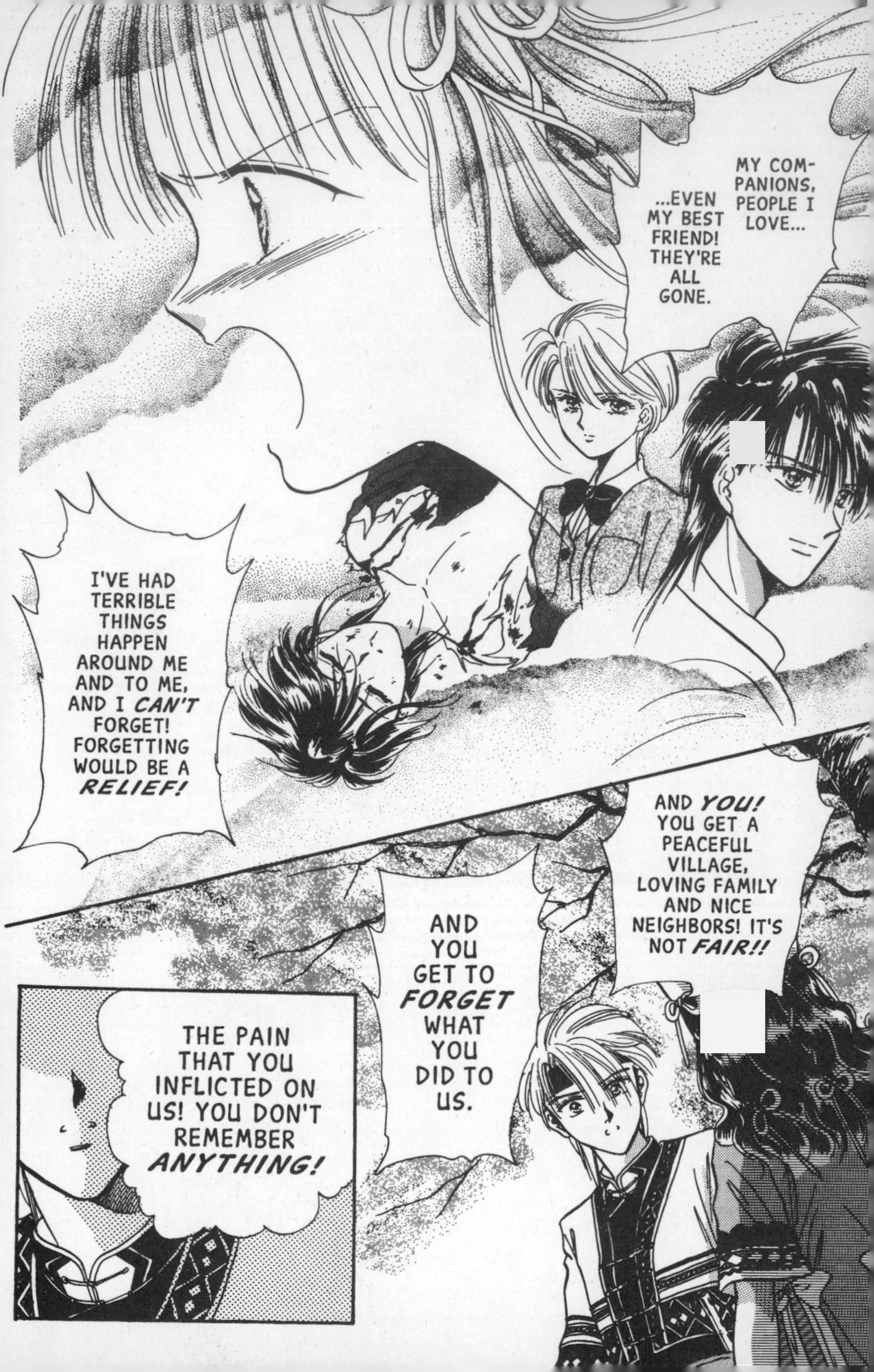
MY COMPANIONS, PEOPLE I LOVE...
...EVEN MY BEST FRIEND! THEY'RE ALL GONE.
I'VE HAD TERRIBLE THINGS HAPPEN AROUND ME AND TO ME, AND I *CAN'T* FORGET! FORGETTING WOULD BE A ***RELIEF!***
AND ***YOU!*** YOU GET A PEACEFUL VILLAGE, LOVING FAMILY AND NICE NEIGHBORS! IT'S NOT ***FAIR!!***
AND YOU GET TO ***FORGET*** WHAT YOU DID TO US.
THE PAIN THAT YOU INFLICTED ON US! YOU DON'T REMEMBER ***ANYTHING!***

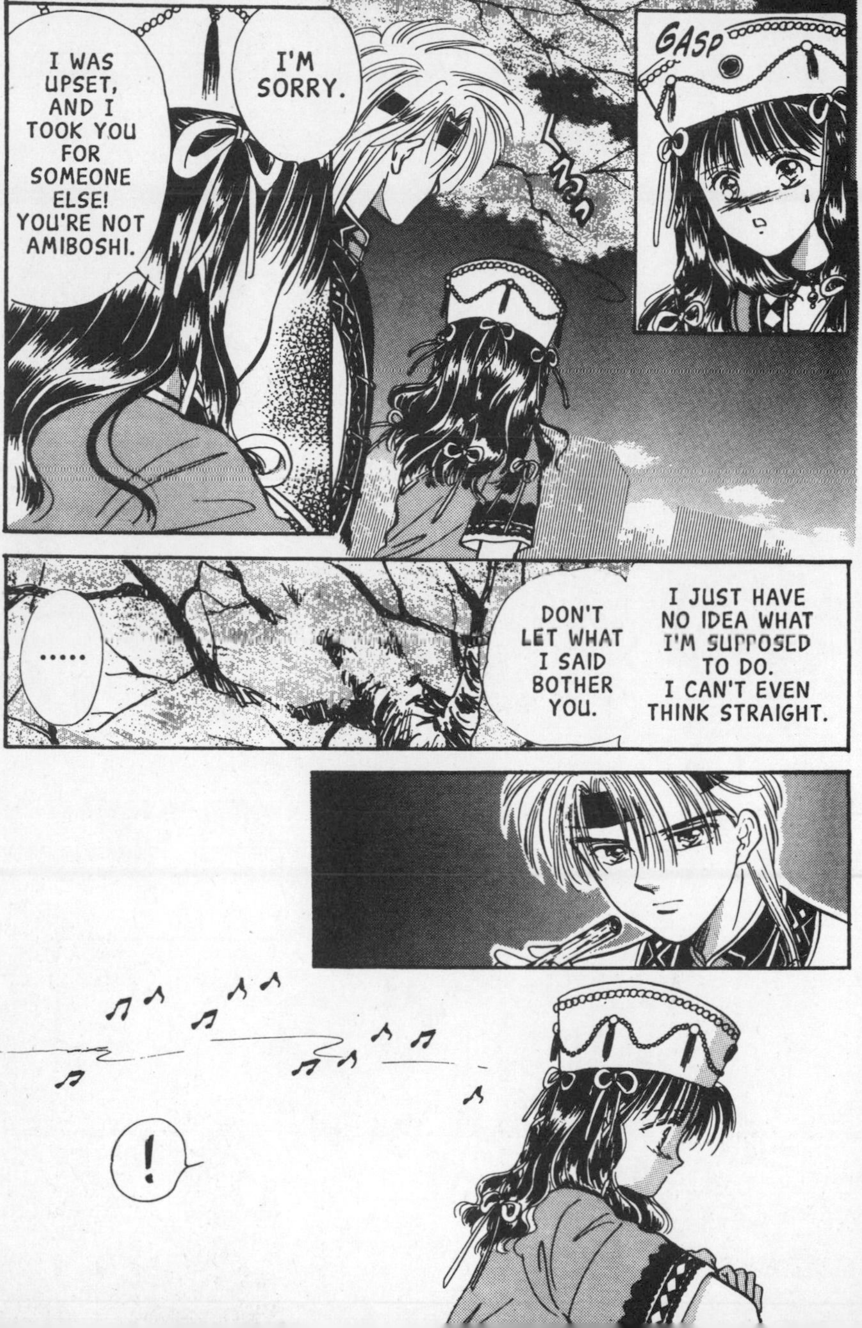
GASP
I'M SORRY.
I WAS UPSET, AND I TOOK YOU FOR SOMEONE ELSE! YOU'RE NOT AMIBOSHI.
I JUST HAVE NO IDEA WHAT I'M SUPPOSED TO DO. I CAN'T EVEN THINK STRAIGHT.
DON'T LET WHAT I SAID BOTHER YOU.
.....
!

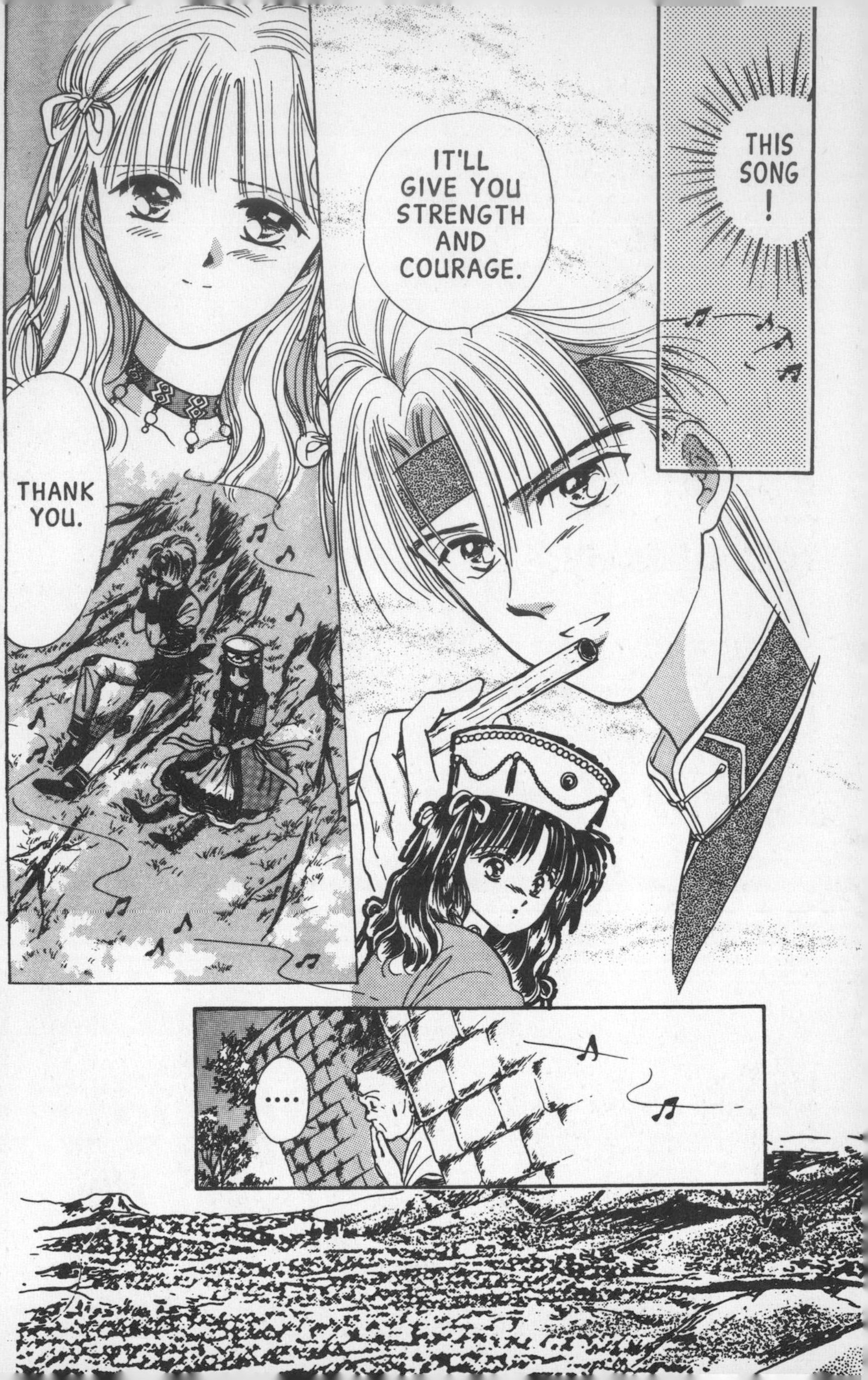
THIS SONG !
IT'LL GIVE YOU STRENGTH AND COURAGE.
THANK YOU.
.....

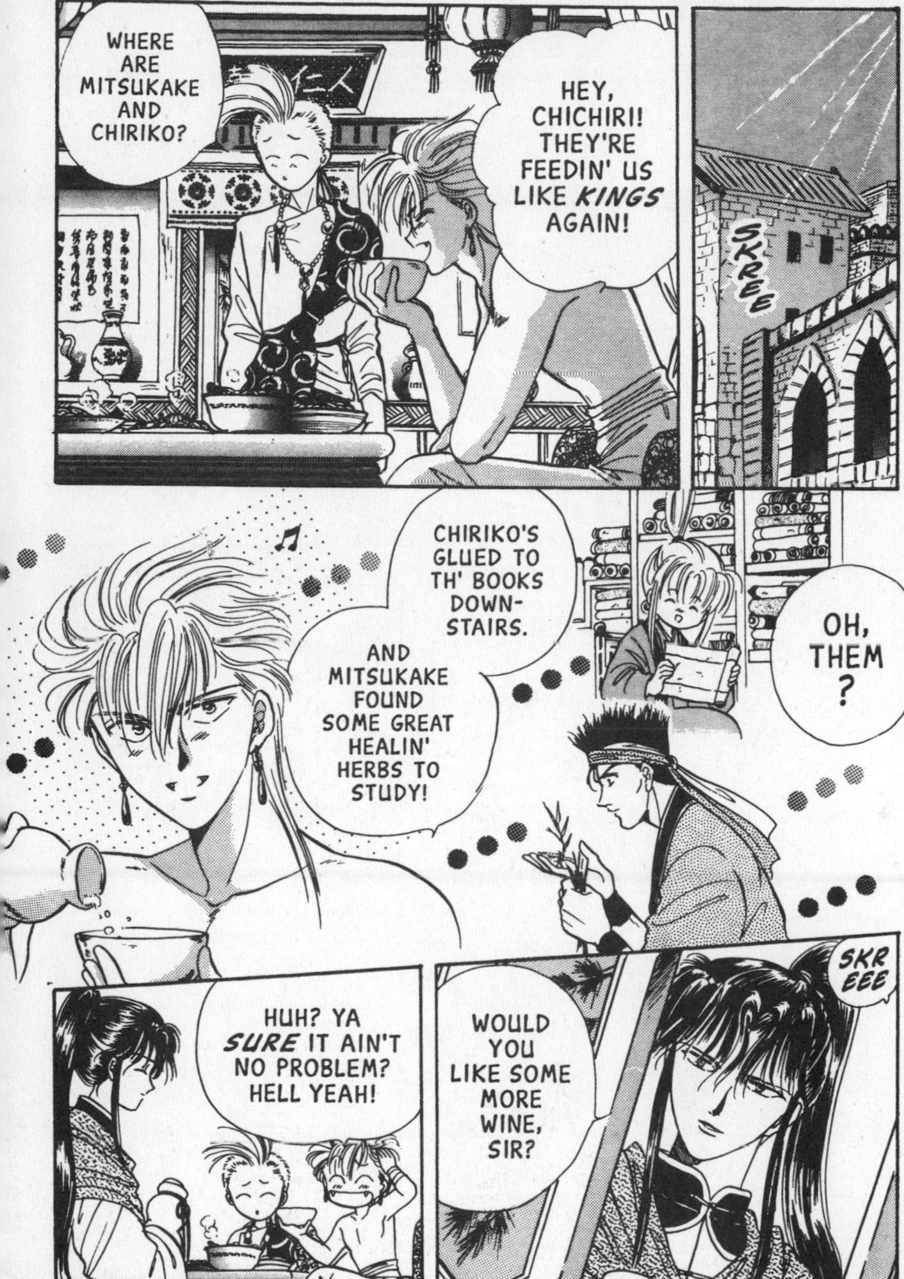
SKREE
HEY, CHICHIRI! THEY'RE FEEDIN' US LIKE KINGS AGAIN!
WHERE ARE MITSUKAKE AND CHIRIKO?
OH, THEM?
CHIRIKO'S GLUED TO TH' BOOKS DOWN-STAIRS.
AND MITSUKAKE FOUND SOME GREAT HEALIN' HERBS TO STUDY!
SKREEE
WOULD YOU LIKE SOME MORE WINE, SIR?
HUH? YA SURE IT AIN'T NO PROBLEM? HELL YEAH!

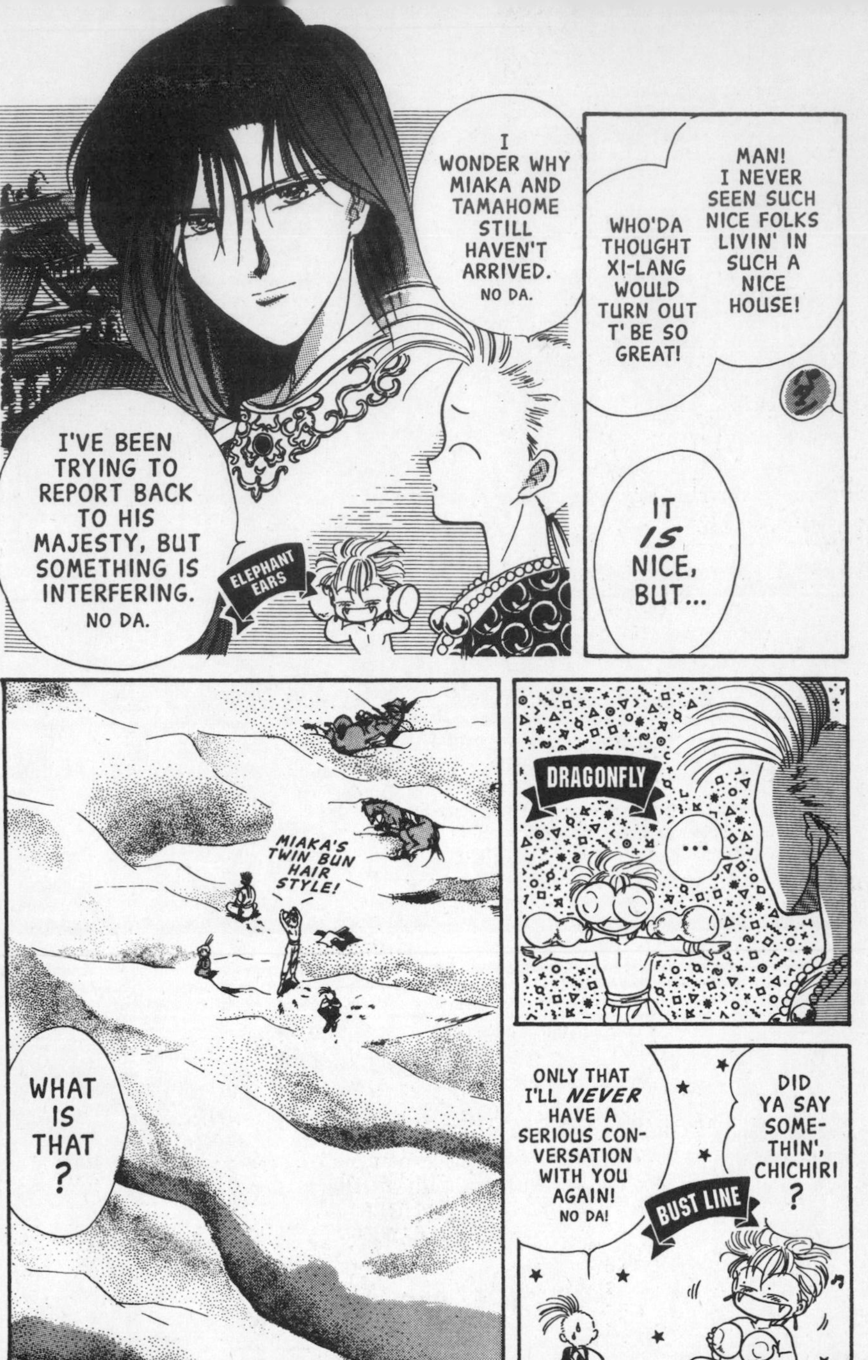
MAN! I NEVER SEEN SUCH NICE FOLKS LIVIN' IN SUCH A NICE HOUSE!
WHO'DA THOUGHT XI-LANG WOULD TURN OUT T' BE SO GREAT!
IT *IS* NICE, BUT...
I WONDER WHY MIAKA AND TAMAHOME STILL HAVEN'T ARRIVED. NO DA.
I'VE BEEN TRYING TO REPORT BACK TO HIS MAJESTY, BUT SOMETHING IS INTERFERING. NO DA.
ELEPHANT EARS
DRAGONFLY
...
DID YA SAY SOME-THIN', CHICHIRI?
ONLY THAT I'LL *NEVER* HAVE A SERIOUS CON-VERSATION WITH YOU AGAIN! NO DA!
BUST LINE
MIAKA'S TWIN BUN HAIR STYLE!
WHAT IS THAT?

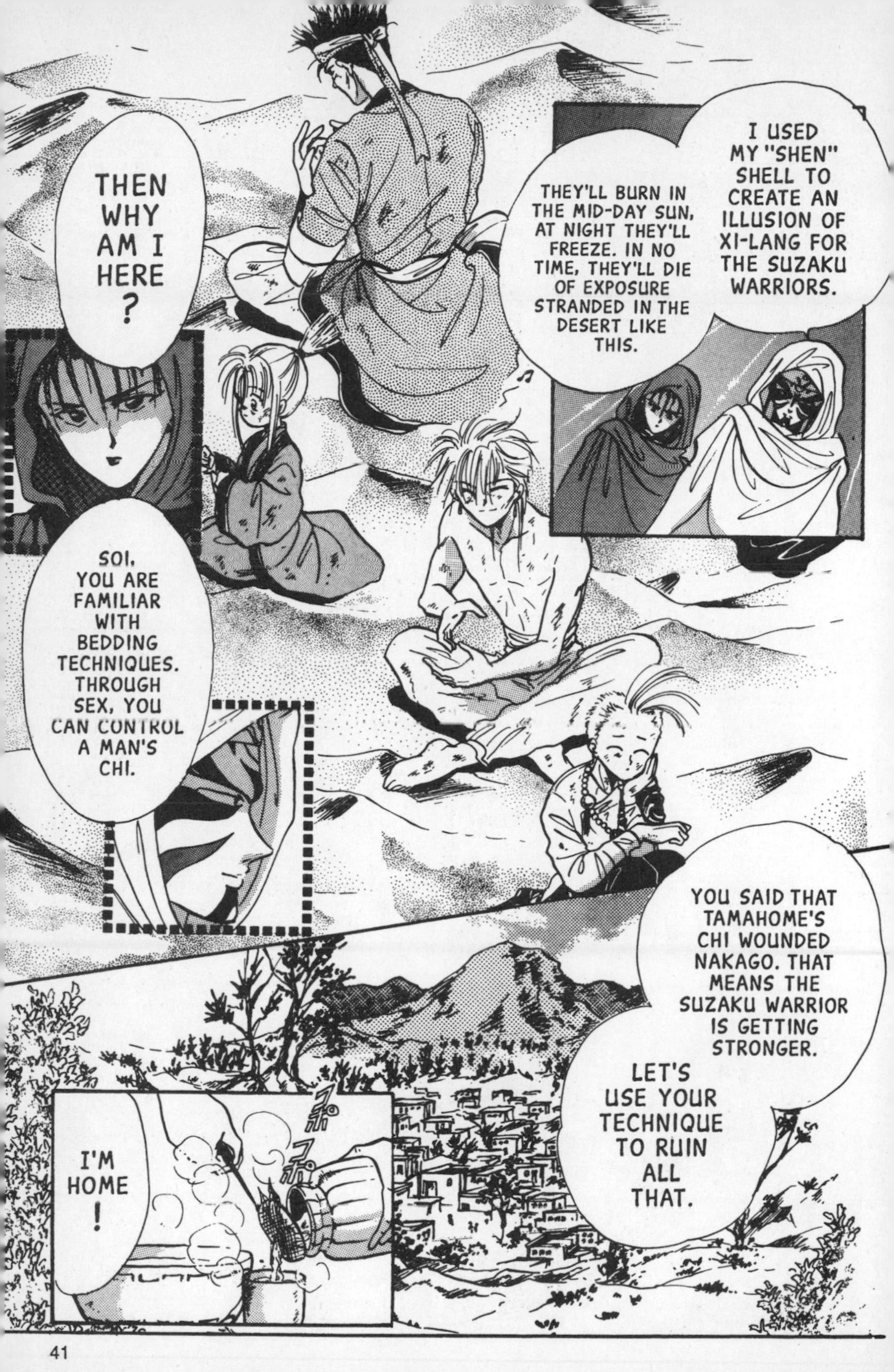
I USED MY "SHEN" SHELL TO CREATE AN ILLUSION OF XI-LANG FOR THE SUZAKU WARRIORS.
THEY'LL BURN IN THE MID-DAY SUN, AT NIGHT THEY'LL FREEZE. IN NO TIME, THEY'LL DIE OF EXPOSURE STRANDED IN THE DESERT LIKE THIS.
THEN WHY AM I HERE?
SOI. YOU ARE FAMILIAR WITH BEDDING TECHNIQUES. THROUGH SEX, YOU CAN CONTROL A MAN'S CHI.
YOU SAID THAT TAMAHOME'S CHI WOUNDED NAKAGO. THAT MEANS THE SUZAKU WARRIOR IS GETTING STRONGER.
LET'S USE YOUR TECHNIQUE TO RUIN ALL THAT.
I'M HOME!

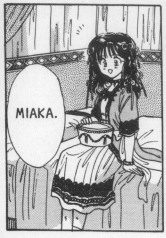

SORRY I TOOK SO LONG.
I'LL GO DRAW SOME WATER.
URK!
O-OH! WEL-COME BACK!
MIAKA.
I'M SORRY FOR CRYING AND CARRYING ON!
O-OH, NO! IT'S QUITE ALL RIGHT. HERE, HAVE SOME SOUP. IT'S GOOD FOR YOU!
OH! THANK YOU!
AHH! IT'S DELICIOUS!

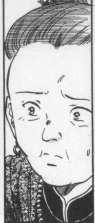

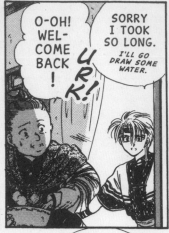

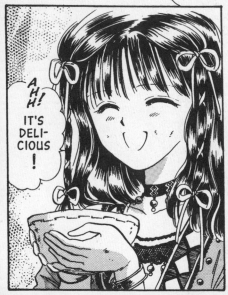

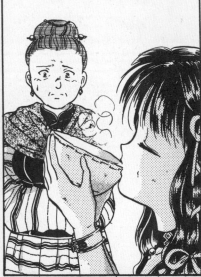

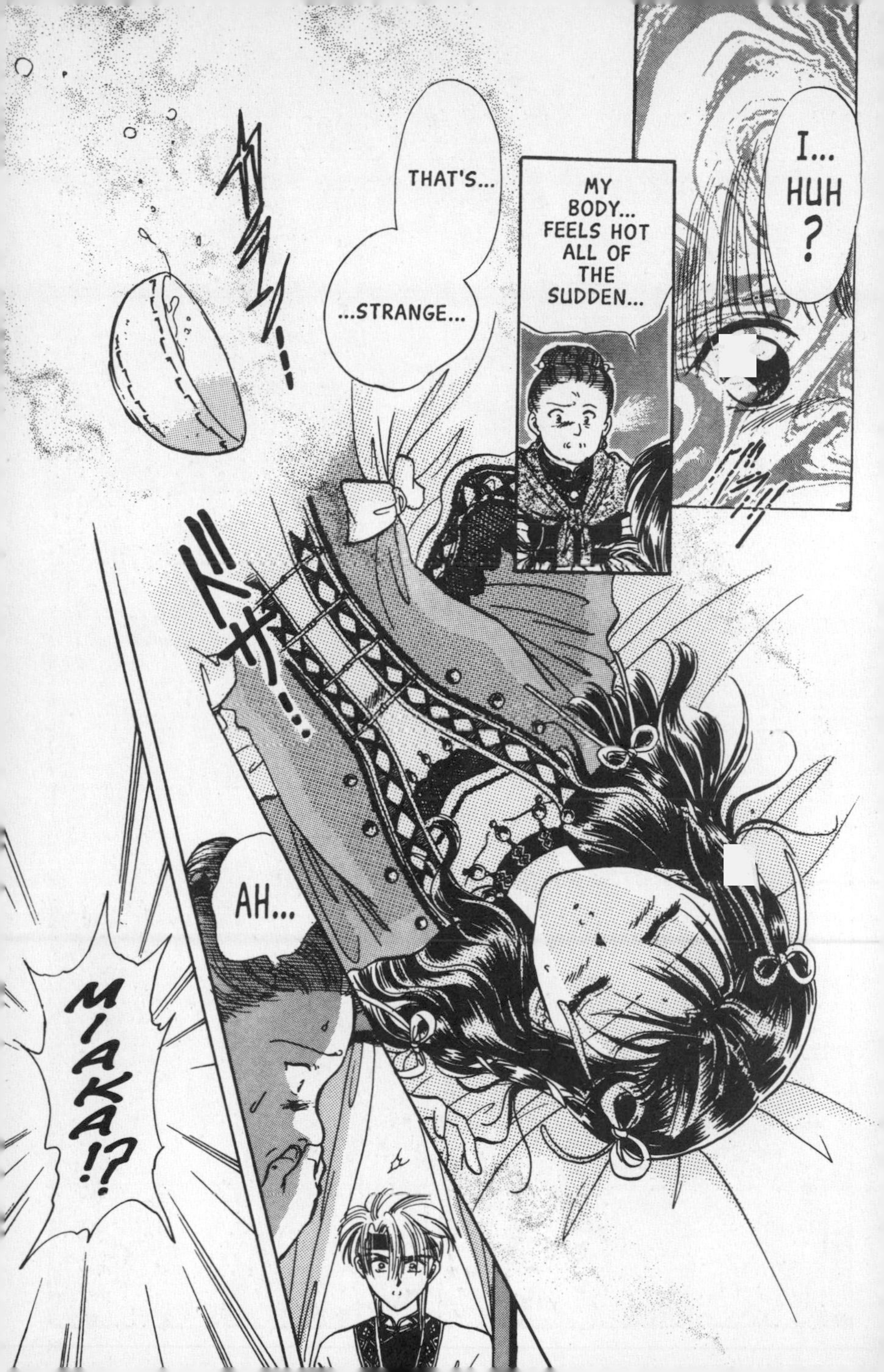
I... HUH?
MY BODY... FEELS HOT ALL OF THE SUDDEN...
THAT'S... ...STRANGE...
AH...
MIAKA!?

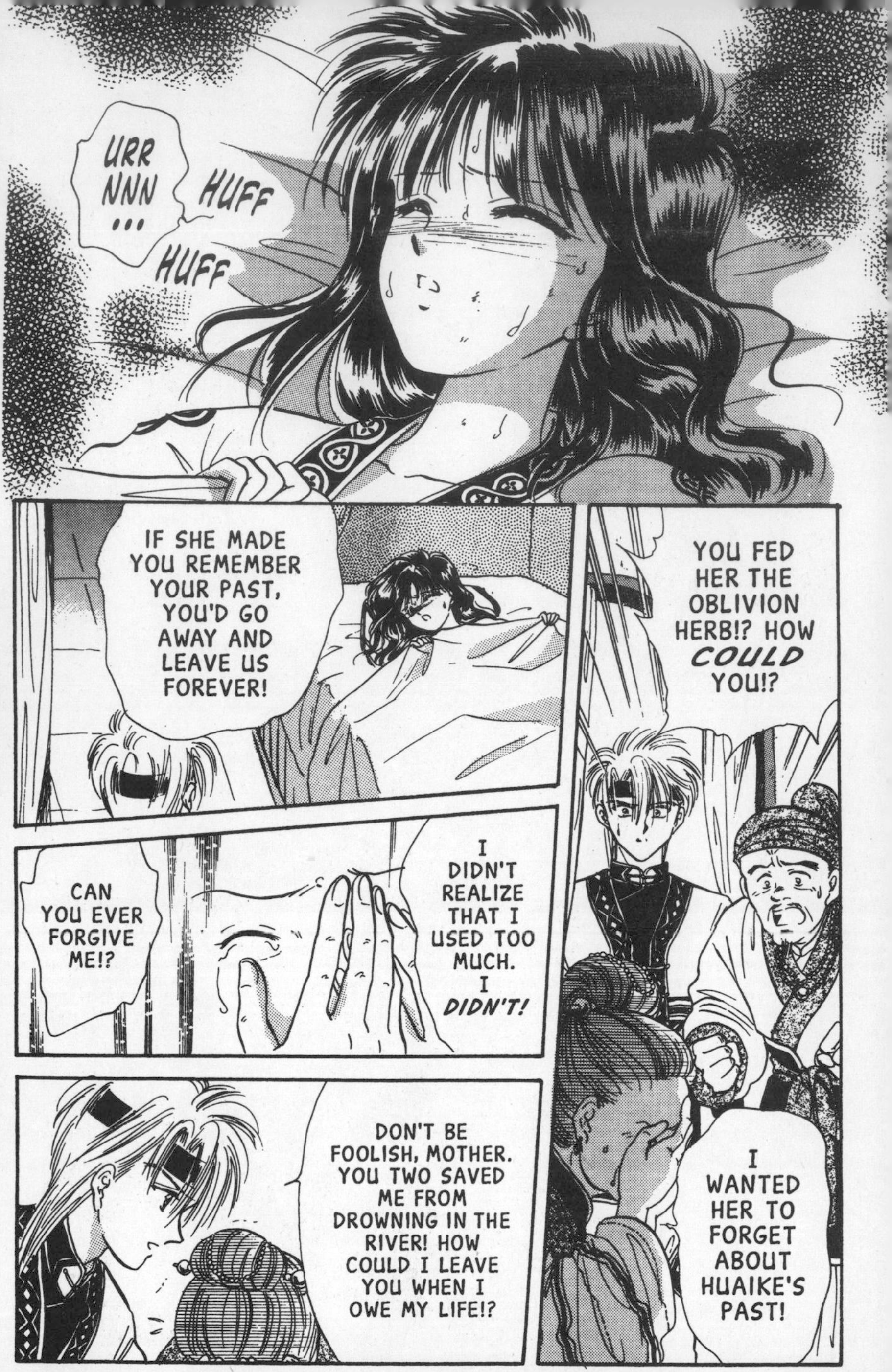
URR NNN ...
HUFF
HUFF
YOU FED HER THE OBLIVION HERB!? HOW *COULD* YOU!?
I WANTED HER TO FORGET ABOUT HUAIKE'S PAST!
IF SHE MADE YOU REMEMBER YOUR PAST, YOU'D GO AWAY AND LEAVE US FOREVER!
I DIDN'T REALIZE THAT I USED TOO MUCH. I *DIDN'T!*
CAN YOU EVER FORGIVE ME!?
DON'T BE FOOLISH, MOTHER. YOU TWO SAVED ME FROM DROWNING IN THE RIVER! HOW COULD I LEAVE YOU WHEN I OWE MY LIFE!?

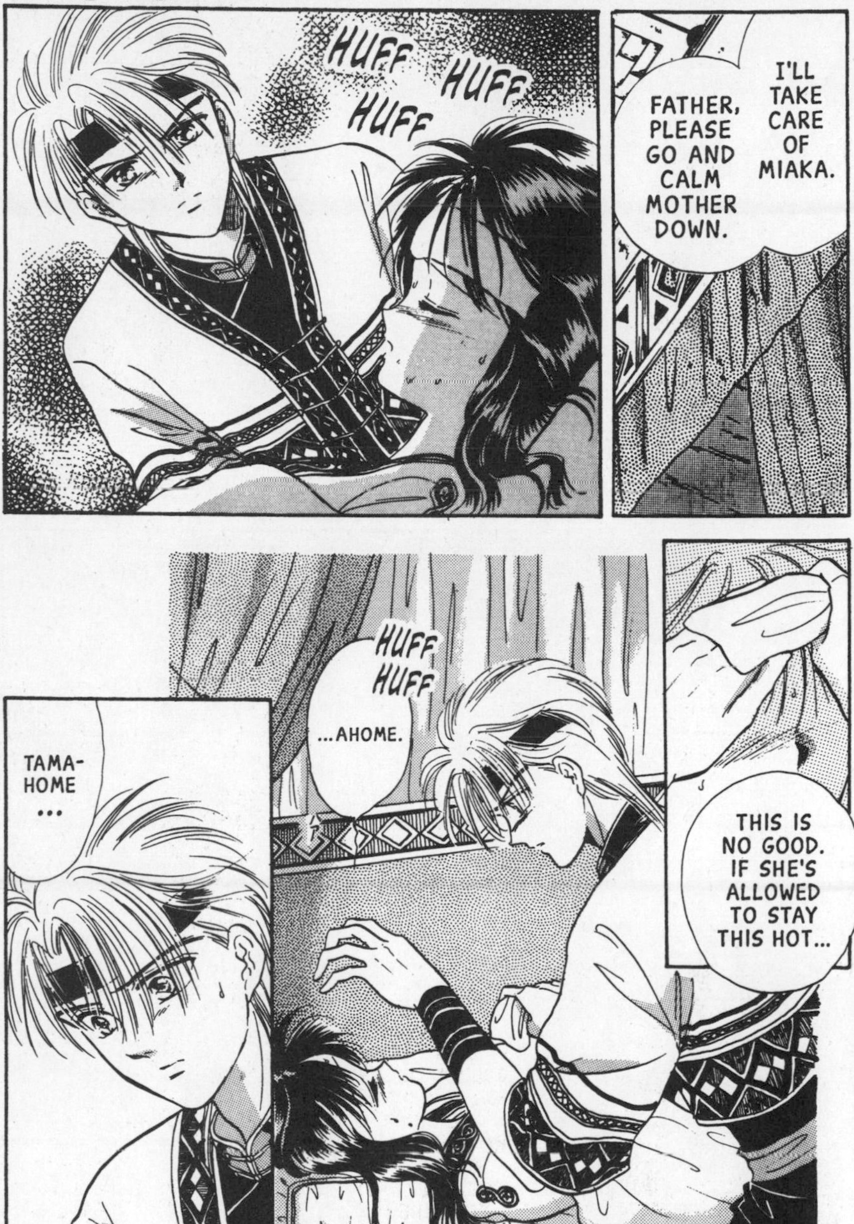
FATHER, PLEASE GO AND CALM MOTHER DOWN. I'LL TAKE CARE OF MIAKA.
HUFF HUFF HUFF
THIS IS NO GOOD. IF SHE'S ALLOWED TO STAY THIS HOT...
HUFF HUFF
...AHOME.
TAMA-HOME ...

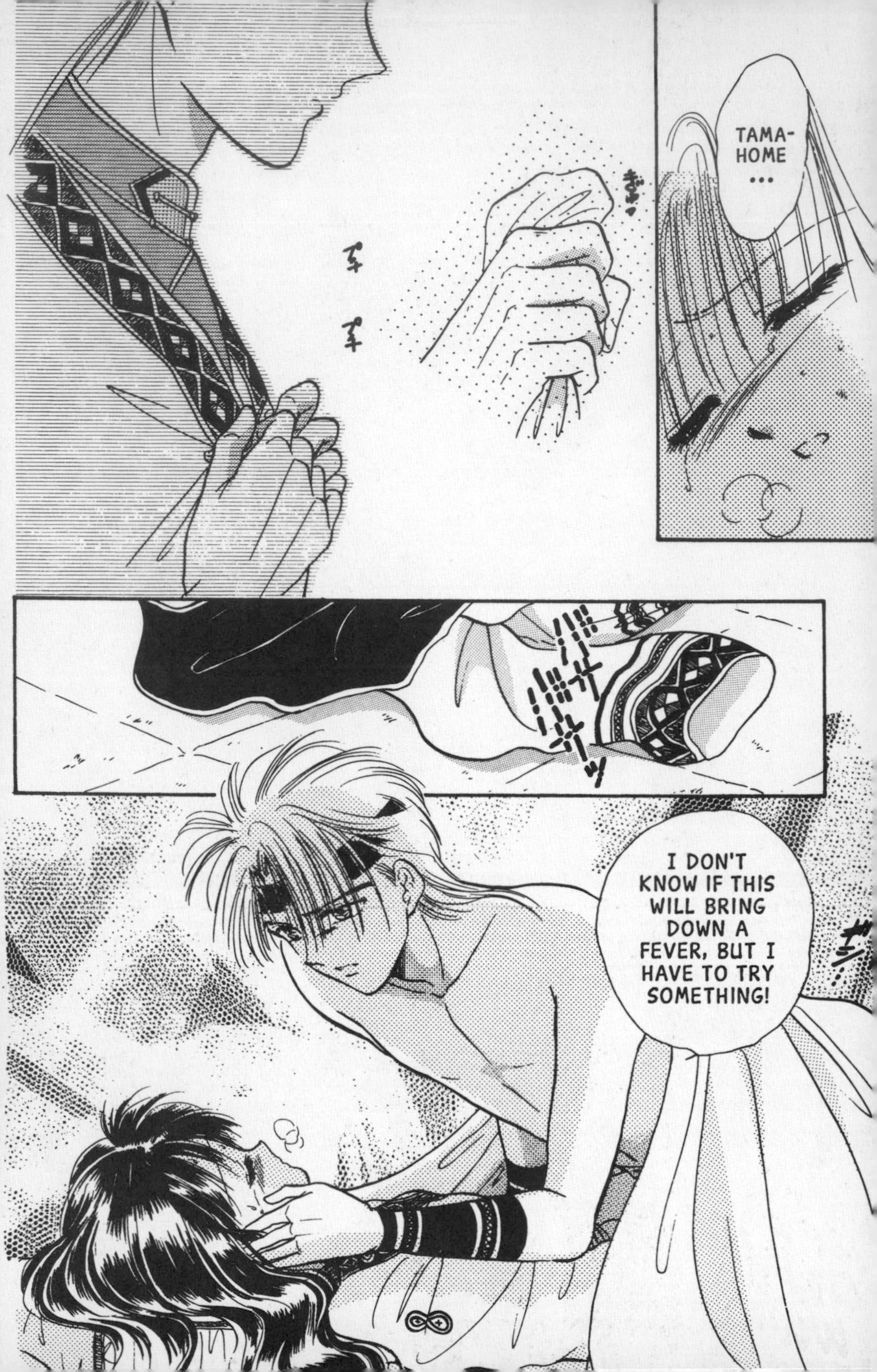
TAMA-HOME ...
I DON'T KNOW IF THIS WILL BRING DOWN A FEVER, BUT I HAVE TO TRY SOMETHING!

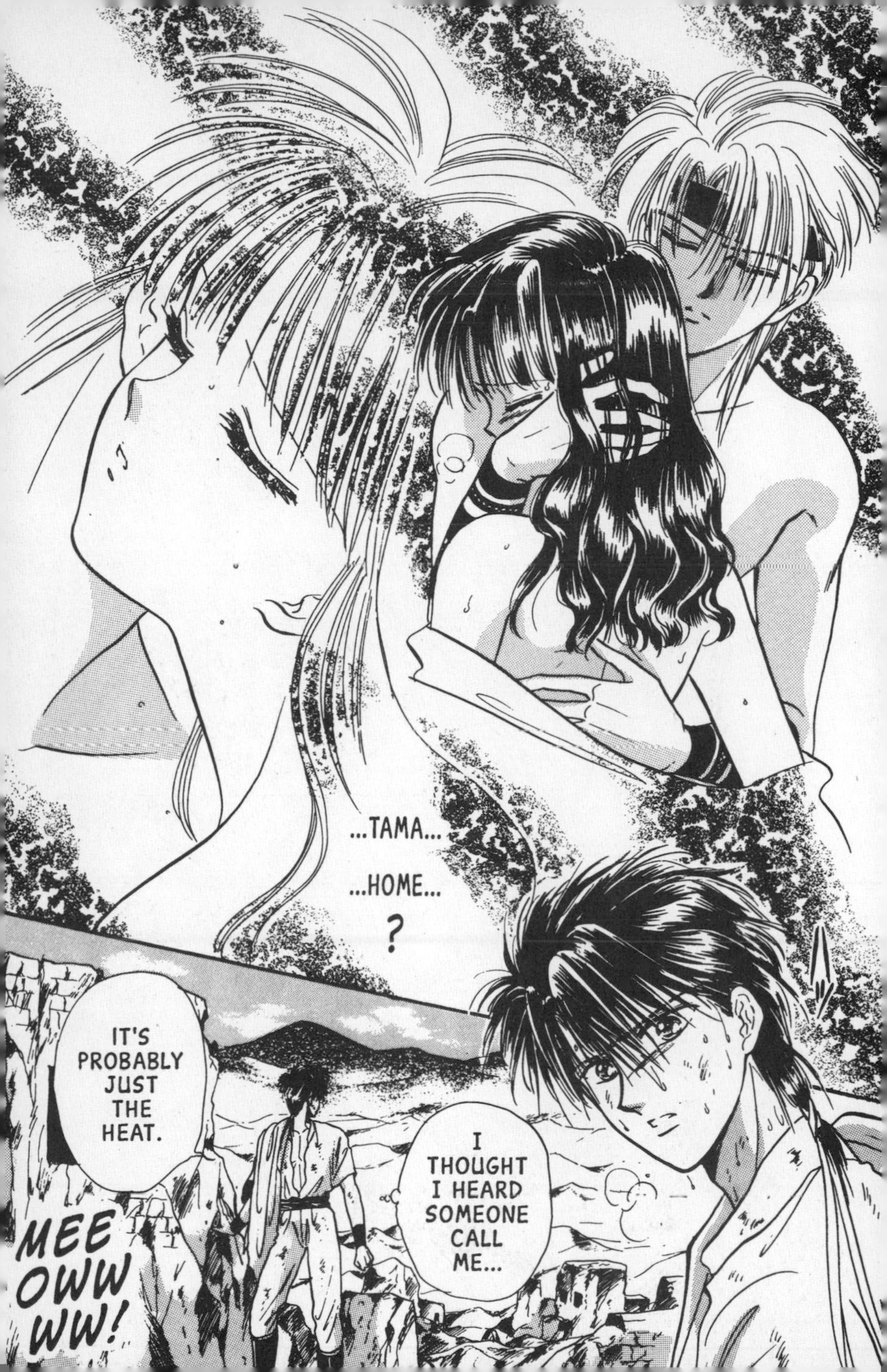
...TAMA...
...HOME...
?
I THOUGHT I HEARD SOMEONE CALL ME...
IT'S PROBABLY JUST THE HEAT.
MEE OWW WW!

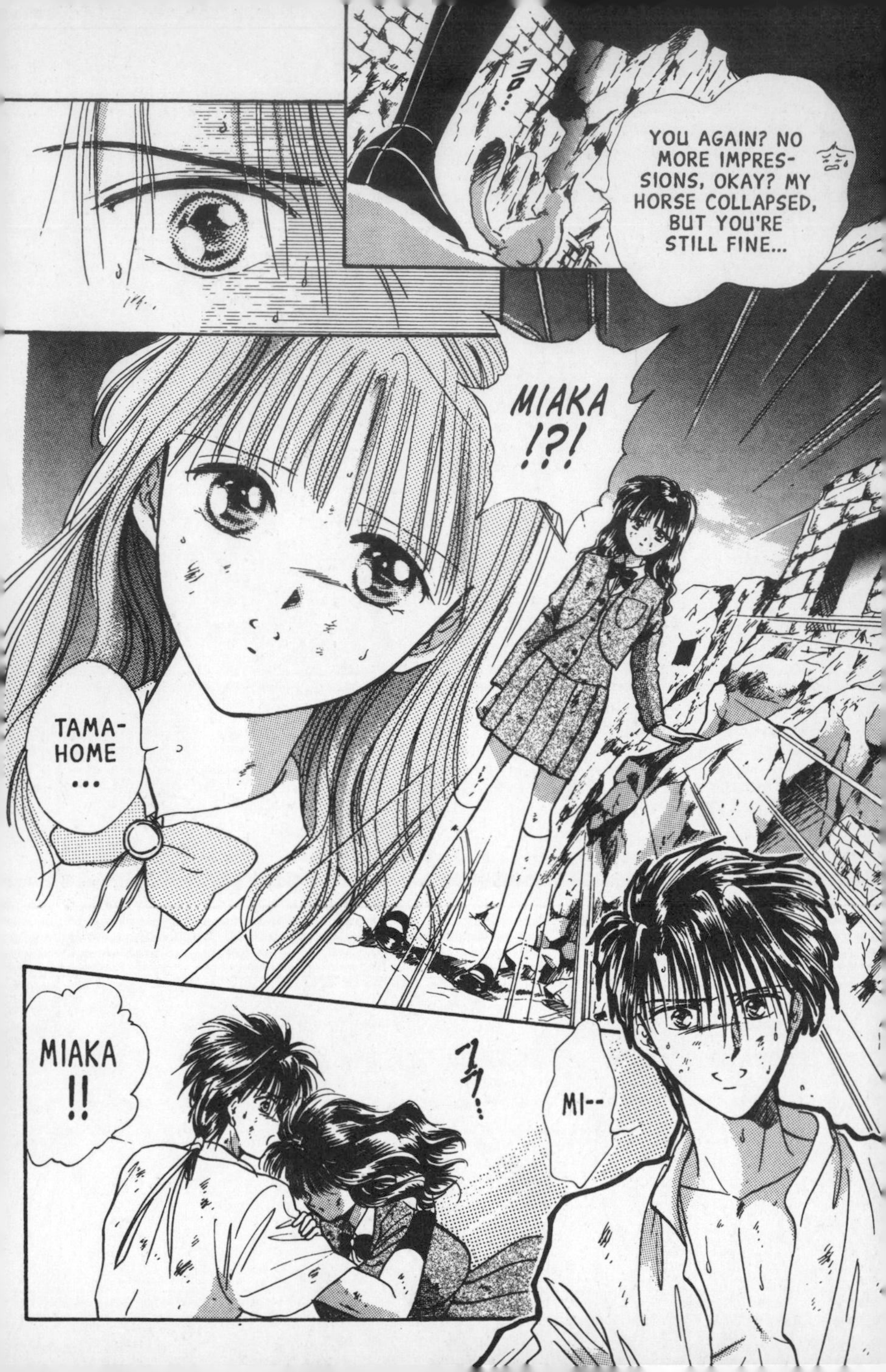
YOU AGAIN? NO MORE IMPRES- SIONS, OKAY? MY HORSE COLLAPSED, BUT YOU'RE STILL FINE...
MIAKA !?!
TAMA- HOME ...
MI--
MIAKA !!

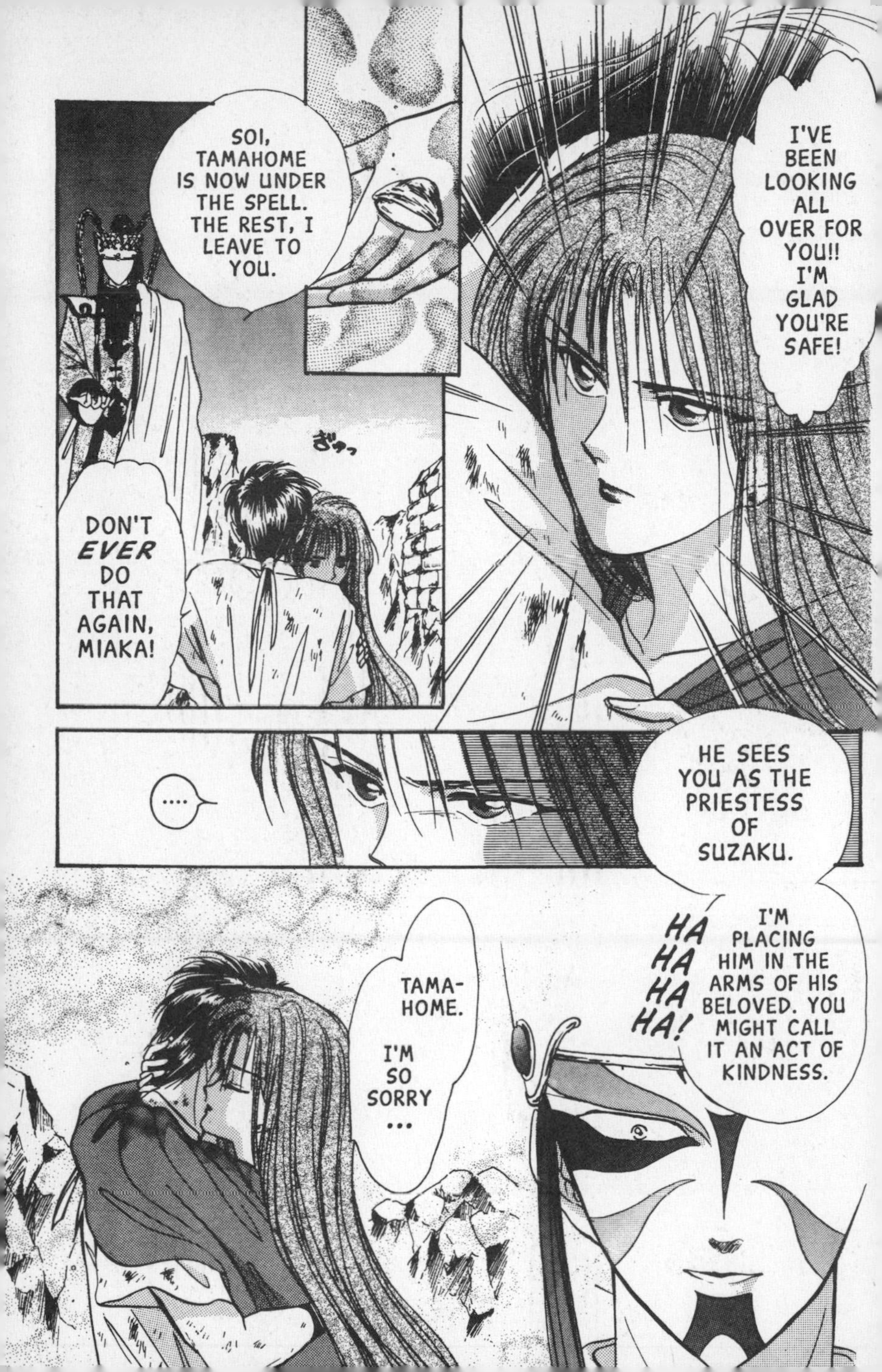
I'VE BEEN LOOKING ALL OVER FOR YOU!! I'M GLAD YOU'RE SAFE!
SOI, TAMAHOME IS NOW UNDER THE SPELL. THE REST, I LEAVE TO YOU.
DON'T *EVER* DO THAT AGAIN, MIAKA!
HE SEES YOU AS THE PRIESTESS OF SUZAKU.
....
I'M PLACING HIM IN THE ARMS OF HIS BELOVED. YOU MIGHT CALL IT AN ACT OF KINDNESS.
HA HA HA HA!
TAMA-HOME.
I'M SO SORRY ...

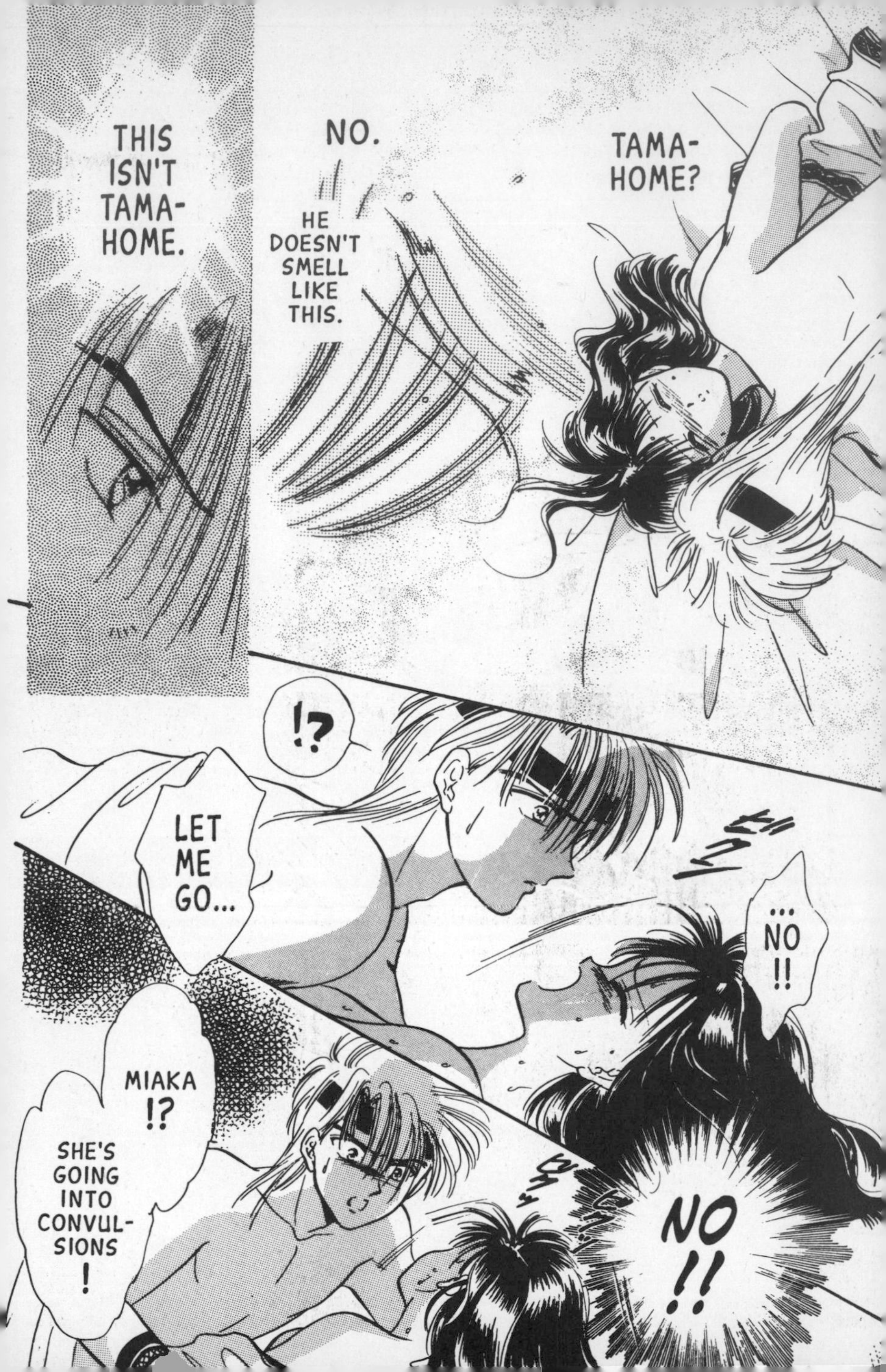
TAMA-HOME?
NO.
HE DOESN'T SMELL LIKE THIS.
THIS ISN'T TAMA-HOME.
!?
...NO!!
LET ME GO...
NO!!
MIAKA!?
SHE'S GOING INTO CONVULSIONS!

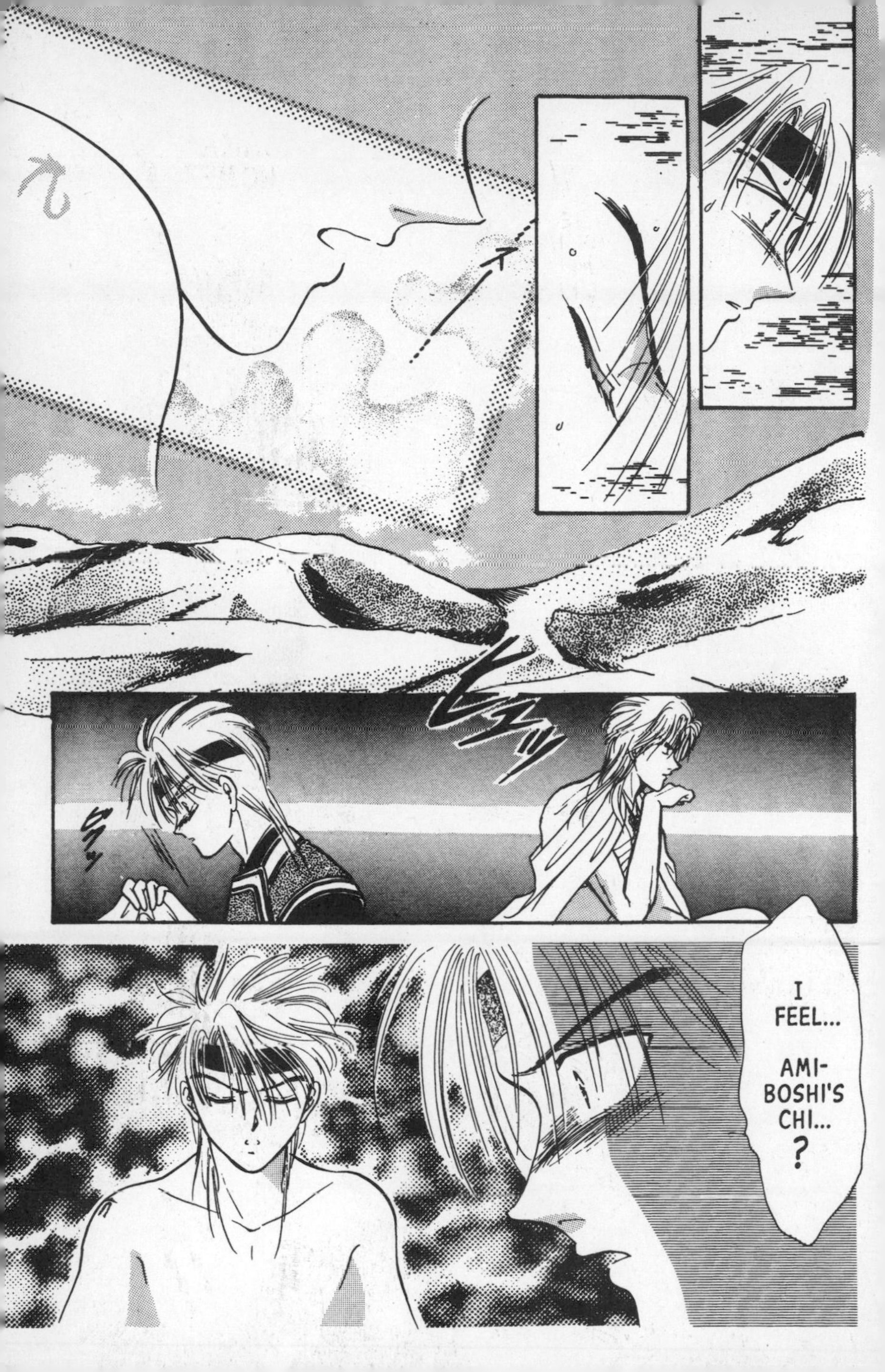
I FEEL...
AMI-BOSHI'S CHI...
?

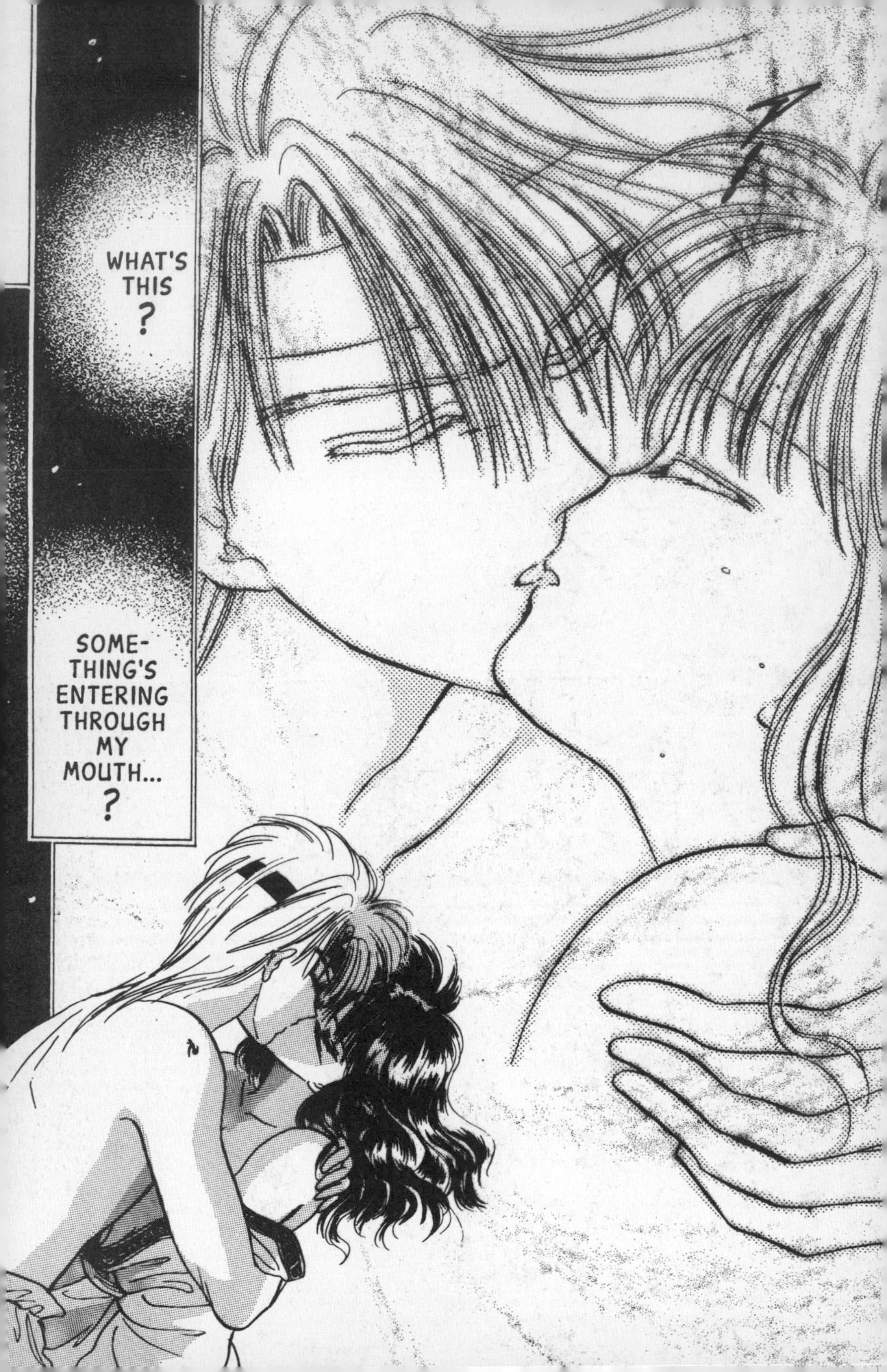
WHAT'S THIS ?
SOME-THING'S ENTERING THROUGH MY MOUTH...?

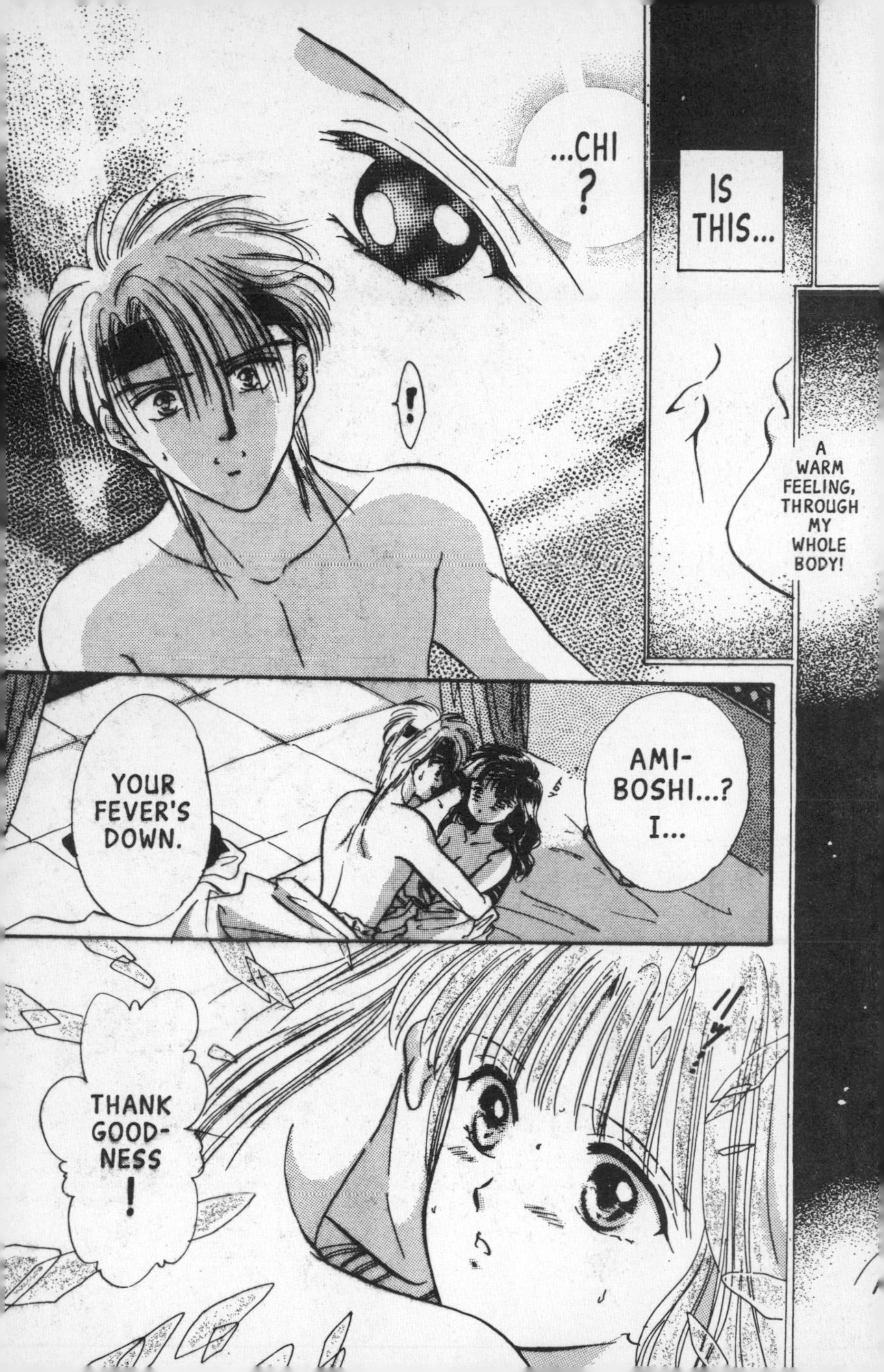
IS THIS...
A WARM FEELING, THROUGH MY WHOLE BODY!
...CHI?
!
AMI-BOSHI...? I...
YOUR FEVER'S DOWN.
THANK GOOD-NESS!

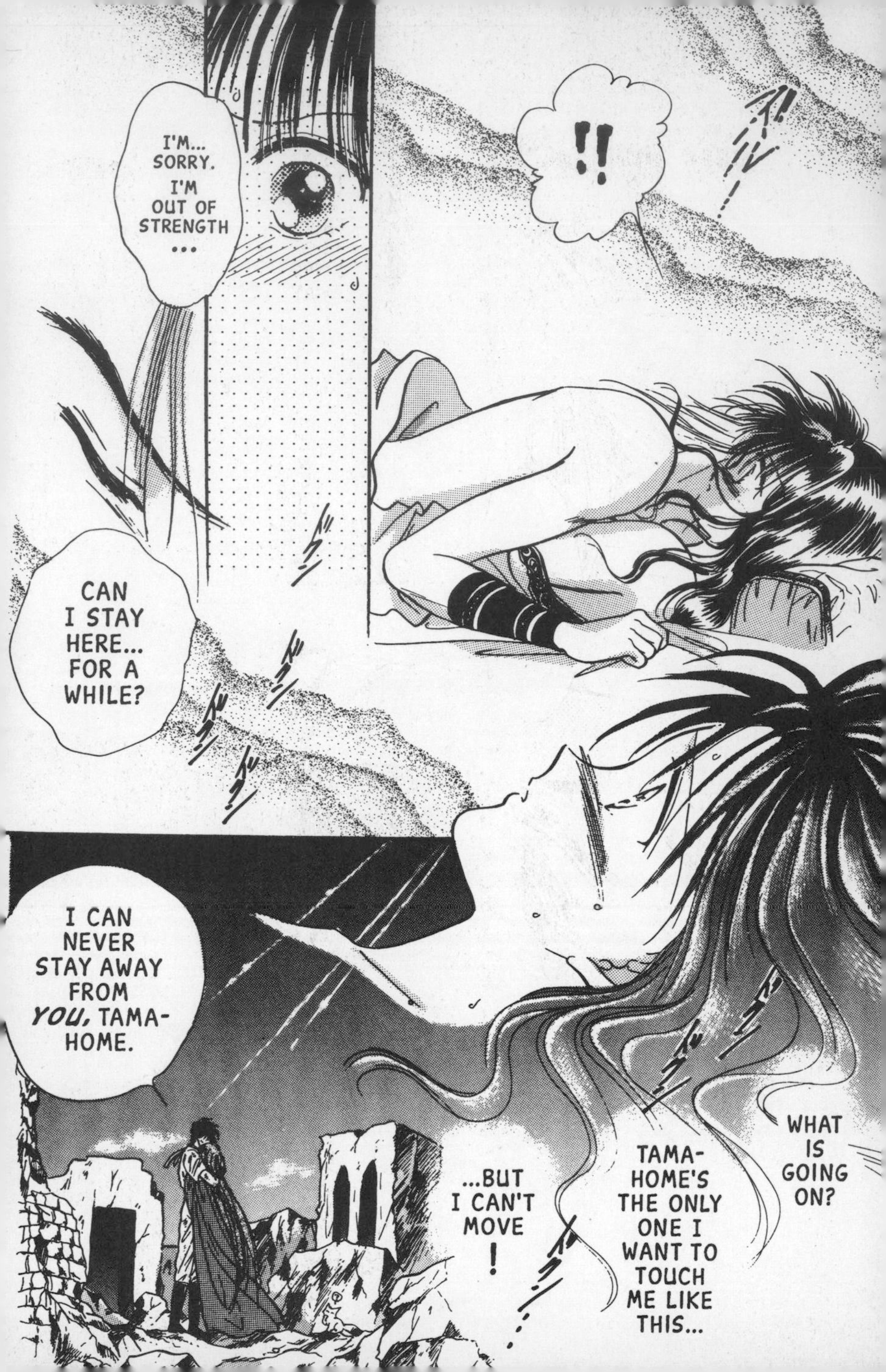
!!
I'M... SORRY. I'M OUT OF STRENGTH...
CAN I STAY HERE... FOR A WHILE?
WHAT IS GOING ON?
TAMA-HOME'S THE ONLY ONE I WANT TO TOUCH ME LIKE THIS...
...BUT I CAN'T MOVE!
I CAN NEVER STAY AWAY FROM *YOU,* TAMA-HOME.

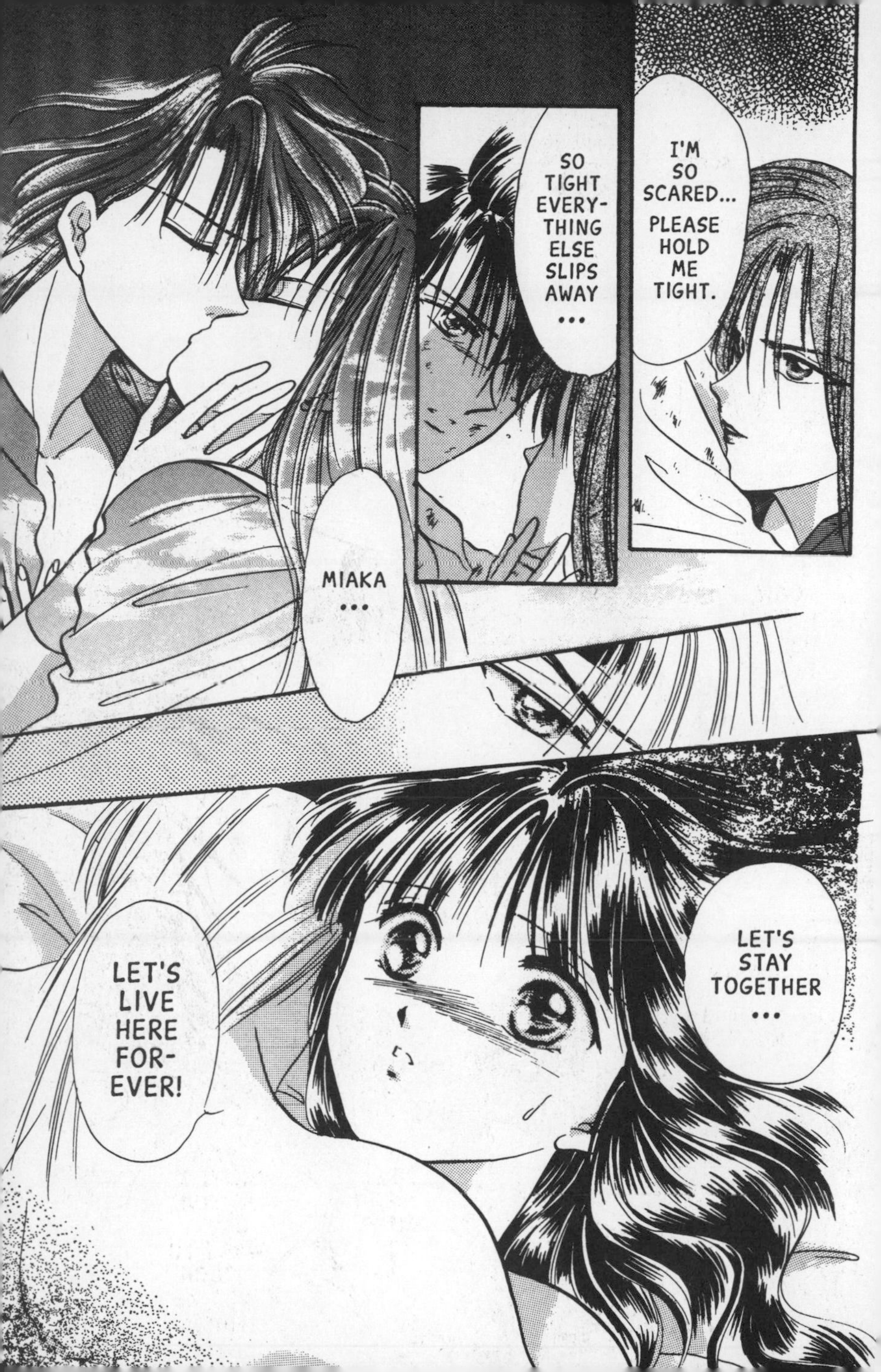
I'M SO SCARED... PLEASE HOLD ME TIGHT.
SO TIGHT EVERYTHING ELSE SLIPS AWAY...
MIAKA...
LET'S STAY TOGETHER...
LET'S LIVE HERE FOREVER!

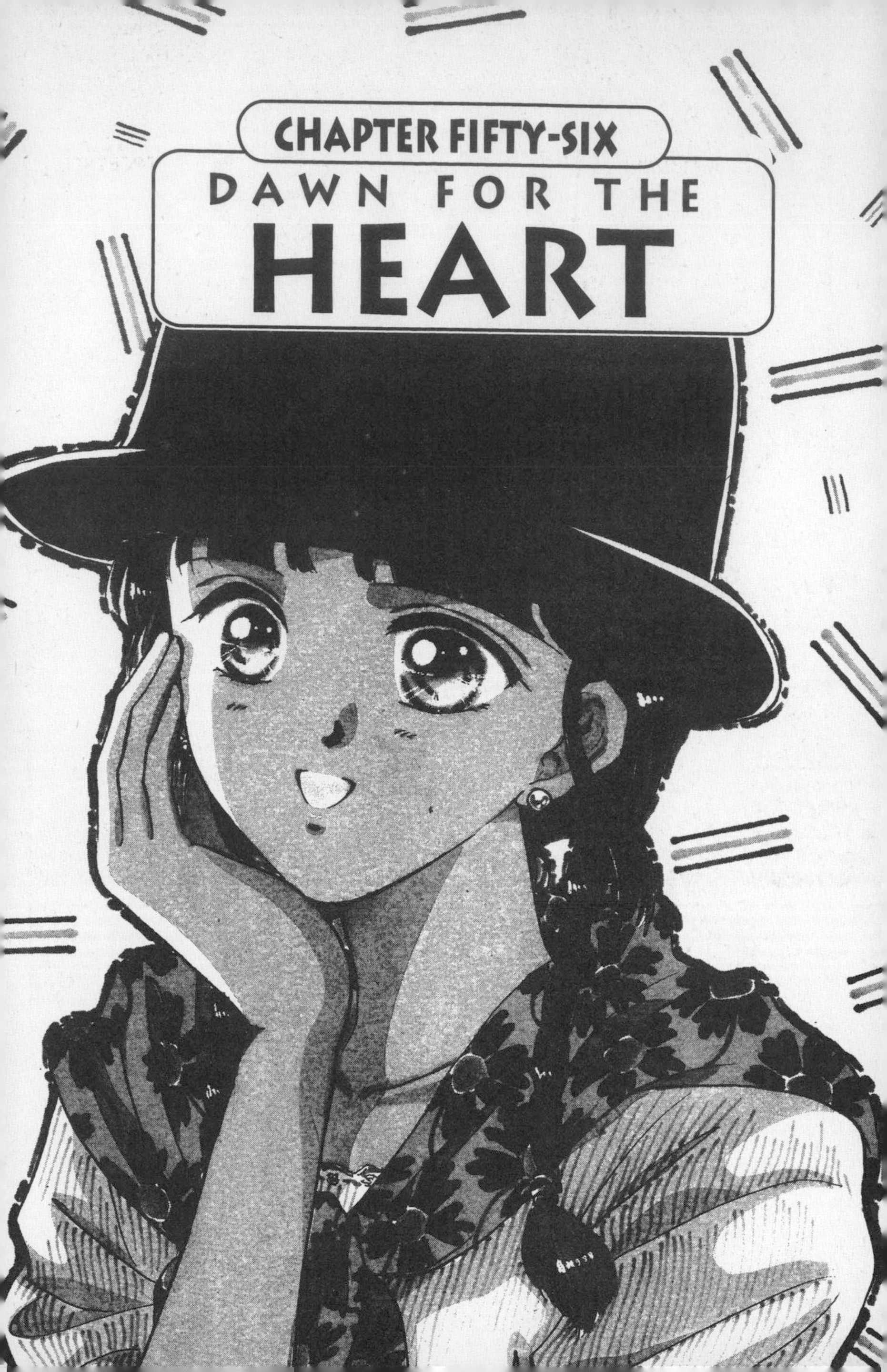
CHAPTER FIFTY-SIX
DAWN FOR THE
HEART

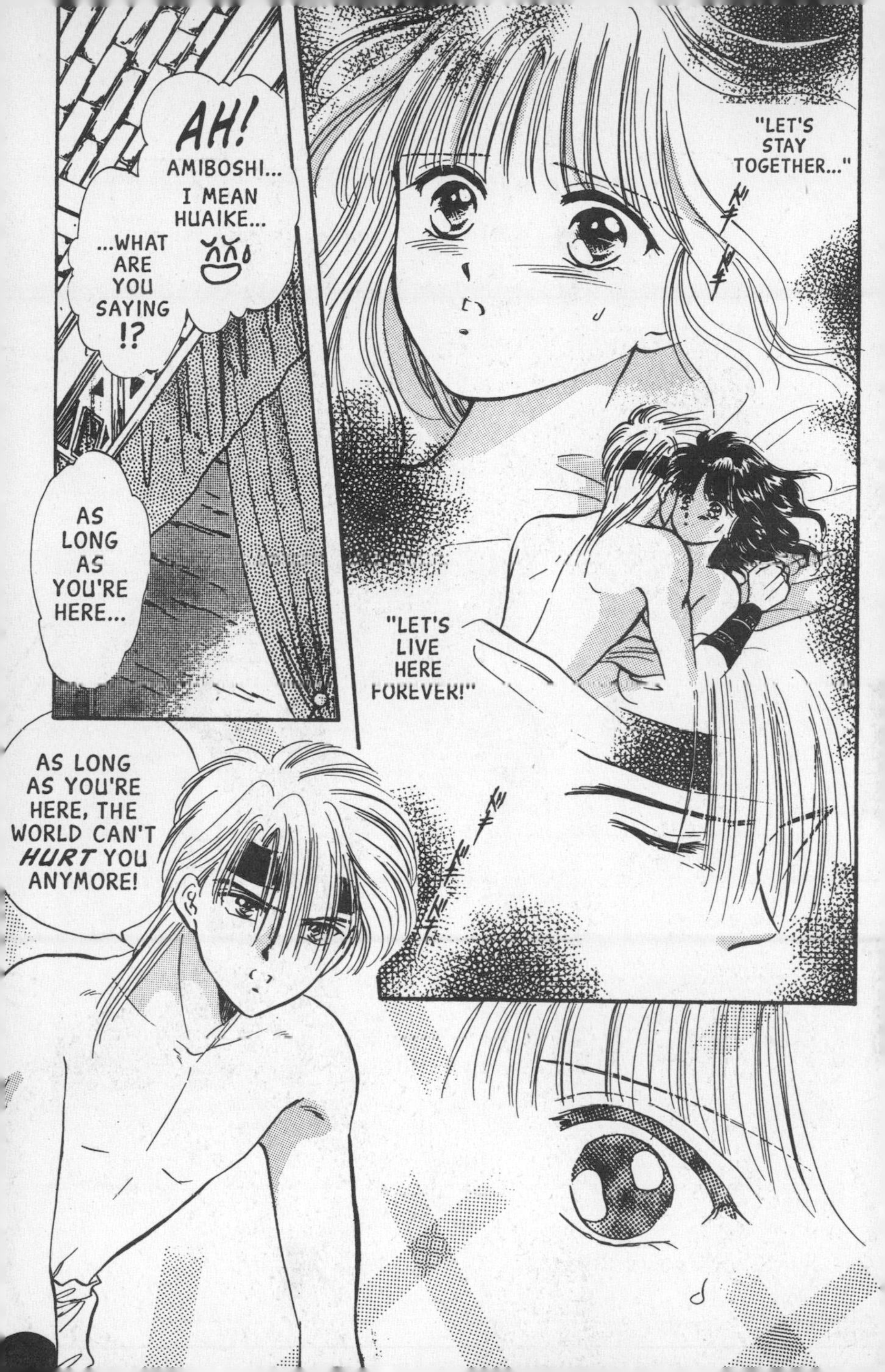
"LET'S STAY TOGETHER..."
"LET'S LIVE HERE FOREVER!"
AH! AMIBOSHI... I MEAN HUAIKE...
...WHAT ARE YOU SAYING!?
AS LONG AS YOU'RE HERE...
AS LONG AS YOU'RE HERE, THE WORLD CAN'T *HURT* YOU ANYMORE!

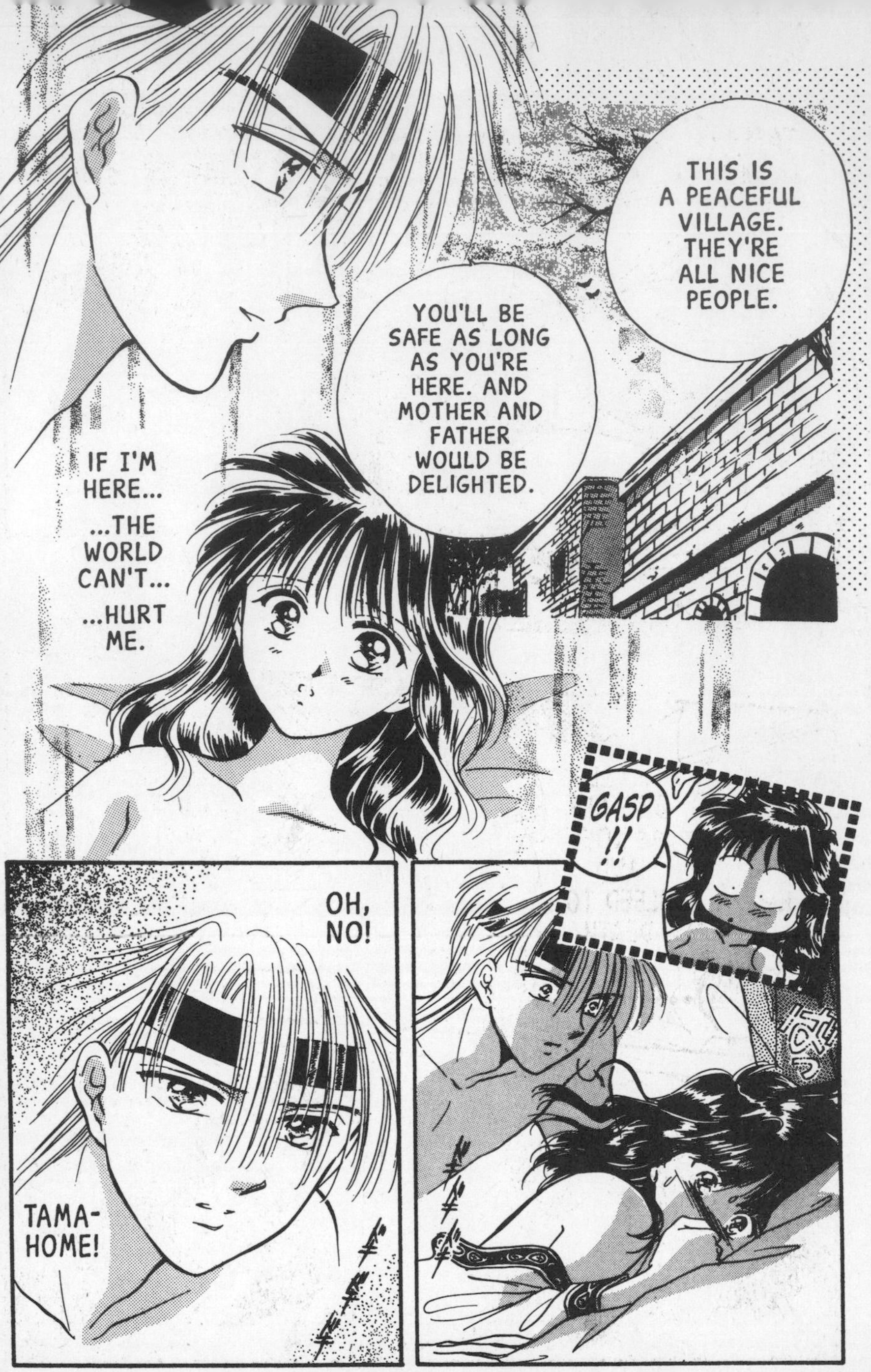
THIS IS A PEACEFUL VILLAGE. THEY'RE ALL NICE PEOPLE.
YOU'LL BE SAFE AS LONG AS YOU'RE HERE. AND MOTHER AND FATHER WOULD BE DELIGHTED.
IF I'M HERE...
...THE WORLD CAN'T...
...HURT ME.
GASP !!
OH, NO!
TAMA-HOME!

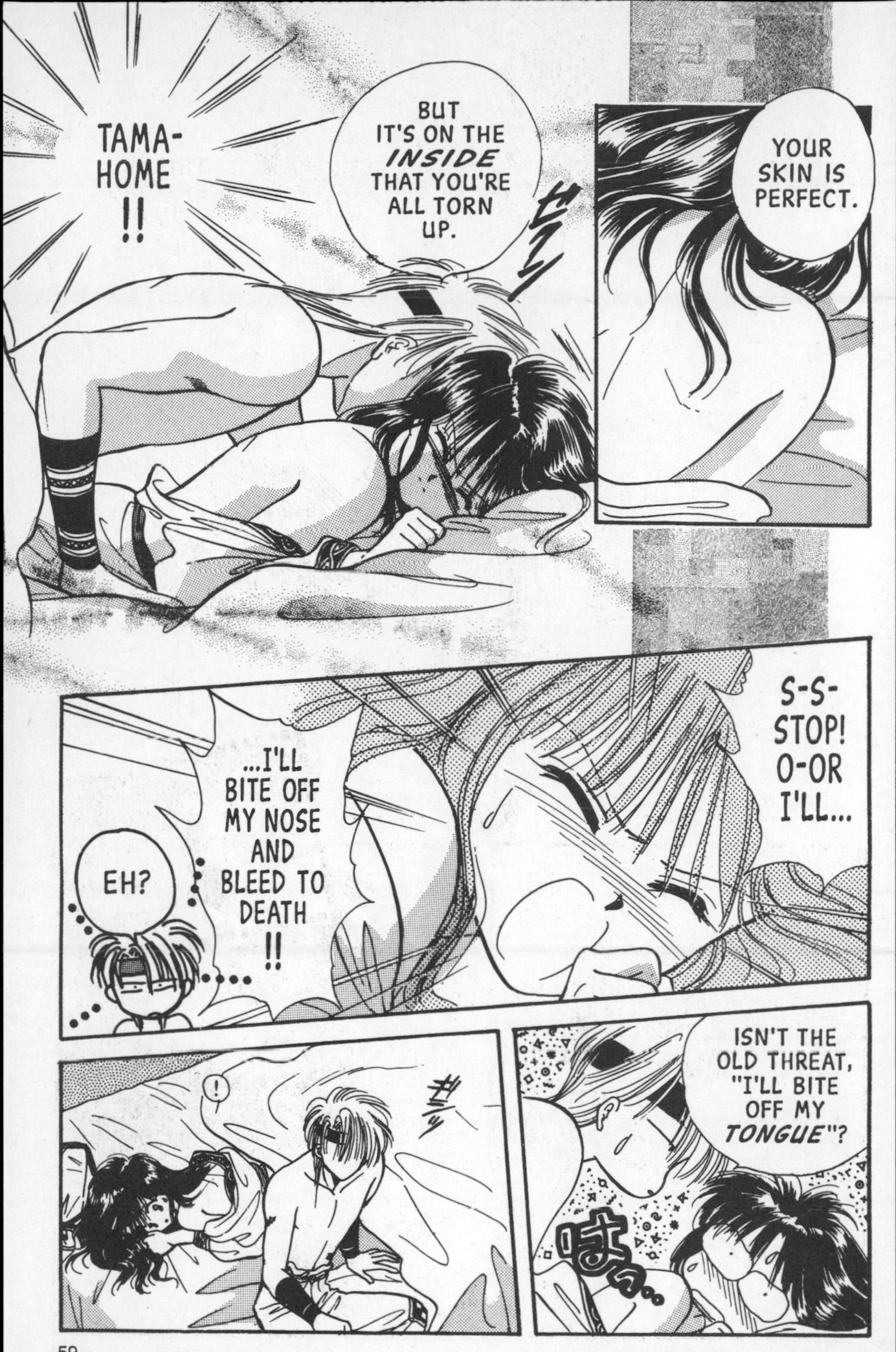
YOUR SKIN IS PERFECT.
BUT IT'S ON THE *INSIDE* THAT YOU'RE ALL TORN UP.
TAMA-HOME !!
S-S-STOP! O-OR I'LL...
...I'LL BITE OFF MY NOSE AND BLEED TO DEATH !!
EH?
ISN'T THE OLD THREAT, "I'LL BITE OFF MY *TONGUE*"?
!

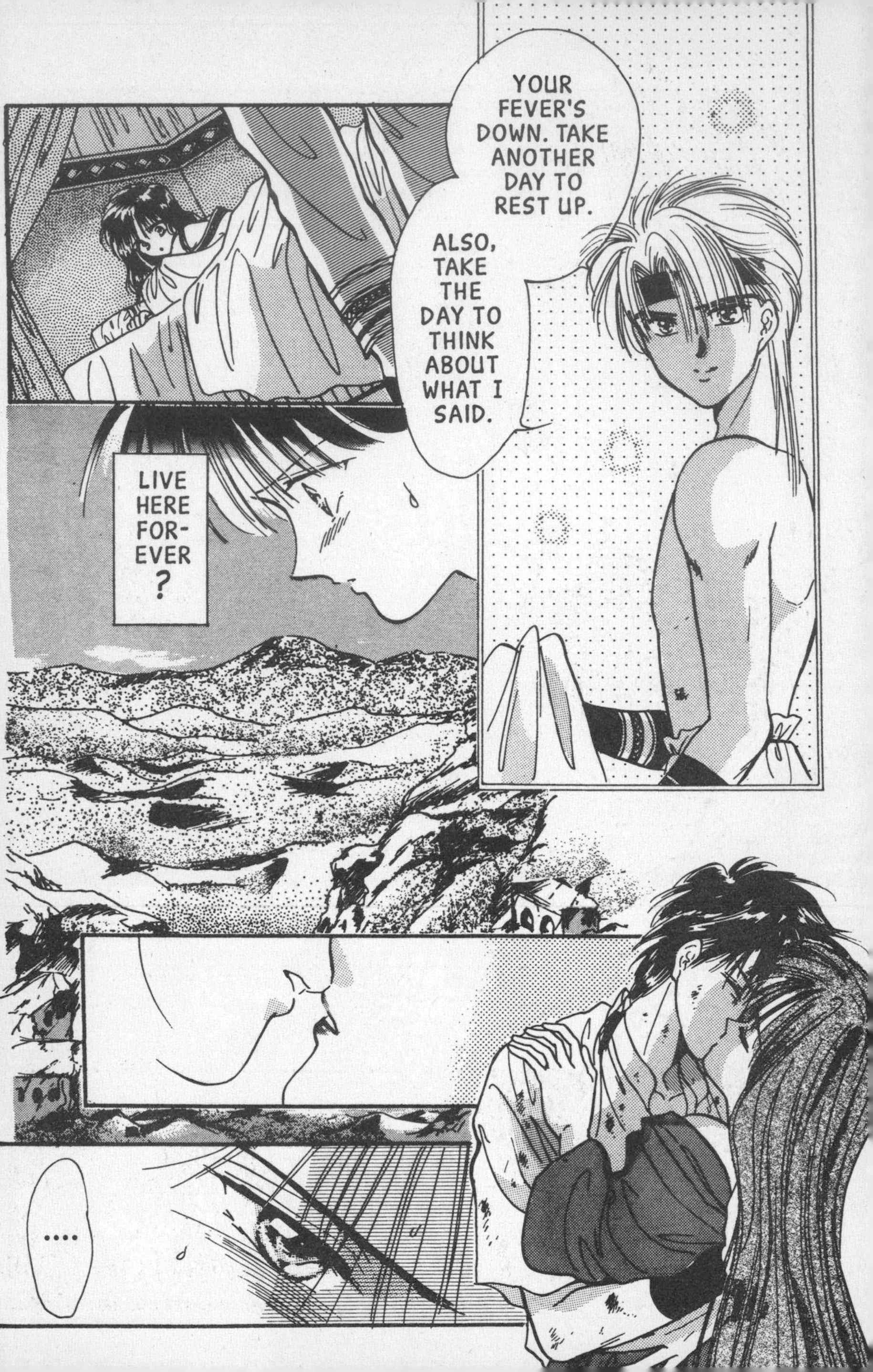
YOUR FEVER'S DOWN. TAKE ANOTHER DAY TO REST UP.
ALSO, TAKE THE DAY TO THINK ABOUT WHAT I SAID.
LIVE HERE FOR-EVER ?
....

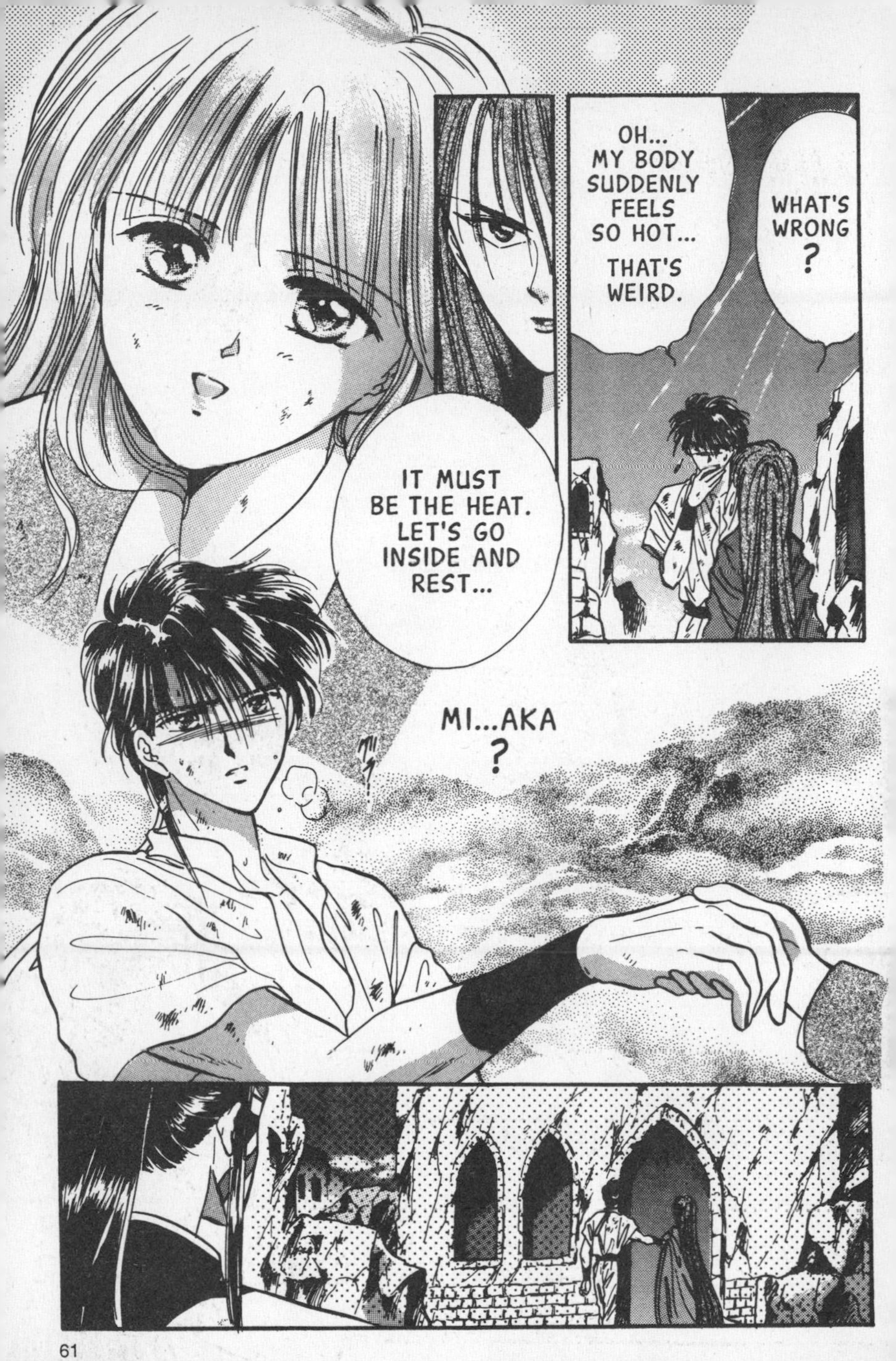
WHAT'S WRONG?
OH... MY BODY SUDDENLY FEELS SO HOT... THAT'S WEIRD.
IT MUST BE THE HEAT. LET'S GO INSIDE AND REST...
MI...AKA?

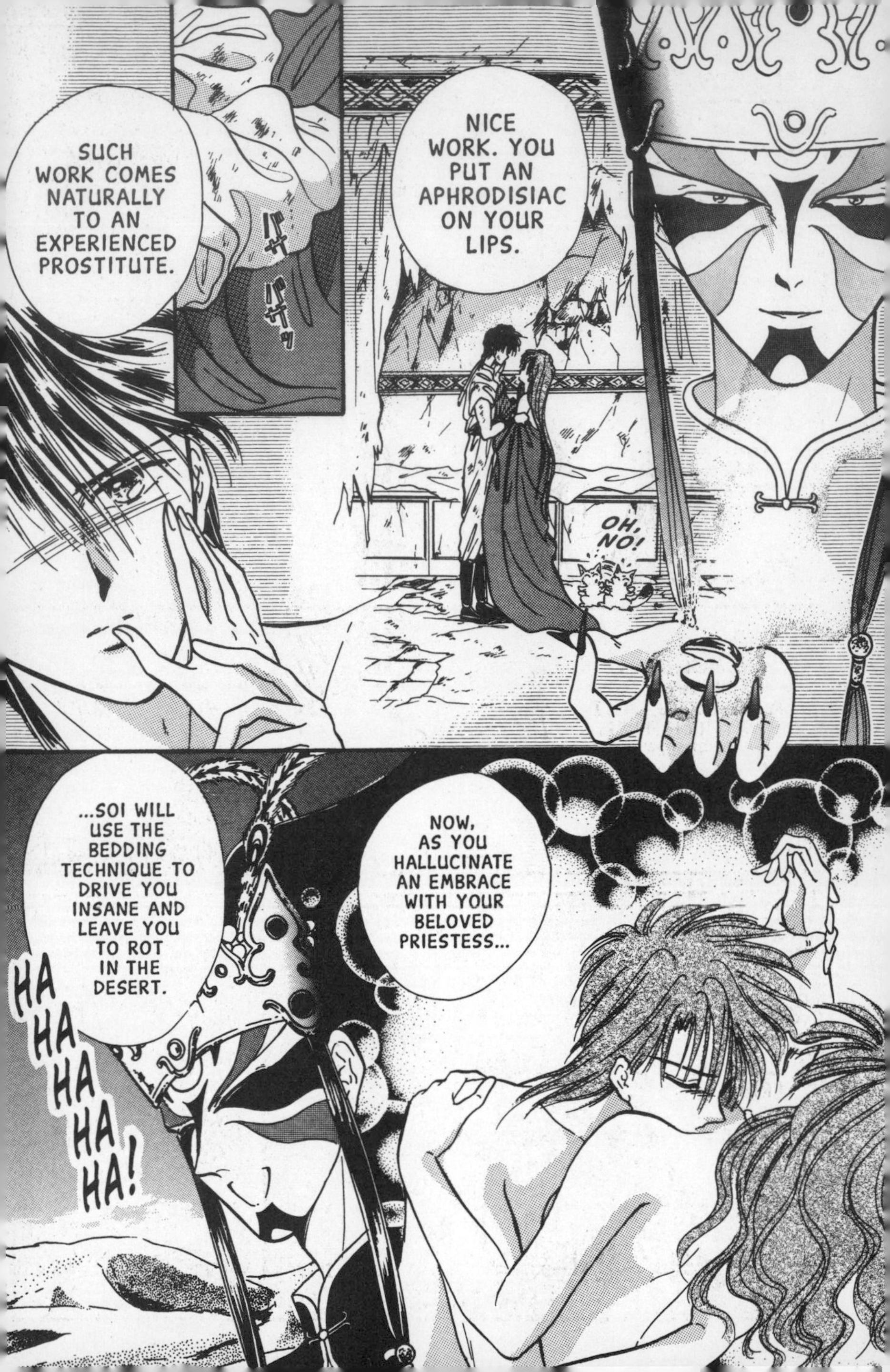
NICE WORK. YOU PUT AN APHRODISIAC ON YOUR LIPS.
OH, NO!
パサ
パサッ
SUCH WORK COMES NATURALLY TO AN EXPERIENCED PROSTITUTE.
NOW, AS YOU HALLUCINATE AN EMBRACE WITH YOUR BELOVED PRIESTESS...
...SOI WILL USE THE BEDDING TECHNIQUE TO DRIVE YOU INSANE AND LEAVE YOU TO ROT IN THE DESERT.
HA HA HA HA HA HA!

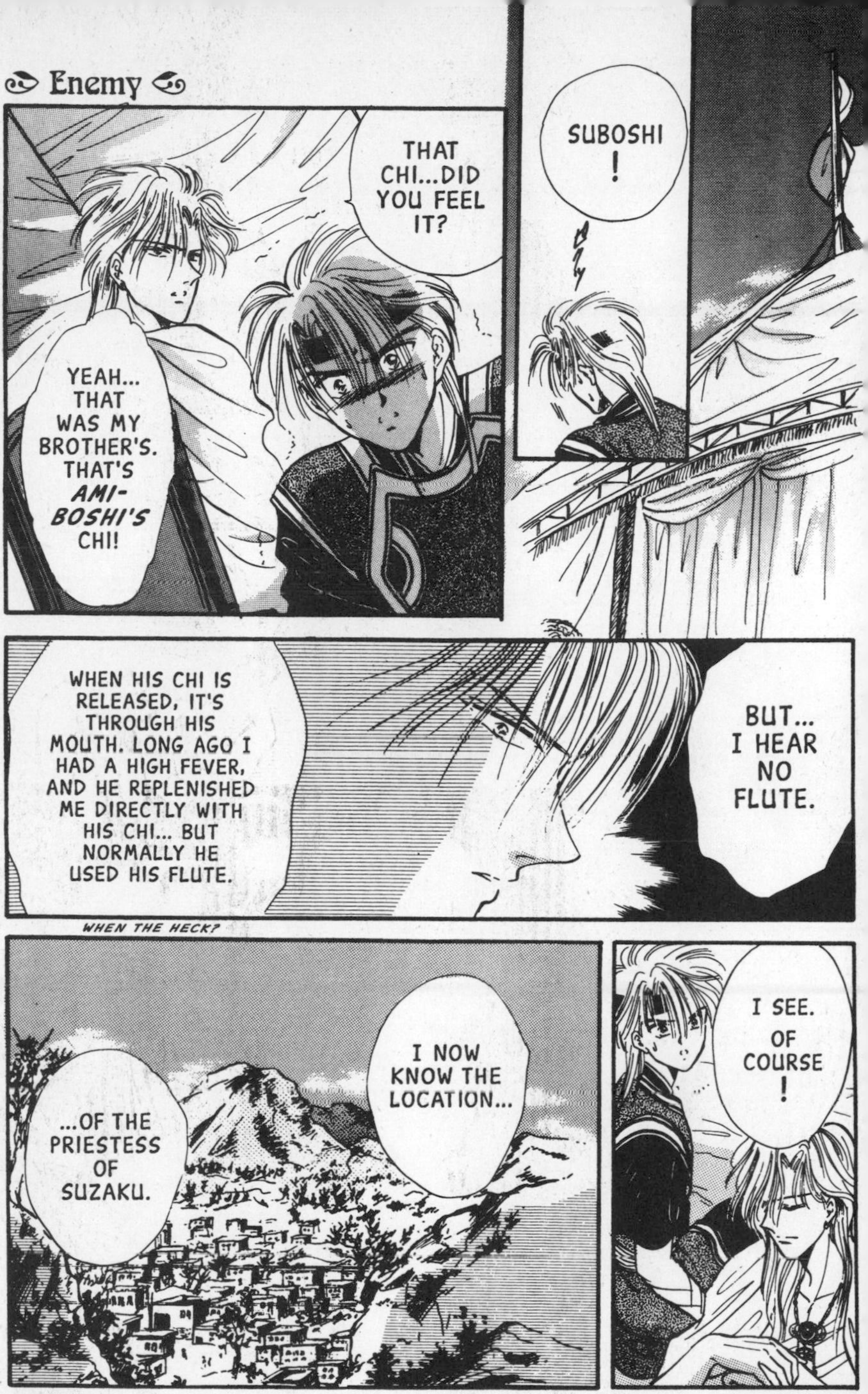
SUBOSHI!
THAT CHI...DID YOU FEEL IT?
YEAH... THAT WAS MY BROTHER'S. THAT'S *AMI-BOSHI'S* CHI!
BUT... I HEAR NO FLUTE.
WHEN HIS CHI IS RELEASED, IT'S THROUGH HIS MOUTH. LONG AGO I HAD A HIGH FEVER, AND HE REPLENISHED ME DIRECTLY WITH HIS CHI... BUT NORMALLY HE USED HIS FLUTE.
WHEN THE HECK?
I SEE. OF COURSE!
I NOW KNOW THE LOCATION...
...OF THE PRIESTESS OF SUZAKU.

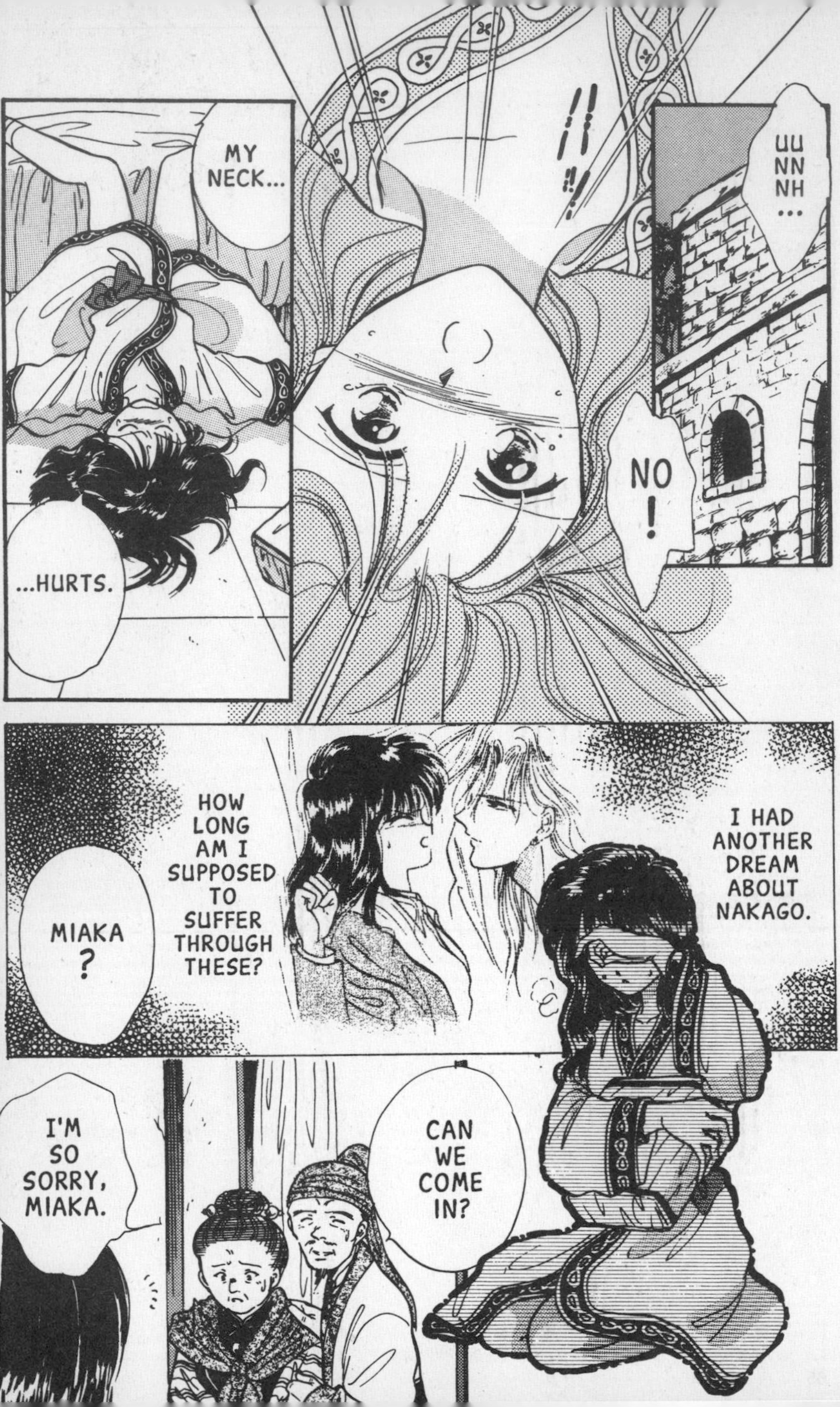
UUNNNH...
NO!
MY NECK...
...HURTS.
I HAD ANOTHER DREAM ABOUT NAKAGO.
HOW LONG AM I SUPPOSED TO SUFFER THROUGH THESE?
MIAKA?
CAN WE COME IN?
I'M SO SORRY, MIAKA.

(Continued)...

Now to continue with the southern Suzaku constellations.

The South had a symbolic meaning for the ancient Chinese emperor. While the Heavenly Ruler (Tai Yi-Jun) took care of the heavens, the earthly emperor was to rule the world from his throne in the south. *H-how lucky can Hotohori get?*

The symbol for the South, the character for "Su" in Suzaku, represented the holy power of eternal life. In other words, the bird of eternal life (the Hō'ō, firebird or Phoenix). Amazingly, it was thought that once Suzaku was summoned, eternal peace would reign over the land!! Is that true, China!? That's the plot of Fushigi Yûgi! I was shocked!

Later this "North Star 28 Constellation Astrology" was applied, not only to the national interests, but to individuals as well. Suzaku guides the fates of love (with the name Hō'ō, the "Hō" part is male, and the "ō" part is female). So the Chinese people used to pray for love to the Suzaku constellations in the south. *Best of luck!*

By the way, I had no idea this kind of astrology even existed in Ancient China. It shocked the heck out of me!

Or maybe it was no coincidence that I chose the Suzaku for Miaka! L-Love? Well, I suppose.

Also, when I began this story, I came up with the characters and assigned each of them to constellations. But much to my surprise, when I casually looked up their meanings, I discovered (this really bowls me over!) that many of the stars corresponded to the characters' personalities!

To be continued...

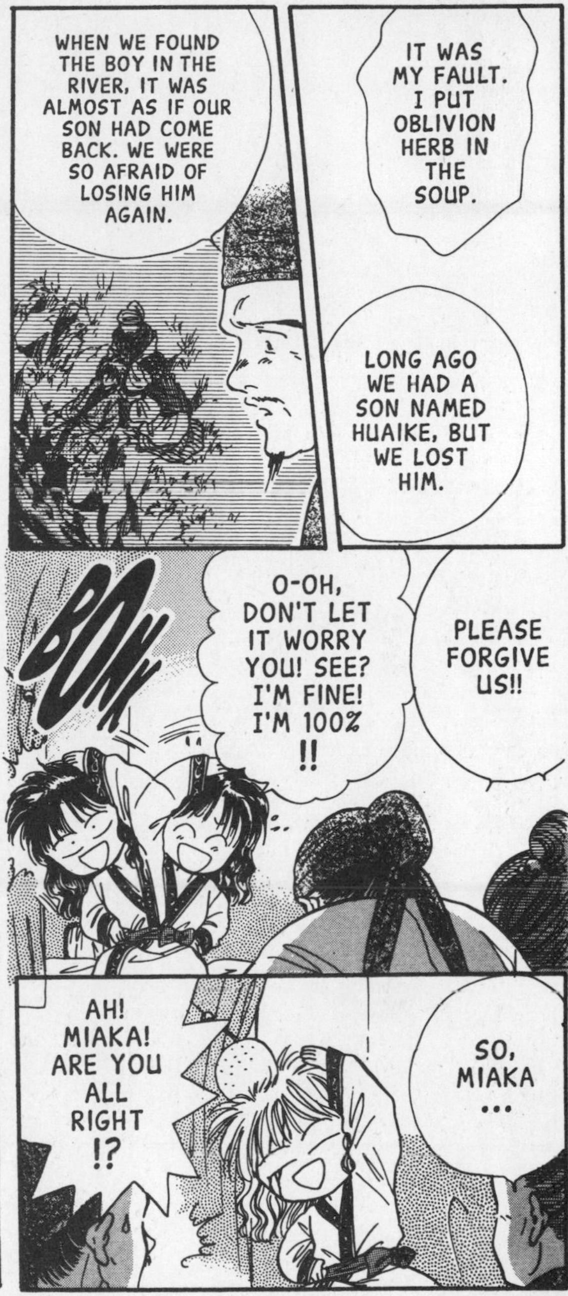
IT WAS MY FAULT. I PUT OBLIVION HERB IN THE SOUP.
LONG AGO WE HAD A SON NAMED HUAIKE, BUT WE LOST HIM.
WHEN WE FOUND THE BOY IN THE RIVER, IT WAS ALMOST AS IF OUR SON HAD COME BACK. WE WERE SO AFRAID OF LOSING HIM AGAIN.
PLEASE FORGIVE US!!
O-OH, DON'T LET IT WORRY YOU! SEE? I'M FINE! I'M 100% !!
BONK
SO, MIAKA ...
AH! MIAKA! ARE YOU ALL RIGHT !?

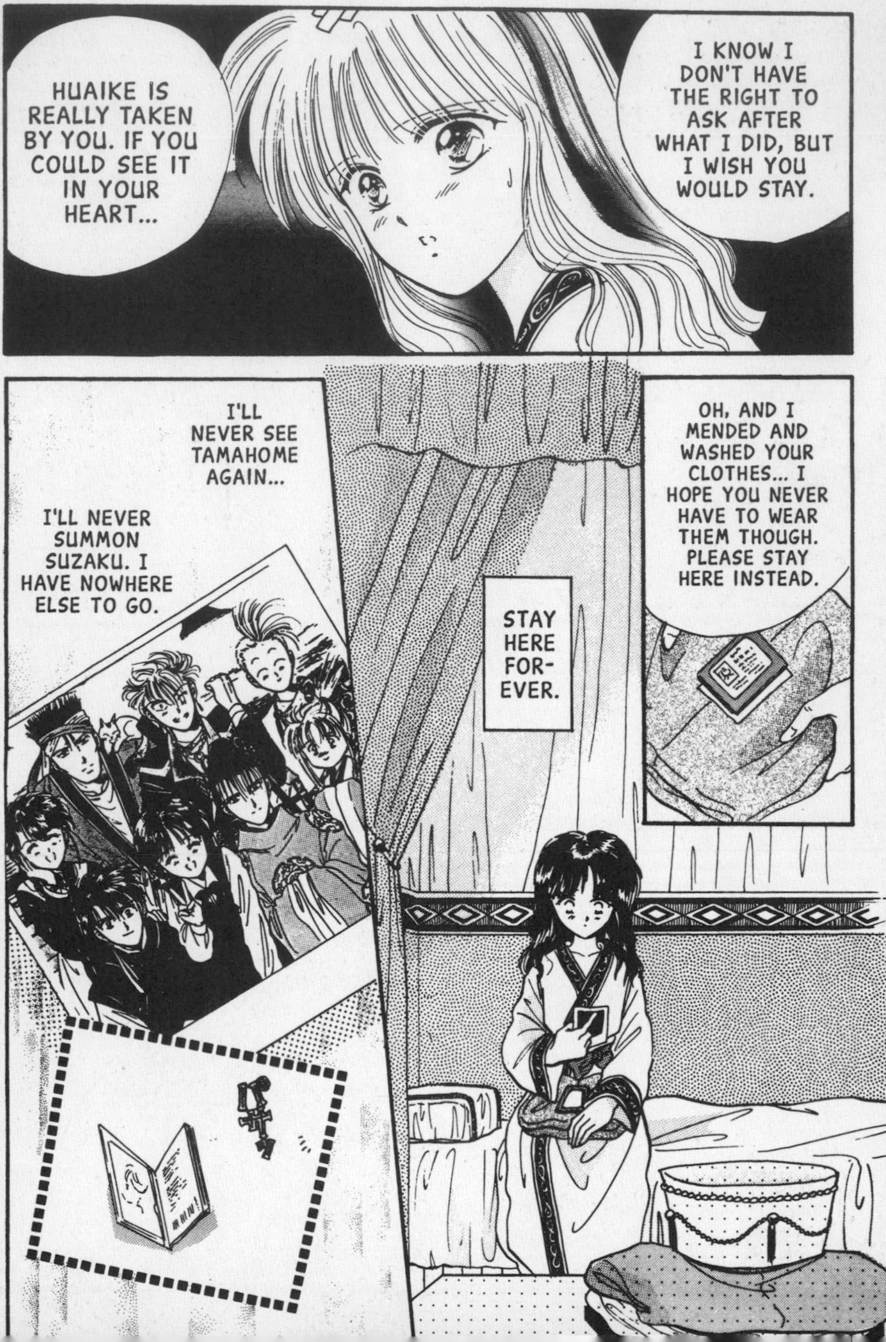
I KNOW I DON'T HAVE THE RIGHT TO ASK AFTER WHAT I DID, BUT I WISH YOU WOULD STAY.
HUAIKE IS REALLY TAKEN BY YOU. IF YOU COULD SEE IT IN YOUR HEART...
OH, AND I MENDED AND WASHED YOUR CLOTHES... I HOPE YOU NEVER HAVE TO WEAR THEM THOUGH. PLEASE STAY HERE INSTEAD.
STAY HERE FOR-EVER.
I'LL NEVER SEE TAMAHOME AGAIN...
I'LL NEVER SUMMON SUZAKU. I HAVE NOWHERE ELSE TO GO.

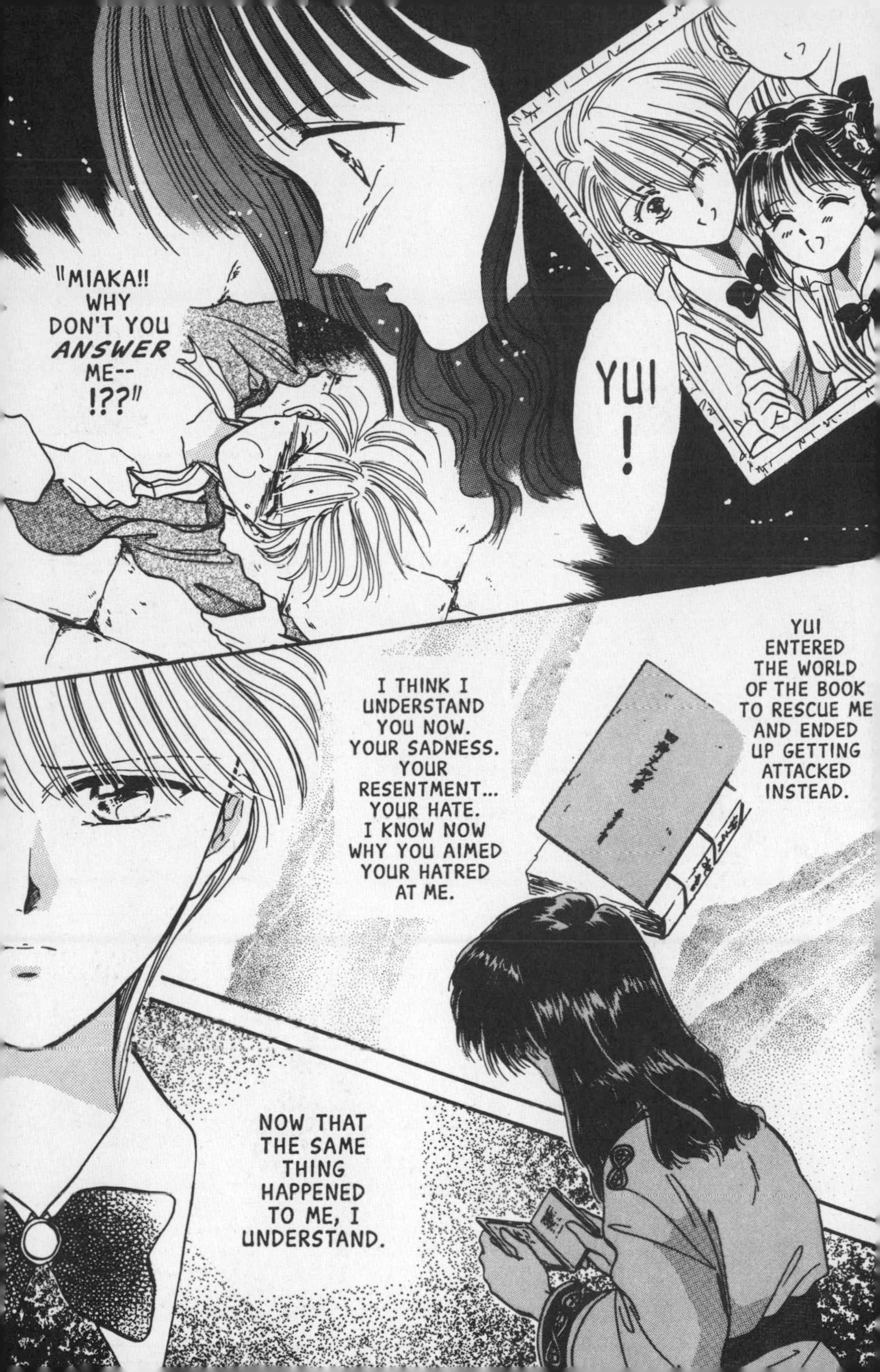
YUI!
"MIAKA!! WHY DON'T YOU *ANSWER* ME--!??"
YUI ENTERED THE WORLD OF THE BOOK TO RESCUE ME AND ENDED UP GETTING ATTACKED INSTEAD.
I THINK I UNDERSTAND YOU NOW. YOUR SADNESS. YOUR RESENTMENT... YOUR HATE. I KNOW NOW WHY YOU AIMED YOUR HATRED AT ME.
NOW THAT THE SAME THING HAPPENED TO ME, I UNDERSTAND.

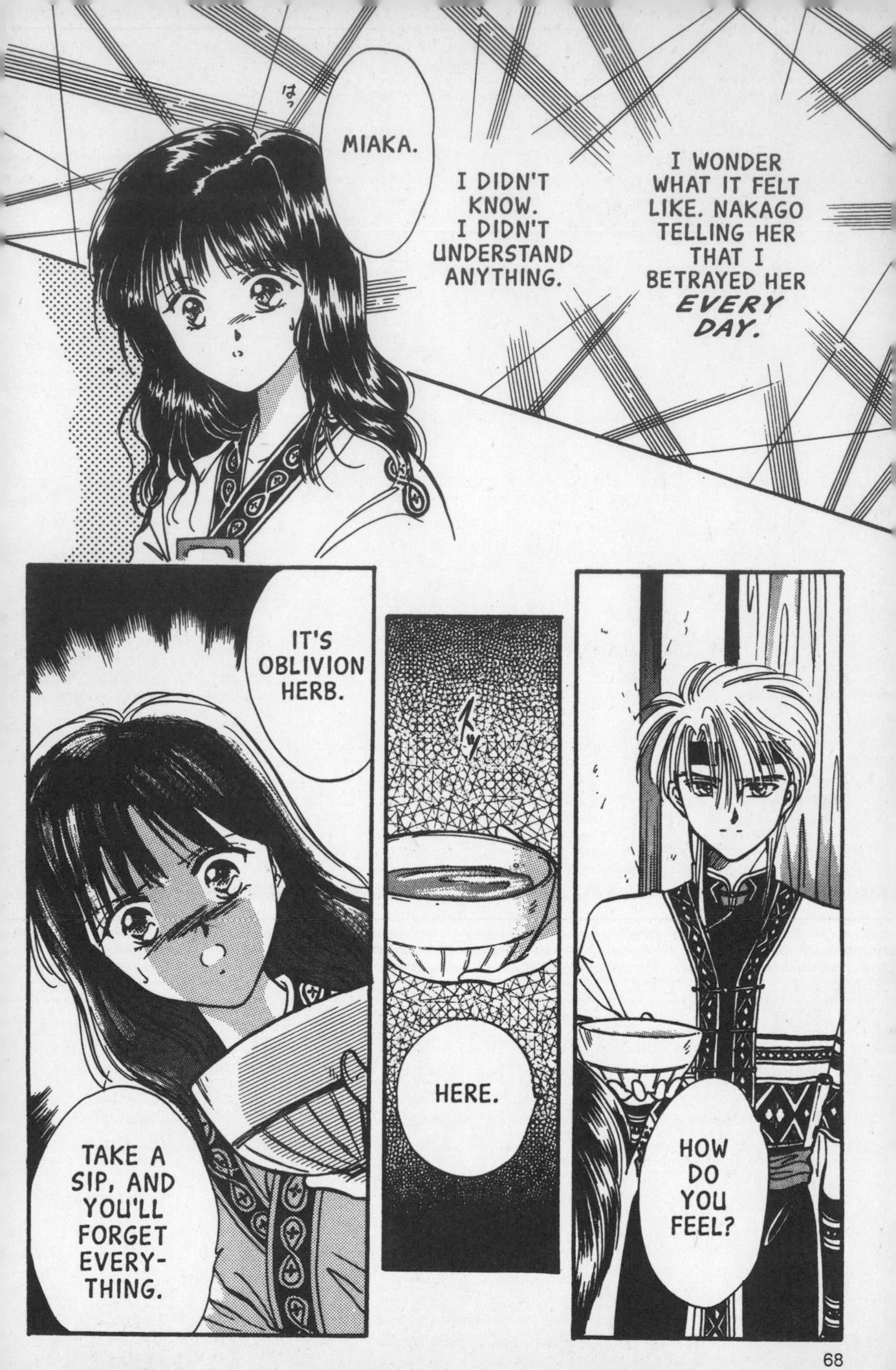
I WONDER WHAT IT FELT LIKE. NAKAGO TELLING HER THAT I BETRAYED HER EVERY DAY.
I DIDN'T KNOW. I DIDN'T UNDERSTAND ANYTHING.
MIAKA.
はっ
HOW DO YOU FEEL?
HERE.
IT'S OBLIVION HERB.
TAKE A SIP, AND YOU'LL FORGET EVERY-THING.

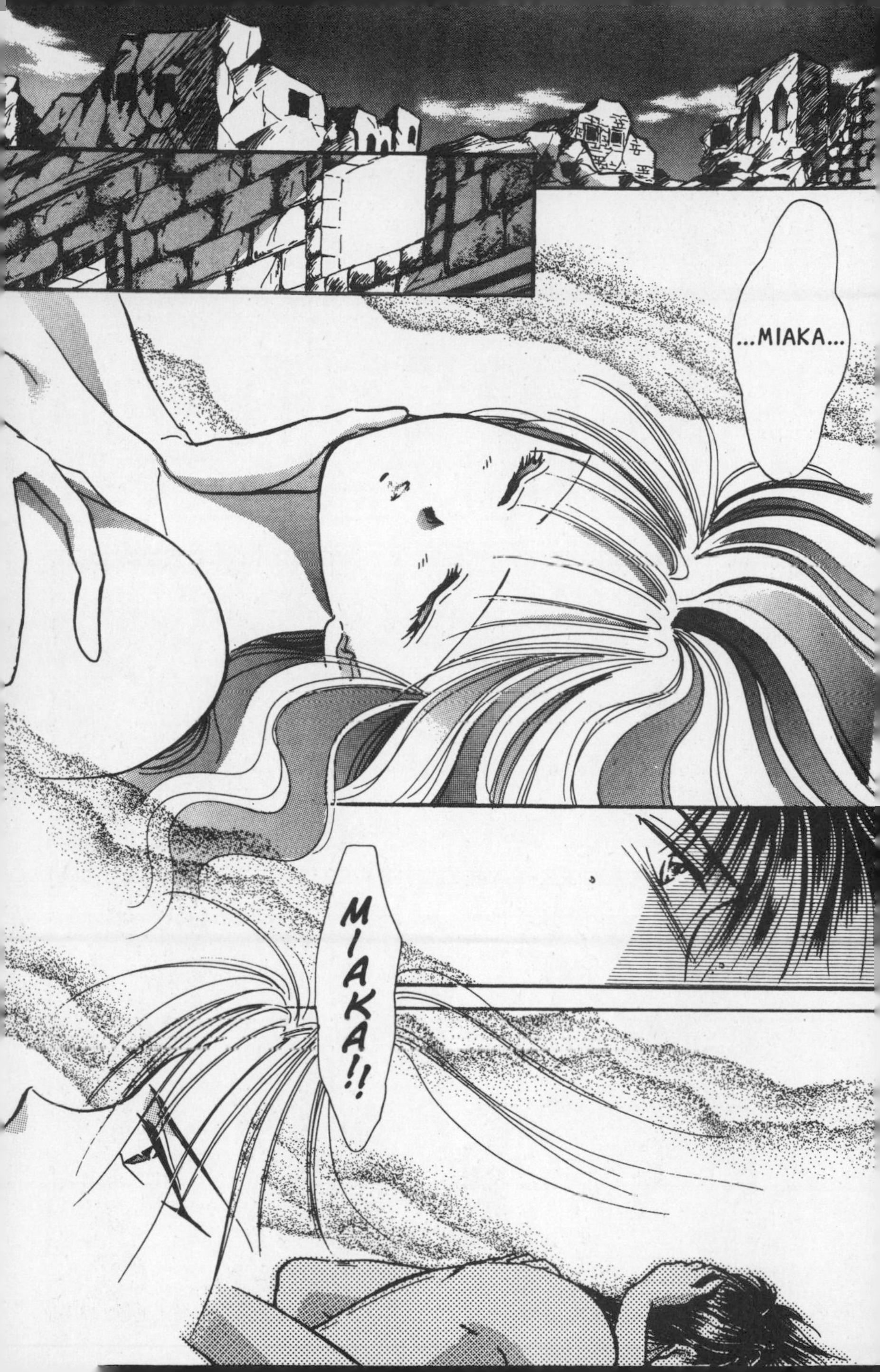
...MIAKA...
MIAKA!!

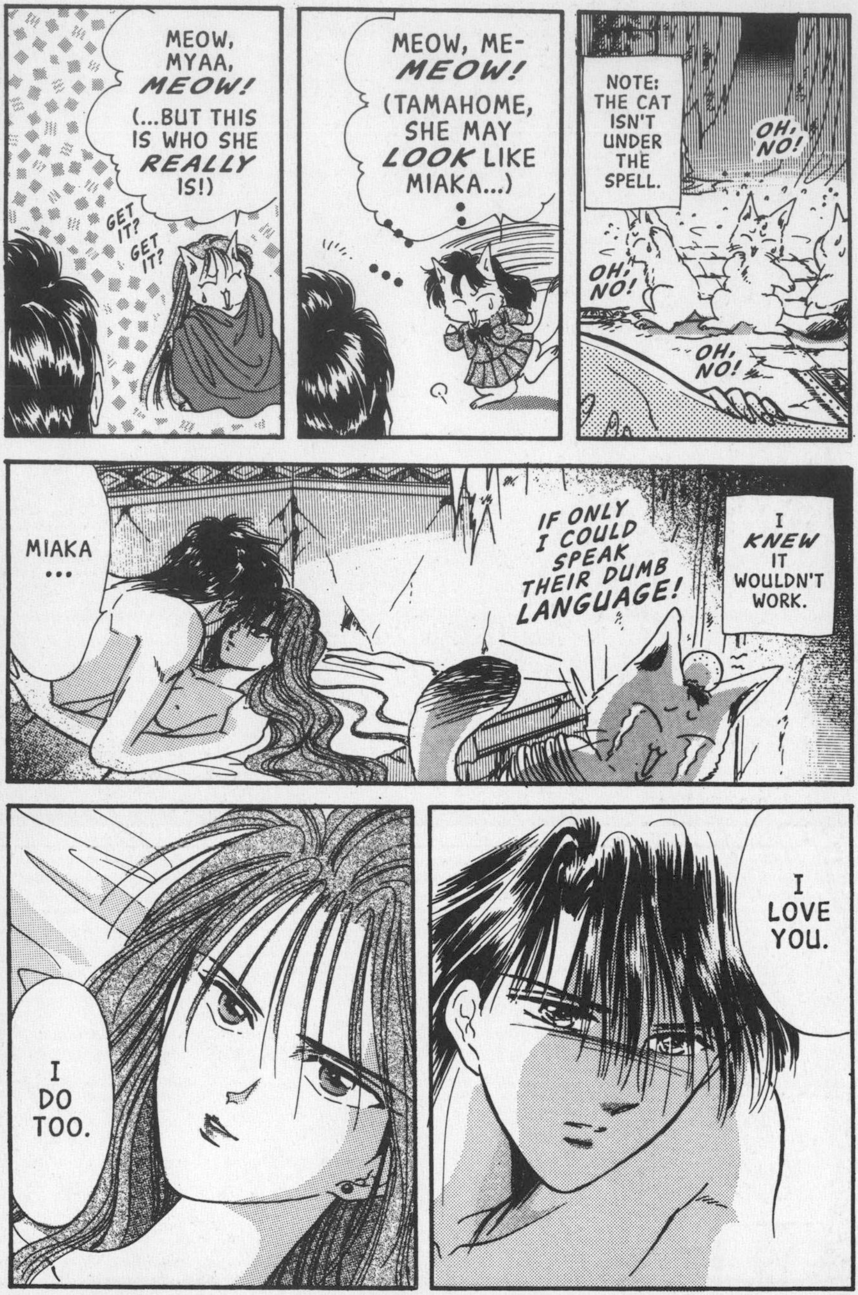
OH, NO!
NOTE: THE CAT ISN'T UNDER THE SPELL.
OH, NO!
OH, NO!
MEOW, ME-MEOW! (TAMAHOME, SHE MAY LOOK LIKE MIAKA...)
...
MEOW, MYAA, MEOW! (...BUT THIS IS WHO SHE REALLY IS!)
GET IT? GET IT?
I KNEW IT WOULDN'T WORK.
IF ONLY I COULD SPEAK THEIR DUMB LANGUAGE!
MIAKA ...
I LOVE YOU.
I DO TOO.

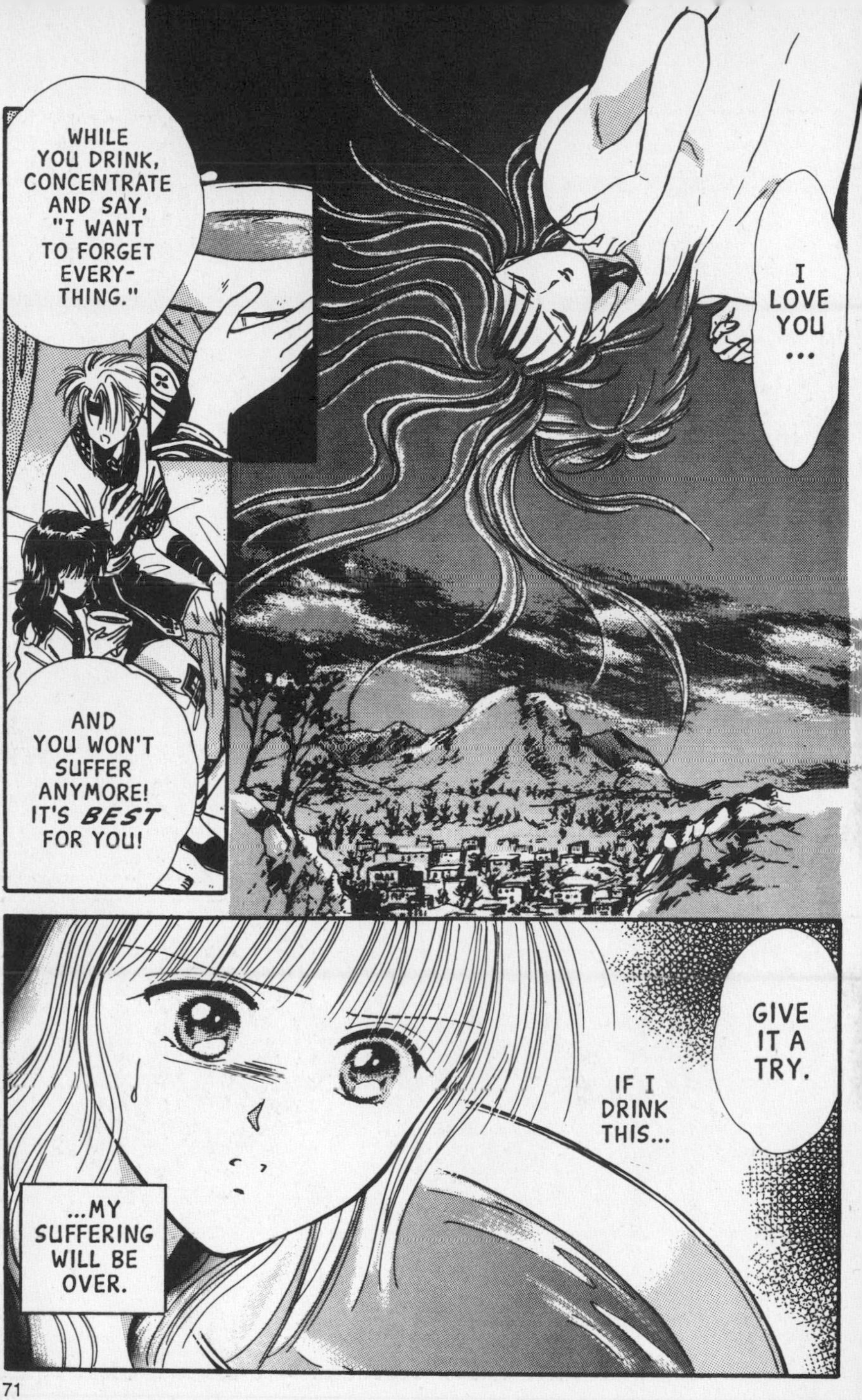
I LOVE YOU ...
WHILE YOU DRINK, CONCENTRATE AND SAY, "I WANT TO FORGET EVERY-THING."
AND YOU WON'T SUFFER ANYMORE! IT'S *BEST* FOR YOU!
GIVE IT A TRY.
IF I DRINK THIS...
...MY SUFFERING WILL BE OVER.

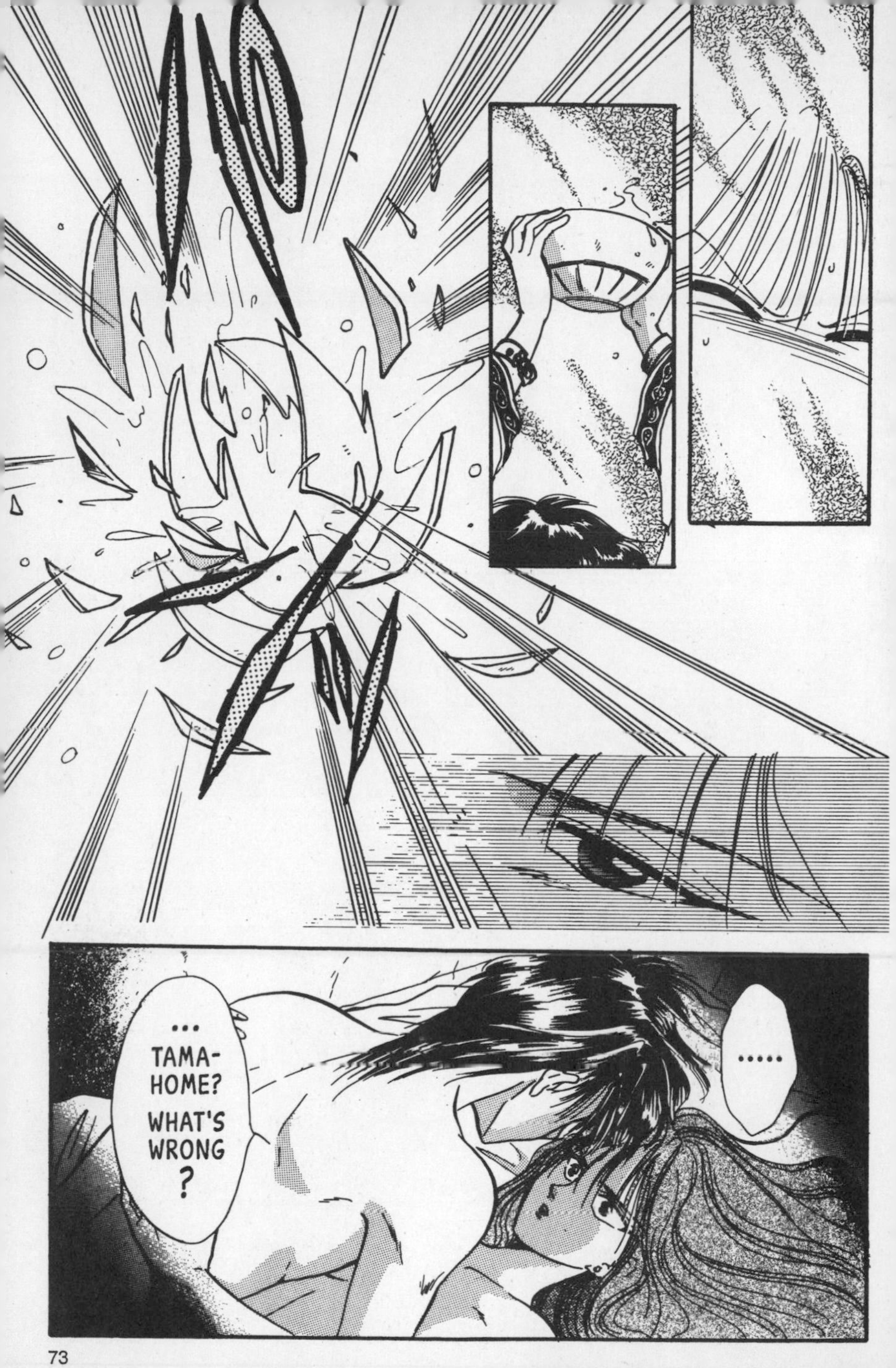
......
... TAMA-HOME? WHAT'S WRONG?

77

...I FELT THAT IT WAS A MISTAKE.

WHEN I BECAME A SPY POSING AS CHIRIKO AND LIVING AS A SUZAKU WARRIOR...

UNLIKE HONG-NAN, MY HOMELAND QU-DONG IS IN A STATE OF CONSTANT CIVIL STRIFE... MY BROTHER SUBOSHI AND I WERE ORPHANS.

WHEN HER EMINENCE YUI APPEARED FROM THE OTHER WORLD, I FIRMLY BELIEVED THAT ONCE SEIRYU WAS SUMMONED, QU-DONG WOULD FIND PEACE.

BUT THEN I REALIZED... THAT QU-DONG'S INTENTIONS WERE TO USE SEIRYU TO DOMINATE NOT ONLY HONG-NAN, BUT BEI-JIA AND XI-LANG AS WELL.

!!

NAKAGO!

NAKAGO INSISTED THAT YOUR SUMMONING OF SUZAKU WOULD PREVENT THAT PEACE.

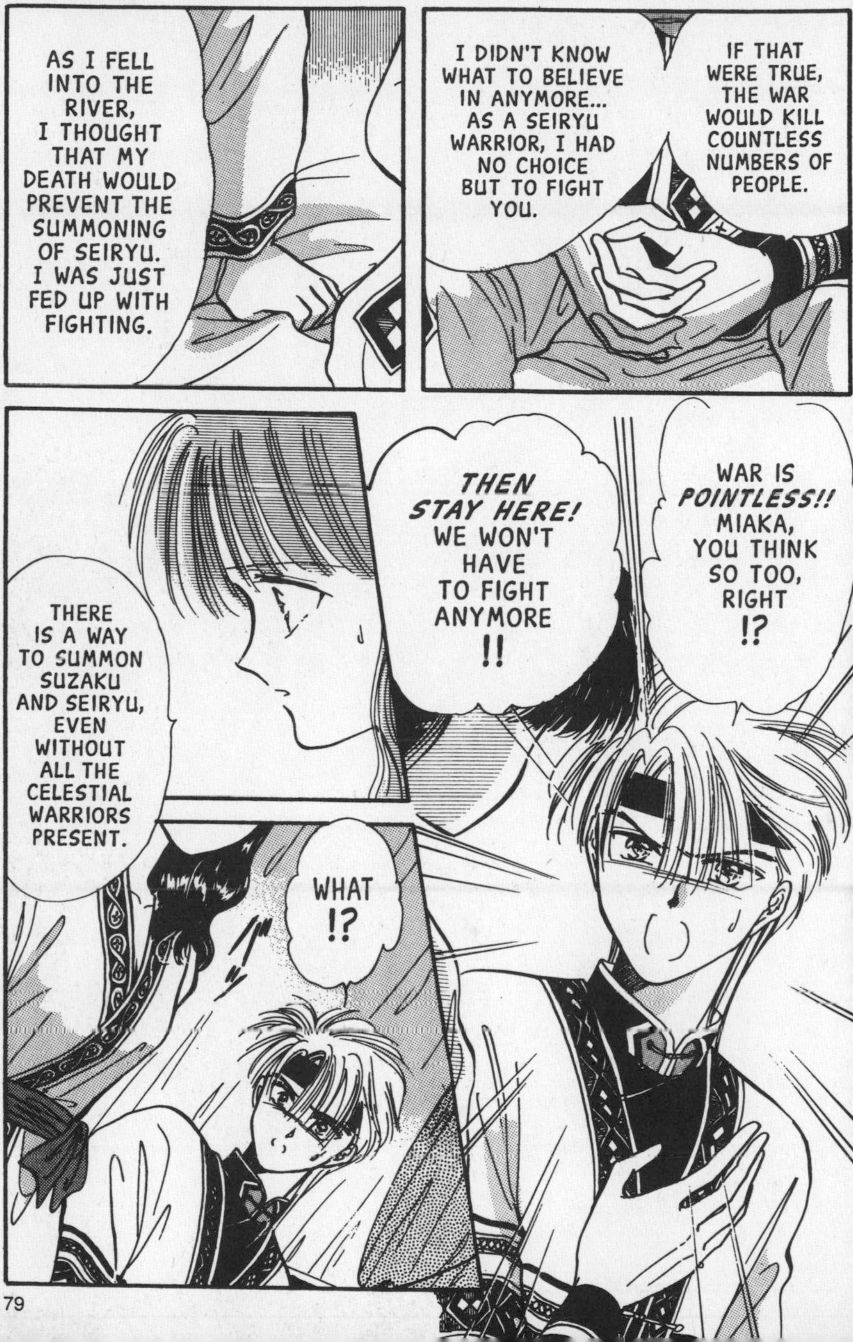
IF THAT WERE TRUE, THE WAR WOULD KILL COUNTLESS NUMBERS OF PEOPLE.
I DIDN'T KNOW WHAT TO BELIEVE IN ANYMORE... AS A SEIRYU WARRIOR, I HAD NO CHOICE BUT TO FIGHT YOU.
AS I FELL INTO THE RIVER, I THOUGHT THAT MY DEATH WOULD PREVENT THE SUMMONING OF SEIRYU. I WAS JUST FED UP WITH FIGHTING.
WAR IS *POINTLESS!!* MIAKA, YOU THINK SO TOO, RIGHT !?
THEN STAY HERE! WE WON'T HAVE TO FIGHT ANYMORE !!
THERE IS A WAY TO SUMMON SUZAKU AND SEIRYU, EVEN WITHOUT ALL THE CELESTIAL WARRIORS PRESENT.
WHAT !?

IF YUI REALIZED HOW NAKAGO WAS DECEIVING HER, SHE'D UNDERSTAND! AFTER THAT SHE'D NEVER LISTEN TO NAKAGO OR THE QU-DONG RULERS!

I CAN'T SUMMON SUZAKU ANYMORE. BUT SEIRYU CAN BE SUMMONED, RIGHT!?

WHAT!?

NO, I'VE GOT A BETTER IDEA... I'LL HAVE YUI SUMMON SEIRYU!

YOU'RE GOING ALONE? RIGHT INTO THE ENEMY'S CAMP? AREN'T YOU AFRAID!?

YOU MAY BE RIGHT ABOUT THAT, BUT...

A LONG TIME AGO, SOMEBODY TOLD ME...

IF YOU RUN AWAY BECAUSE YOU "CAN'T DO IT" OR BECAUSE YOU THINK SOMETHING'S "IMPOSSIBLE"... THEN YOU'LL BECOME A COWARD AS AN ADULT.

...THE KANJI CHARACTERS FOR "BATTLE" AND "RUNNING AWAY" DIFFER BY ONLY A FEW LINES...AND YET THEIR MEANINGS ARE EXACTLY OPPOSITE.

IS THIS MAN...

...SO MUCH IN *LOVE* WITH THE PRIESTESS OF SUZAKU!?

HOW CAN HE DO IT?

I DON'T BELIEVE THIS! IT'S MY MOST POWERFUL APHRODISIAC, YET HE'S IN CONTROL!

WHO ARE YOU!?

PERHAPS YOUR SEDUCTION SKILLS HAVE ATROPHIED.

SOI, YOU FAILED.

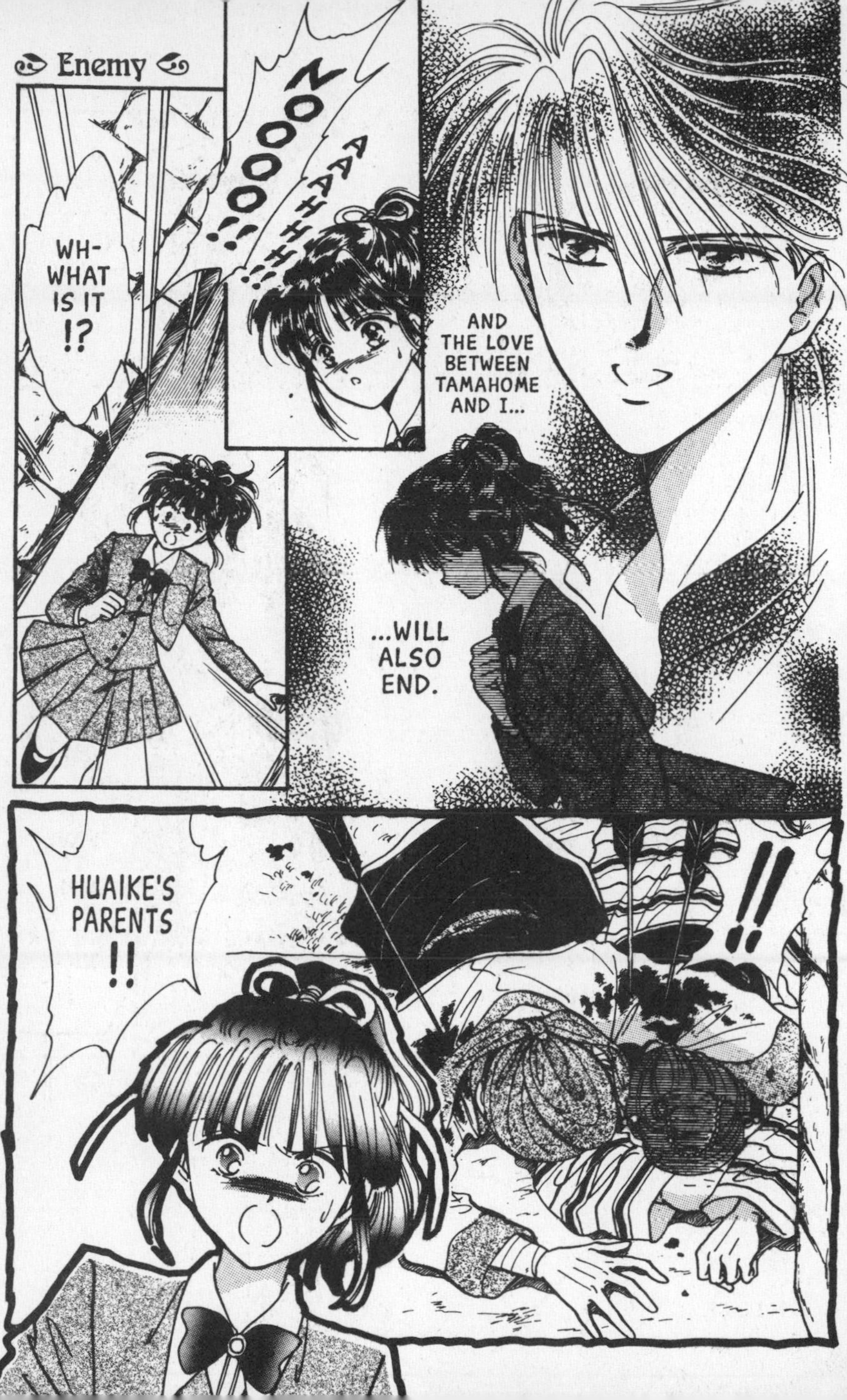
AND THE LOVE BETWEEN TAMAHOME AND I...
...WILL ALSO END.
NOOOO!!
AAAHHH!!
WH-WHAT IS IT !?
!!
HUAIKE'S PARENTS !!

From Volume 7 (Ah, the memories!)

Long Overdue - Fushigi Akugi The Malicious Play (8)

I'LL HOLD YOU UNTIL YOU'RE FINISHED

URGH.

Thank you for sending me all those dōjinshi and tapes, Ms. Haruta (great parody!). It was all really interesting! The Tasuki novel and the notebook with all your friends' drawings! I also received a "Ranma 1/2" video and cute illustrations from someone who is now an animator. I'd like to have all the fan art and character portraits from you readers displayed somewhere. Can I?

The idea came from several readers ... I-I still don't know your names! Sorry! ♡

Why am I always in these dōjinshi !?

It never ends! They call me Akago, Inago, Mukago, Chicago ...

Are you that jealous, Nakago? Then why don't you cuddle up with Tamahome ... (krak)

.....

SUBOSHI ...

I WANNA DO THAT !

BGM: Final Fantasy IV (3 CD set)

The names of each celestial warrior were written on each of these handmade chocolates!

The box was home made too.

Seven Celestial Chocolates

I had quite a few that were home made. Here are two samples.

I ran out of space to write it in Volume 9, but I wanted to thank you for all the Valentine's Day chocolates! (Come on, that was so long ago!) Thank you so much!

There were so many others I received. Even ones that had love letters (?) to Fushigi characters. Everyone was so thrilled! There was one that was called "Nuriko in Heaven." A note to the fan who sent a gift to Mitsukake, in the CD Book II, he talks a lot more than he does in the manga. In fact he even laughs.

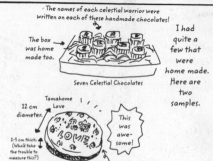

Tamahome Love

12 cm diameter.

2-3 cm thick. (Who'd take the trouble to measure this?)

This was awesome!

All kinds of topping on the strawberry chocolate.

Wow, there's almond inside!

MNCH MNCH

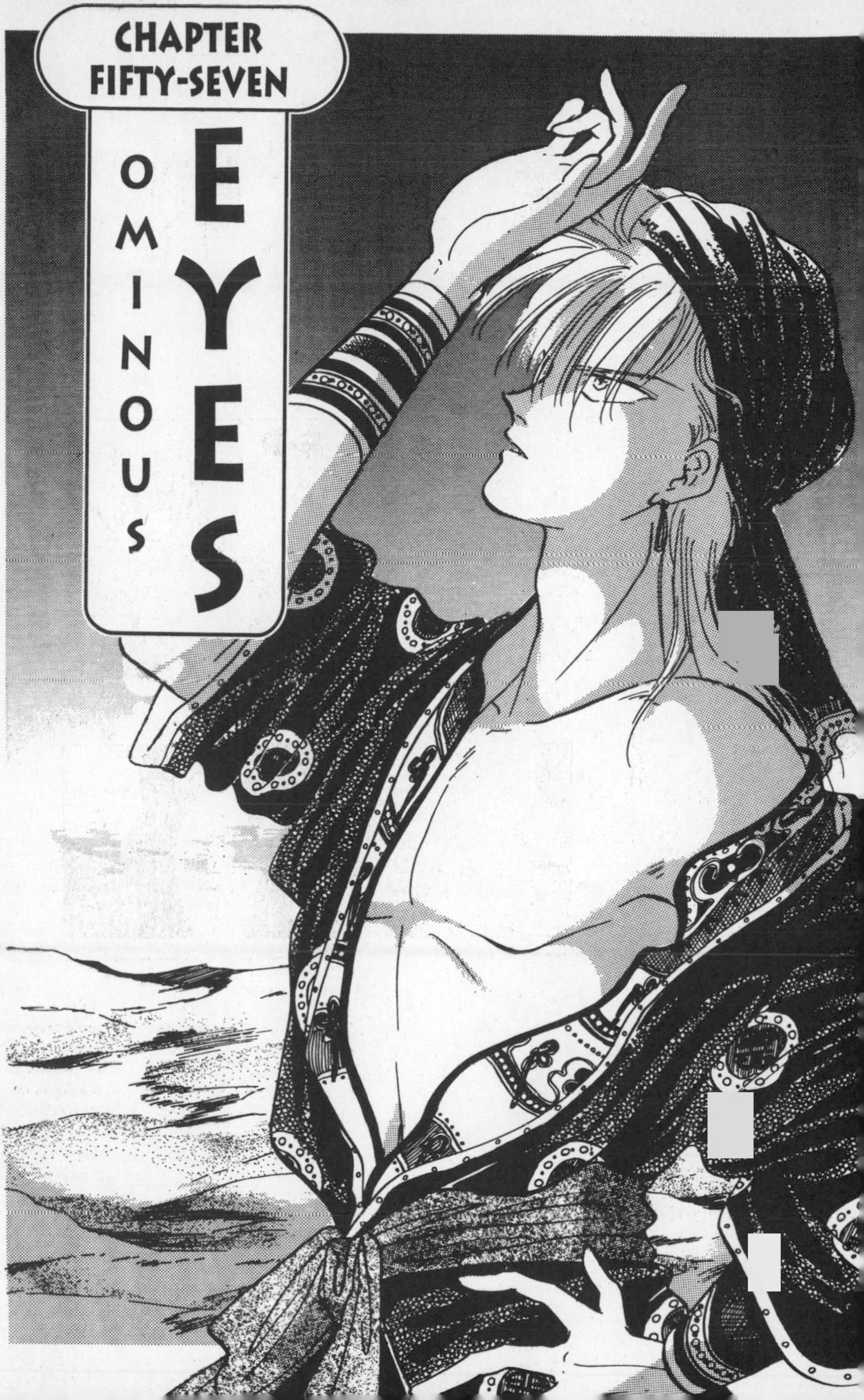
CHAPTER FIFTY-SEVEN
OMINOUS EYES

NAKAGO!

HE DESTROYED THE VILLAGE!

BUT HE'S NOT AFTER YOU, AMIBOSHI...

WHAT?

THIS IS A QU-DONG ARROW! SO THEY *DID* FIND ME!

NAKAGO MUST HAVE DETECTED IT... AND FOUND ME.

I USED MY CHI TO EASE YOUR FEVER.

BUT WHY? HE'S DEFILED ME. I CAN'T SUMMON SUZAKU ANYMORE.

HE WANTS ME! NAKAGO REALIZED I WAS HERE!

SO YOU *ARE* HERE, PRIESTESS OF SUZAKU!

ATTACKING INNOCENT VILLAGERS LIKE THIS ...

IN ANY CASE, THIS IS TOO MUCH!

MIAKA, WAIT! YOU CAN'T GO OUT THERE!

I'M GOING! NAKAGO NEEDS A GOOD PUNCHING OUT!!

STEP BACK, MIAKA! AND... DON'T WATCH THIS!

YOU WILL COME WITH ME!

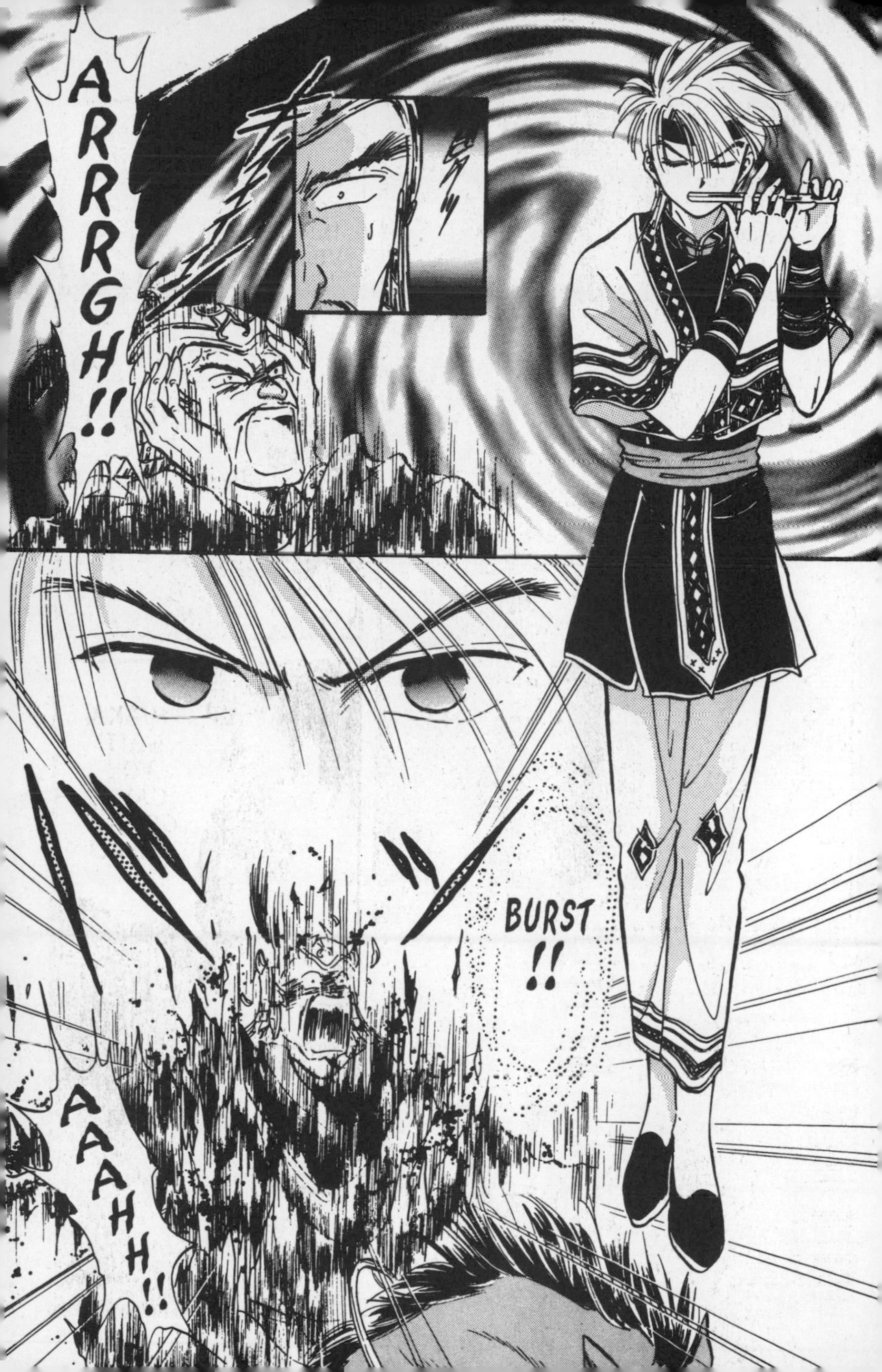
ARRRGH!!
BURST!!
AAAHH!!

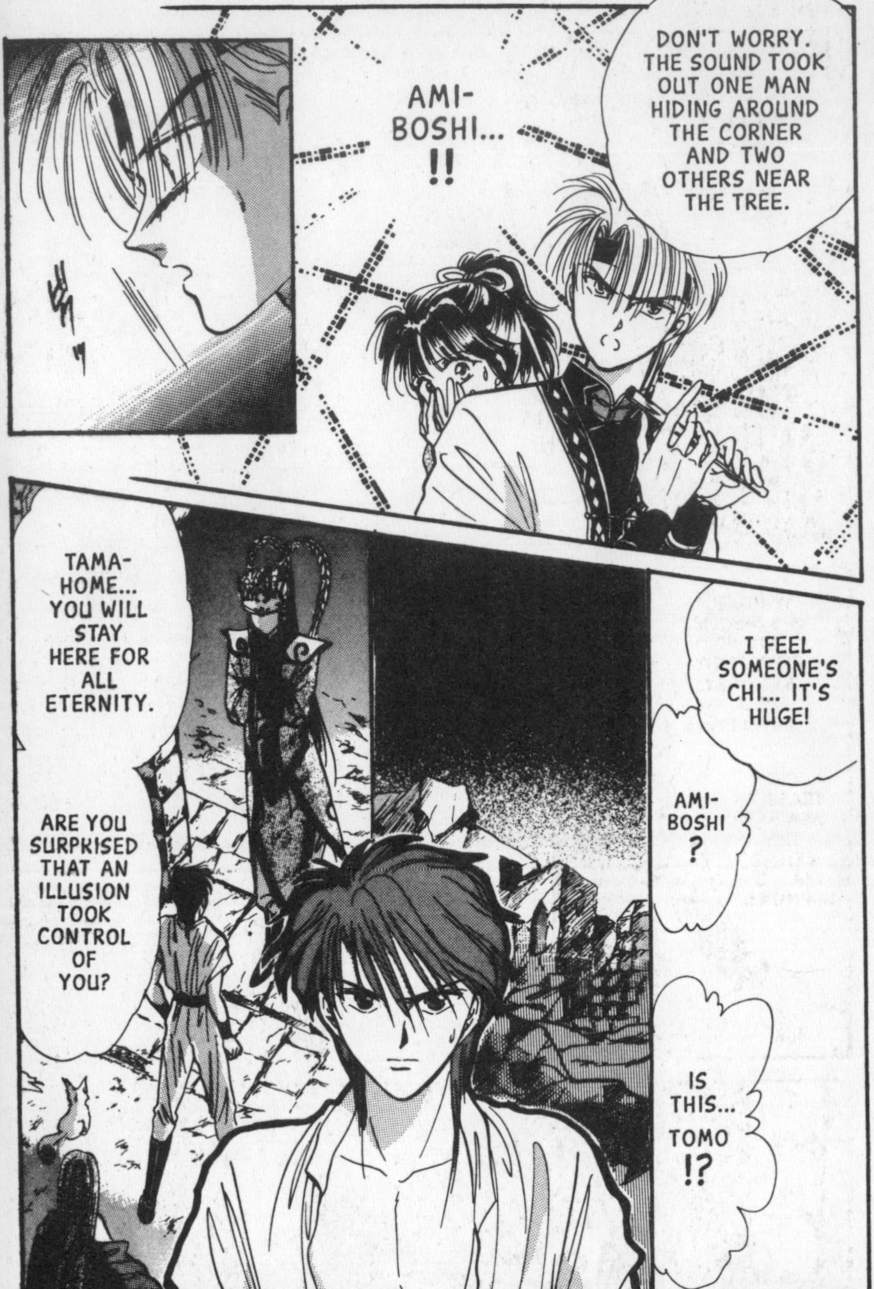
DON'T WORRY. THE SOUND TOOK OUT ONE MAN HIDING AROUND THE CORNER AND TWO OTHERS NEAR THE TREE.
AMI-BOSHI... !!
I FEEL SOMEONE'S CHI... IT'S HUGE!
AMI-BOSHI ?
IS THIS... TOMO !?
TAMA-HOME... YOU WILL STAY HERE FOR ALL ETERNITY.
ARE YOU SURPRISED THAT AN ILLUSION TOOK CONTROL OF YOU?

YOU'RE CALLED... TOMO, AREN'T YOU?

...THAT *CLOWN SUIT* YOU HAVE ON?

DON'T YOU REGRET...

MY MAKEUP IS SYMBOLIC. INDIGO REPRESENTS STRATEGY. BLACK IS LOYALTY...

...CONTRASTED AGAINST THE BRIGHT GOLD OF HARMONY...

...

HEH.

HOW I PITY YOUNG MEN THESE DAYS WITH NO UNDERSTANDING OF TRUE ART.

THOSE FEATHERS ARE SO LAME!

NO SENSE FOR USING MAKEUP!

THOSE GAUDY PRIMARY COLORS!

HOW CAN YOU EVEN STEP OUTSIDE IN THAT GET-UP?

THIS WON'T IMPRESS THE GIRLS!

SEE YA!!

HEY!!

TOMO, TAMAHOME TOOK OFF.

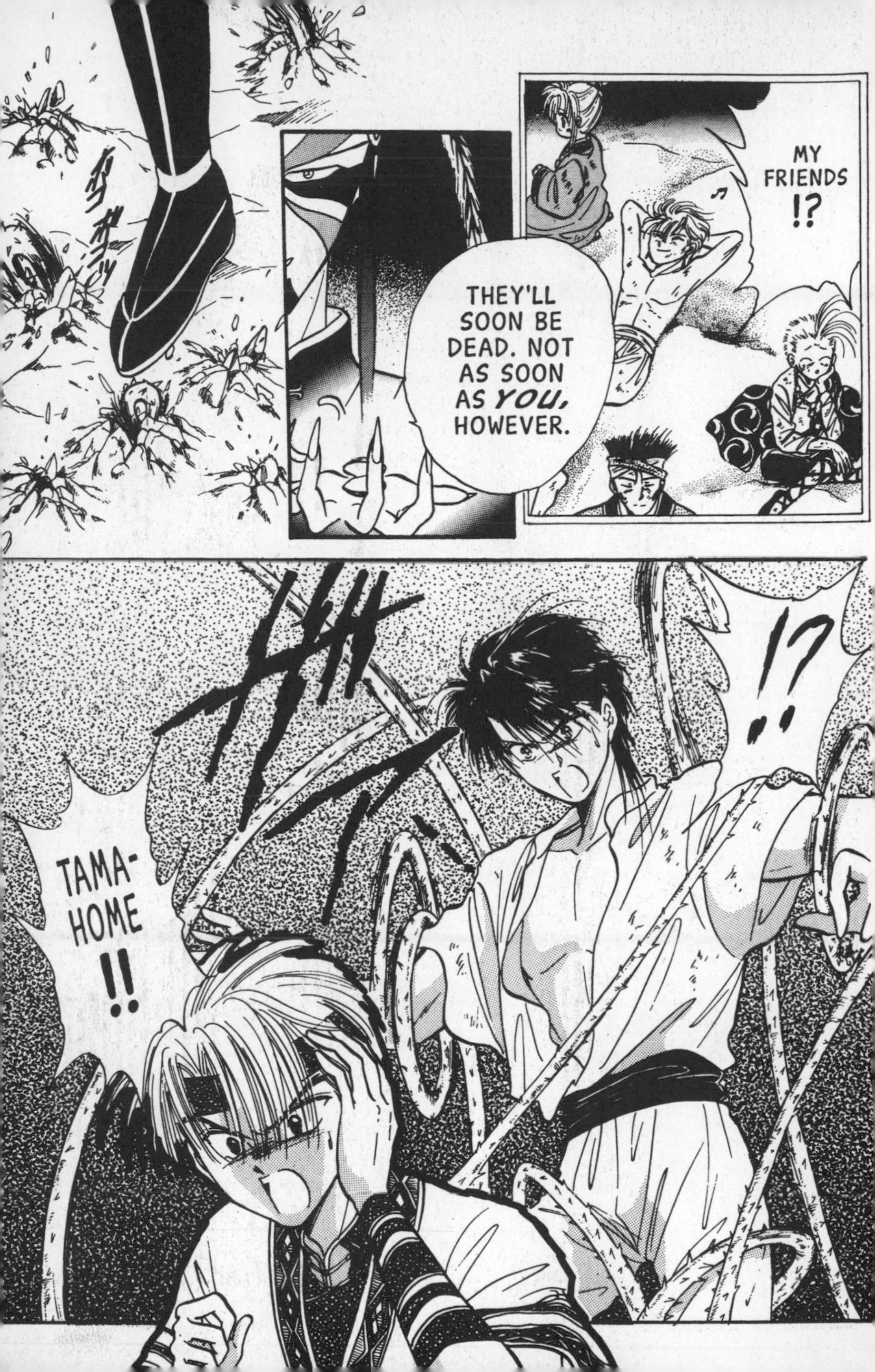
MY FRIENDS !?
THEY'LL SOON BE DEAD. NOT AS SOON AS *YOU,* HOWEVER.
!?
TAMA-HOME !!

MIAKA, TAMA-HOME'S IN TROUBLE!

HE'S VERY CLOSE BY!

I CAN'T TELL YOU. BUT I HAVE NO RIGHT TO BE NEAR HIM.

WH-WHY!?

NO. I CAN'T GO TO HIM.

I'LL BRING HIM, OKAY? YOU *WAIT* FOR US HERE, OKAY?

YOU *HAVE* TO BE TOGETHER!!

THAT DOESN'T MAKE SENSE! YOU TWO WERE IN *LOVE!!*

HUAIKE...

Enemy

Here are the details. First, Tamahome. When I found out the meaning for his character was "man with courage," I stopped short! I started looking up the other characters and burst out laughing.
"Nuriko" = graceful beauty.
"Hotohori" = a highly ranked person.
"Tasuki" = help, assistance, protection.
Then, "Chichiri" means home town. "Chiriko" means to widen and spread. "Mitsukake" means to suffer. As for the Seiryu warriors—*Are you even interested?*—I hadn't checked them before so I'll look them up now! *Watase pulls out her Kanji character dictionary.*
"Su" of "Suboshi" = to compete, fight. *Wow!*
"Ami" of "Amiboshi" = go far, cut off.
"Soi" = to draw near, to be wed
"Tomo" = despicable... Ha ha!
"Ashitare" = back, the end.
"Mi" of "Miboshi" = trash collecting, and...
What the--? Now this is a shock for Watase!! "...sitting cross-legged"!? Those who've been reading FY serialized in the magazine must know how Miboshi has always remained in that sitting position the whole time!! Geez!!
"Nakago" = prudence (strategy, maybe?), center, considerate... hmm. Those are a lot of other meanings, but I highlighted the ones that match him.
Oh yeah, my assistant did a reading of Tamahome's name and found that it signified "poverty, looks after others, loses family, gentle in appearance, but strong inside" (wait, isn't it the other way around?) That really took me by surprise.
You might think I'm lying, but this was all a coincidence. Really! I find it a little frightening myself.

The world can work in mysterious ways...!!

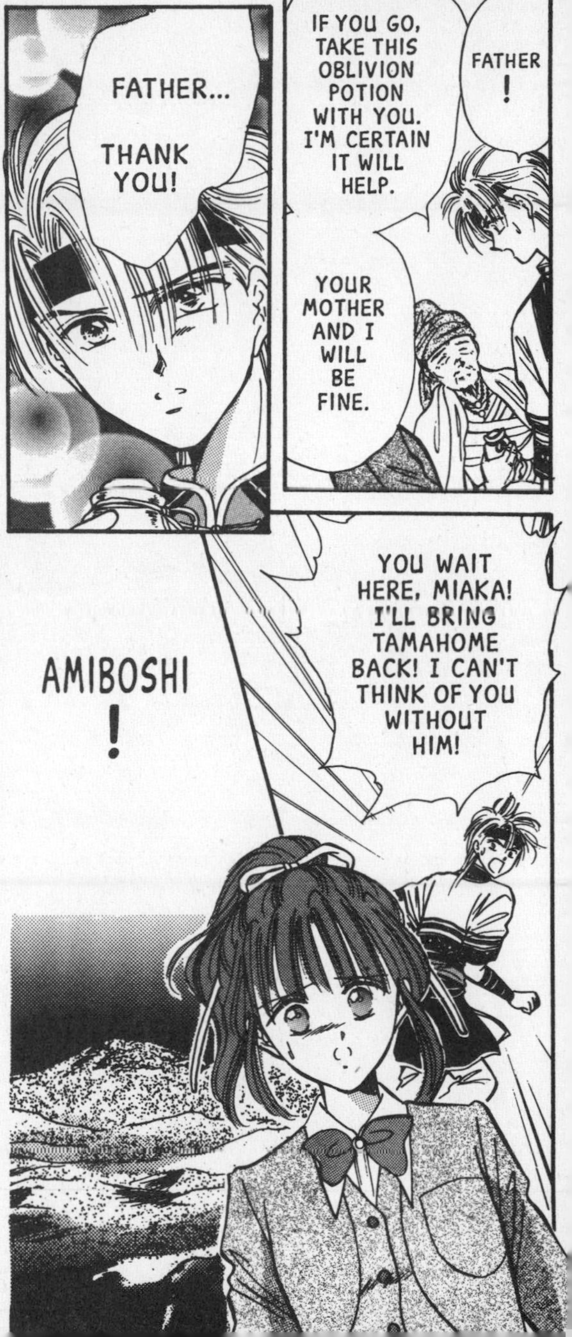
FATHER!
IF YOU GO, TAKE THIS OBLIVION POTION WITH YOU. I'M CERTAIN IT WILL HELP.
YOUR MOTHER AND I WILL BE FINE.
FATHER... THANK YOU!
YOU WAIT HERE, MIAKA! I'LL BRING TAMAHOME BACK! I CAN'T THINK OF YOU WITHOUT HIM!
AMIBOSHI!

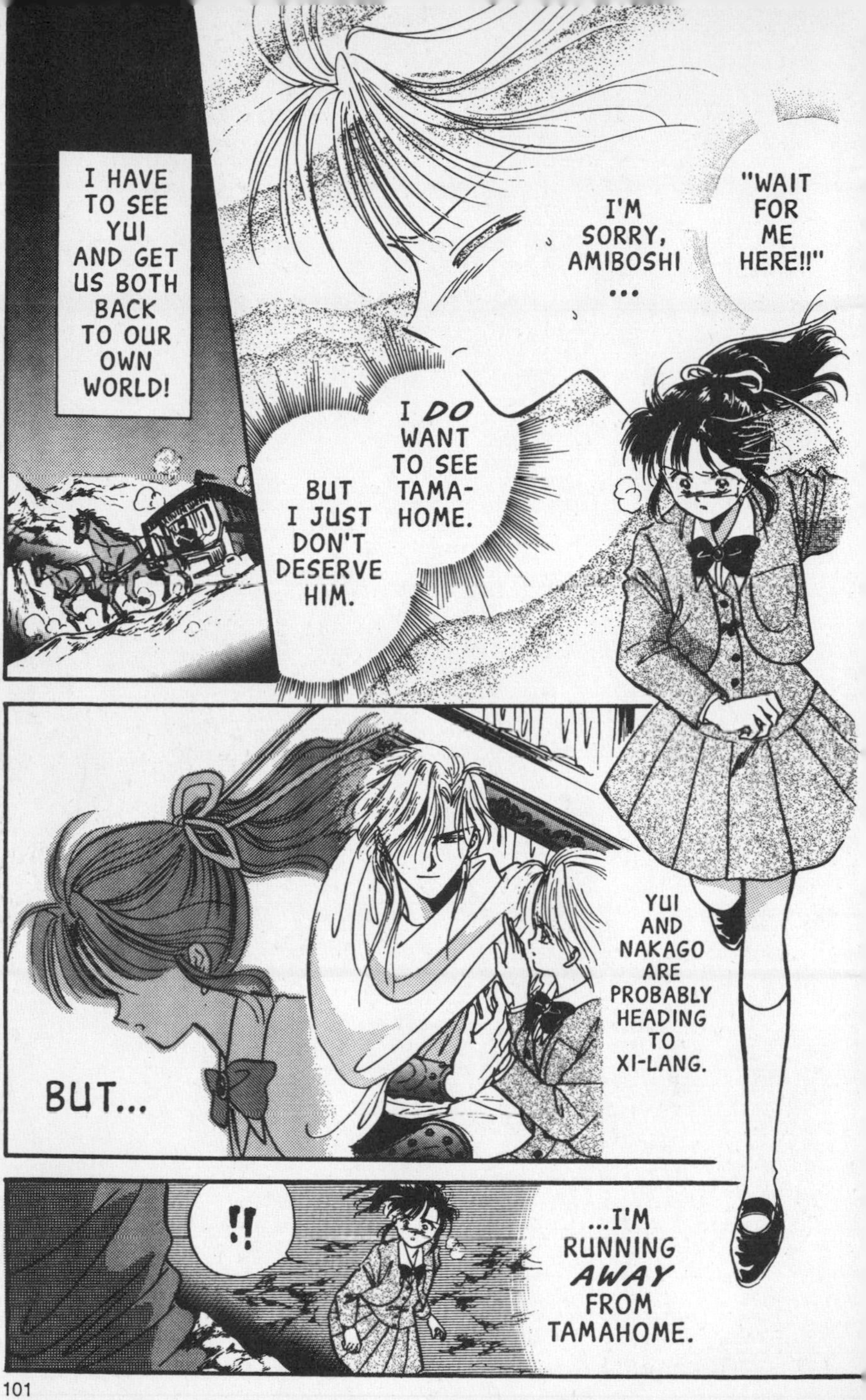
"WAIT FOR ME HERE!!"
I'M SORRY, AMIBOSHI...
I *DO* WANT TO SEE TAMA-HOME.
BUT I JUST DON'T DESERVE HIM.
YUI AND NAKAGO ARE PROBABLY HEADING TO XI-LANG.
I HAVE TO SEE YUI AND GET US BOTH BACK TO OUR OWN WORLD!
BUT...
!!
...I'M RUNNING *AWAY* FROM TAMAHOME.

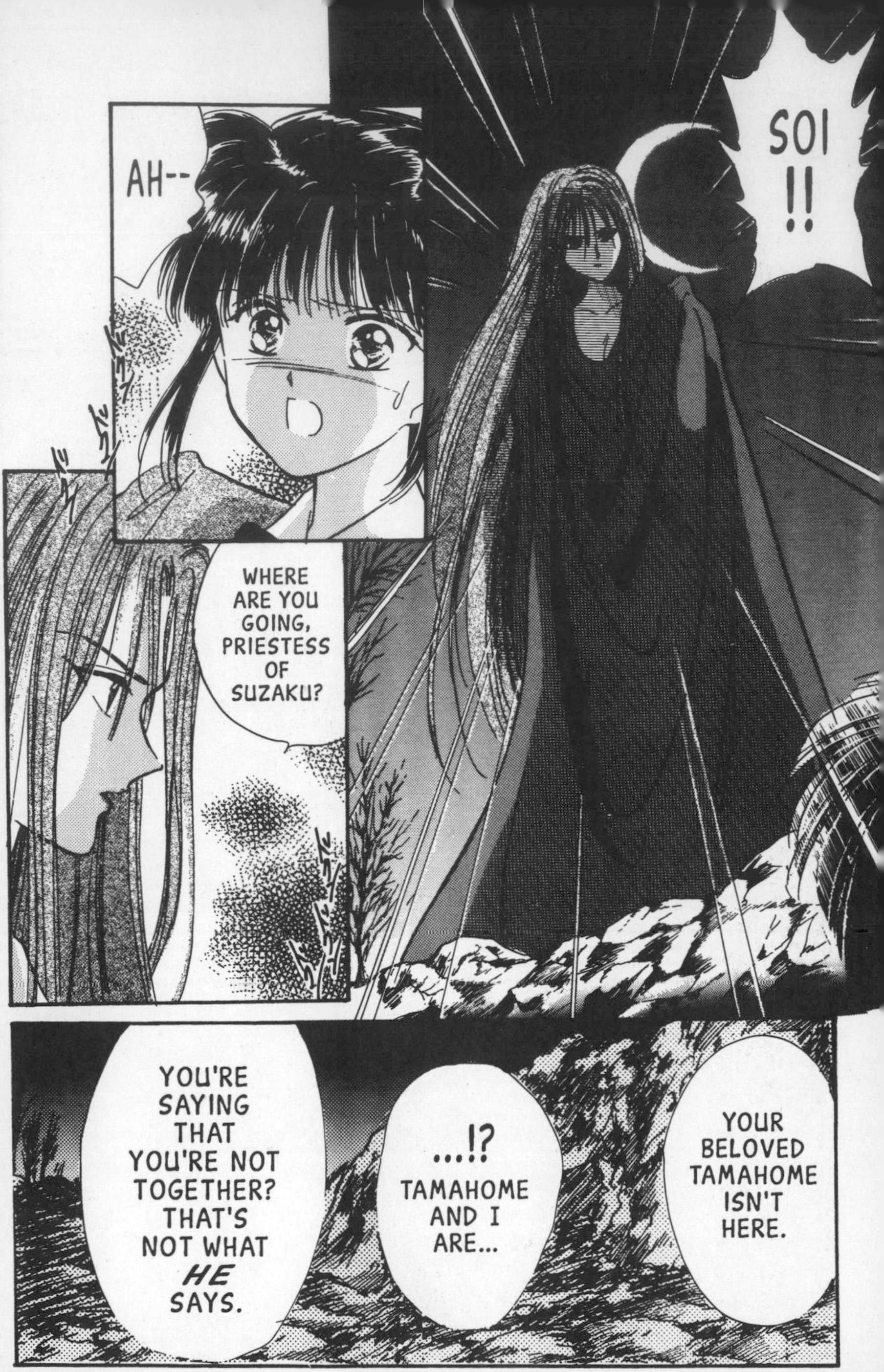
SOI !!
AH--
WHERE ARE YOU GOING, PRIESTESS OF SUZAKU?
YOUR BELOVED TAMAHOME ISN'T HERE.
...!? TAMAHOME AND I ARE...
YOU'RE SAYING THAT YOU'RE NOT TOGETHER? THAT'S NOT WHAT HE SAYS.

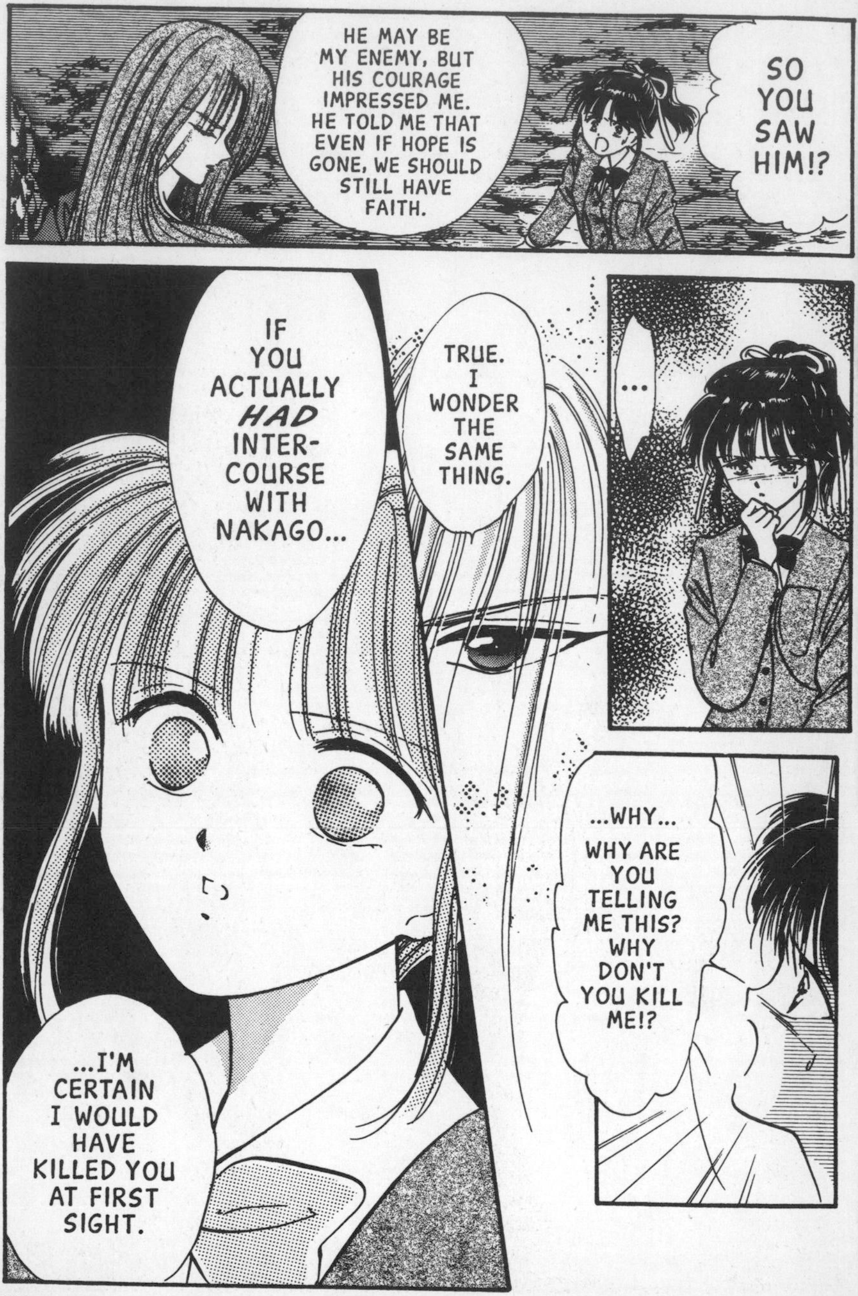
SO YOU SAW HIM!?
HE MAY BE MY ENEMY, BUT HIS COURAGE IMPRESSED ME. HE TOLD ME THAT EVEN IF HOPE IS GONE, WE SHOULD STILL HAVE FAITH.
...
...WHY... WHY ARE YOU TELLING ME THIS? WHY DON'T YOU KILL ME!?
TRUE. I WONDER THE SAME THING.
IF YOU ACTUALLY *HAD* INTER-COURSE WITH NAKAGO...
...I'M CERTAIN I WOULD HAVE KILLED YOU AT FIRST SIGHT.

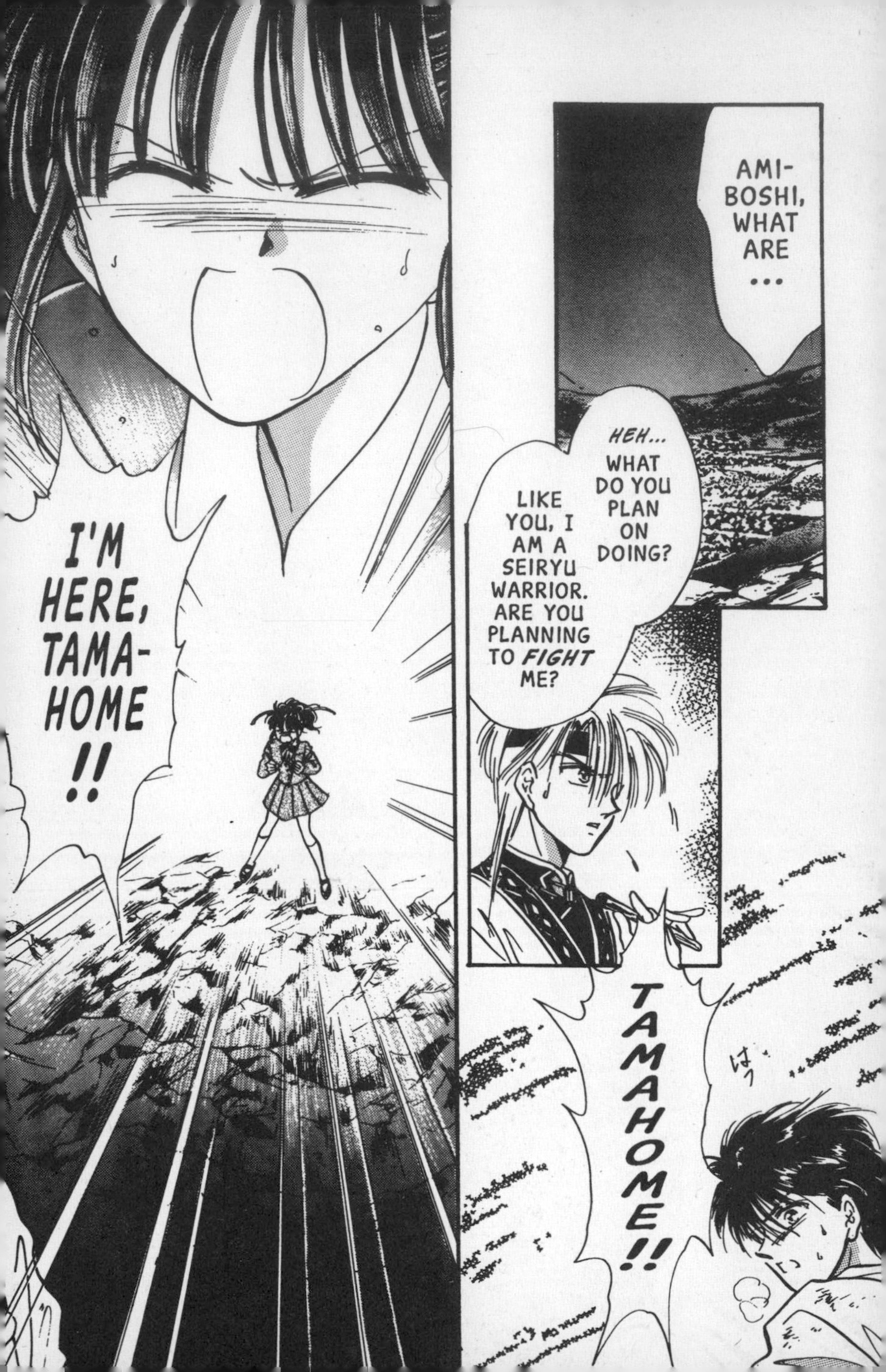
AMI-BOSHI, WHAT ARE ...
HEH... WHAT DO YOU PLAN ON DOING?
LIKE YOU, I AM A SEIRYU WARRIOR. ARE YOU PLANNING TO *FIGHT* ME?
TAMAHOME!!
はっ
I'M HERE, TAMA-HOME !!

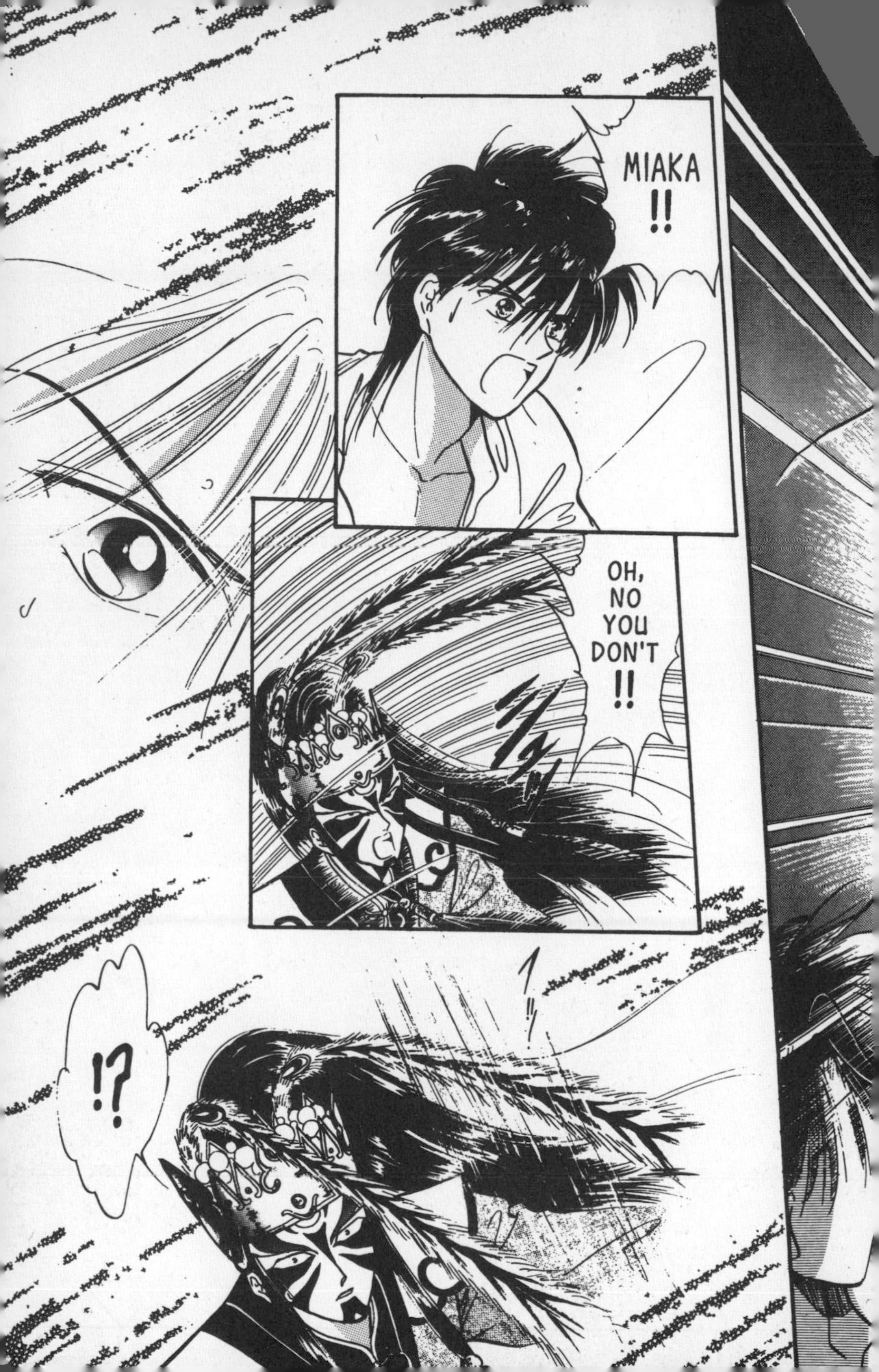
MIAKA!!
OH, NO YOU DON'T!!
!?

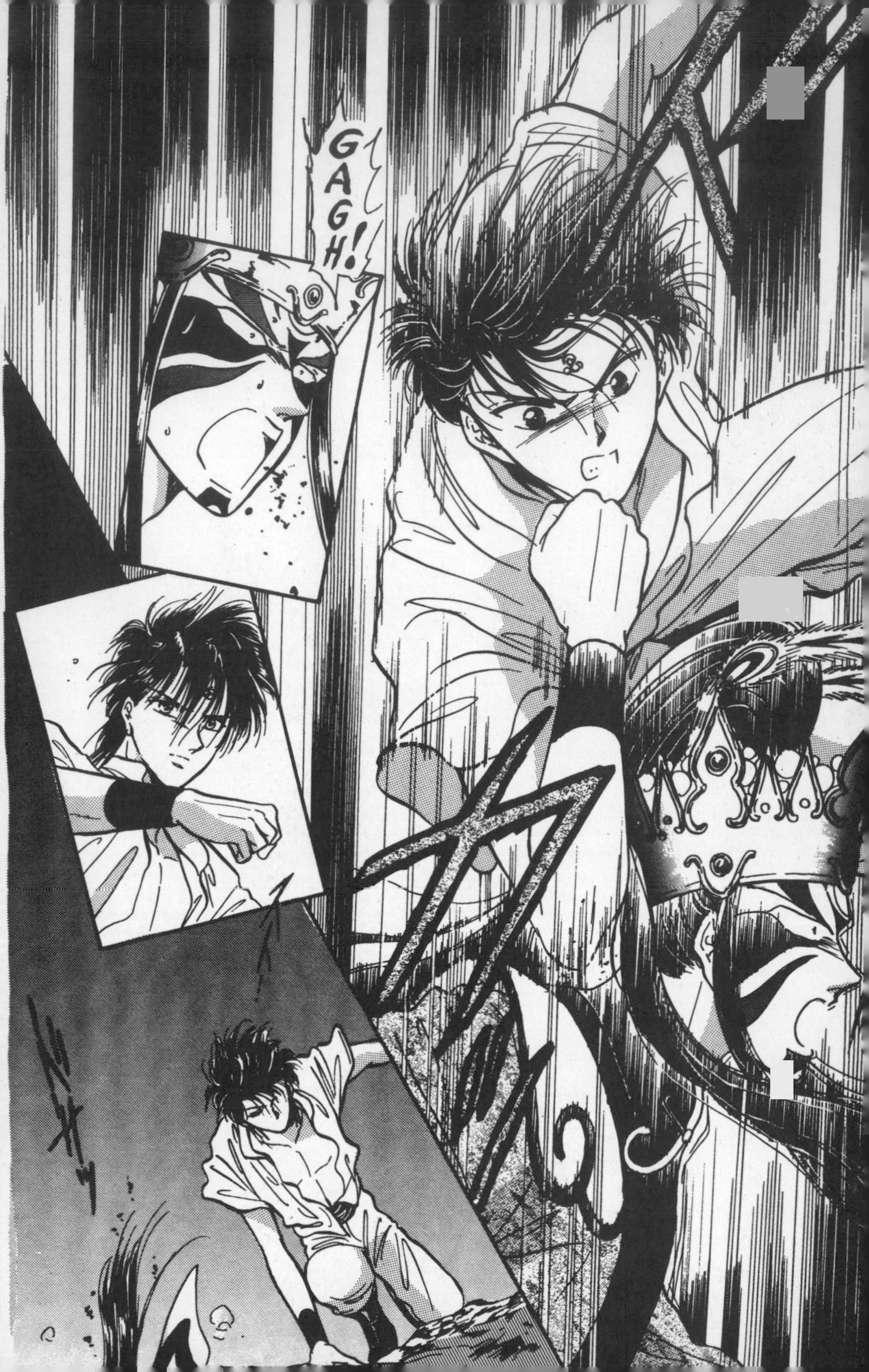
GAGH!

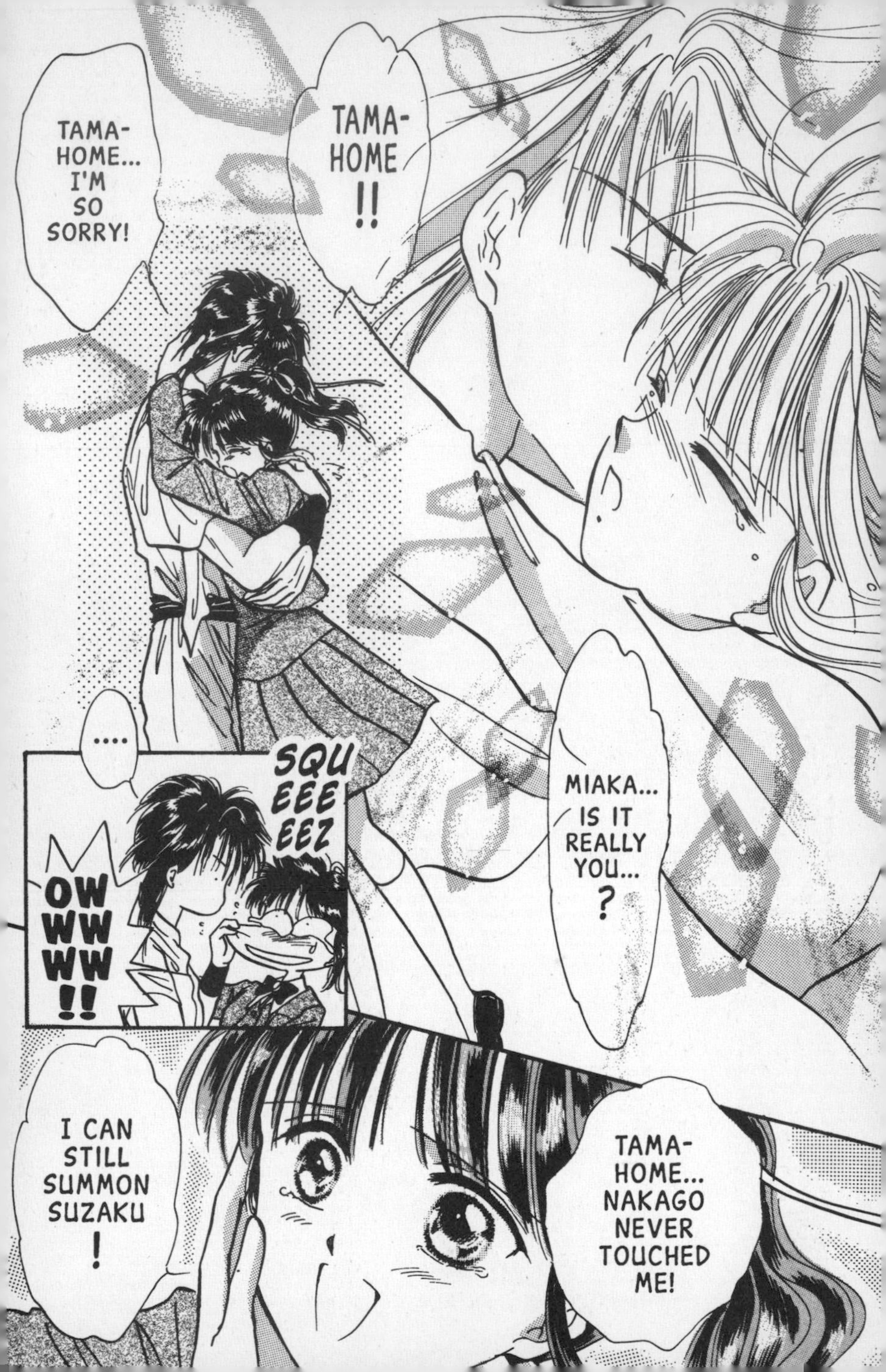
TAMA-HOME !!
TAMA-HOME... I'M SO SORRY!
MIAKA... IS IT REALLY YOU... ?
....
SQUEEEEEZ
OWWWWWW!!
TAMA-HOME... NAKAGO NEVER TOUCHED ME!
I CAN STILL SUMMON SUZAKU !

THAT'S GREAT.

REALLY !?

YES !

...I FELL AND HURT MY LEG. HE RESCUED ME.

AMI-BOSHI...

THAT'S JUST WONDER-FUL !!

....

P-PLEASE FORGIVE MY BETRAYAL AT THE CEREMONY.

HE SWORE TO BRING YOU BACK. HE DID EVERYTHING HE COULD FOR US.

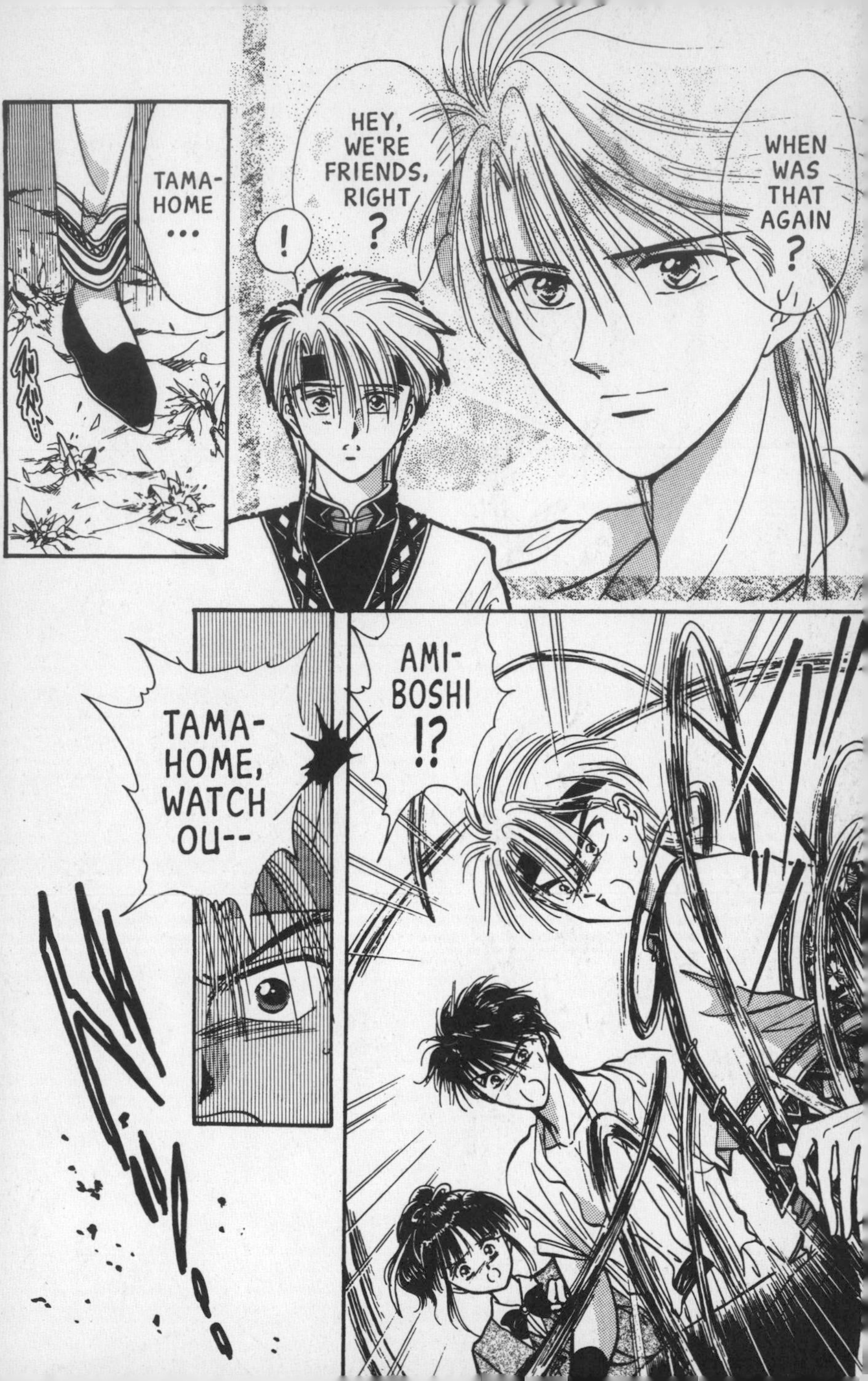

HEY, WE'RE FRIENDS, RIGHT?
WHEN WAS THAT AGAIN?
!
TAMA-HOME...
AMI-BOSHI!?
TAMA-HOME, WATCH OU--

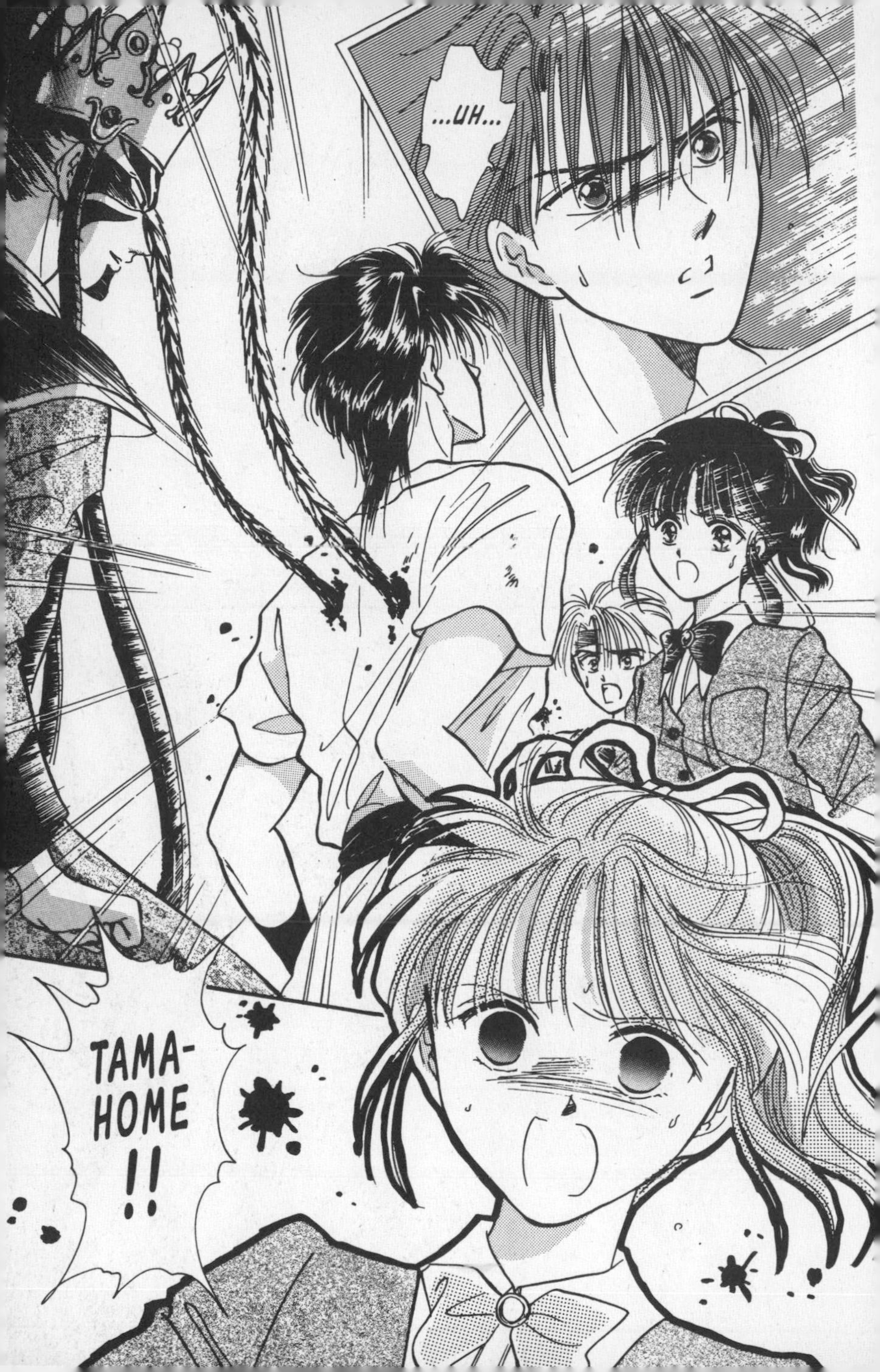
...UH...
TAMA-HOME !!

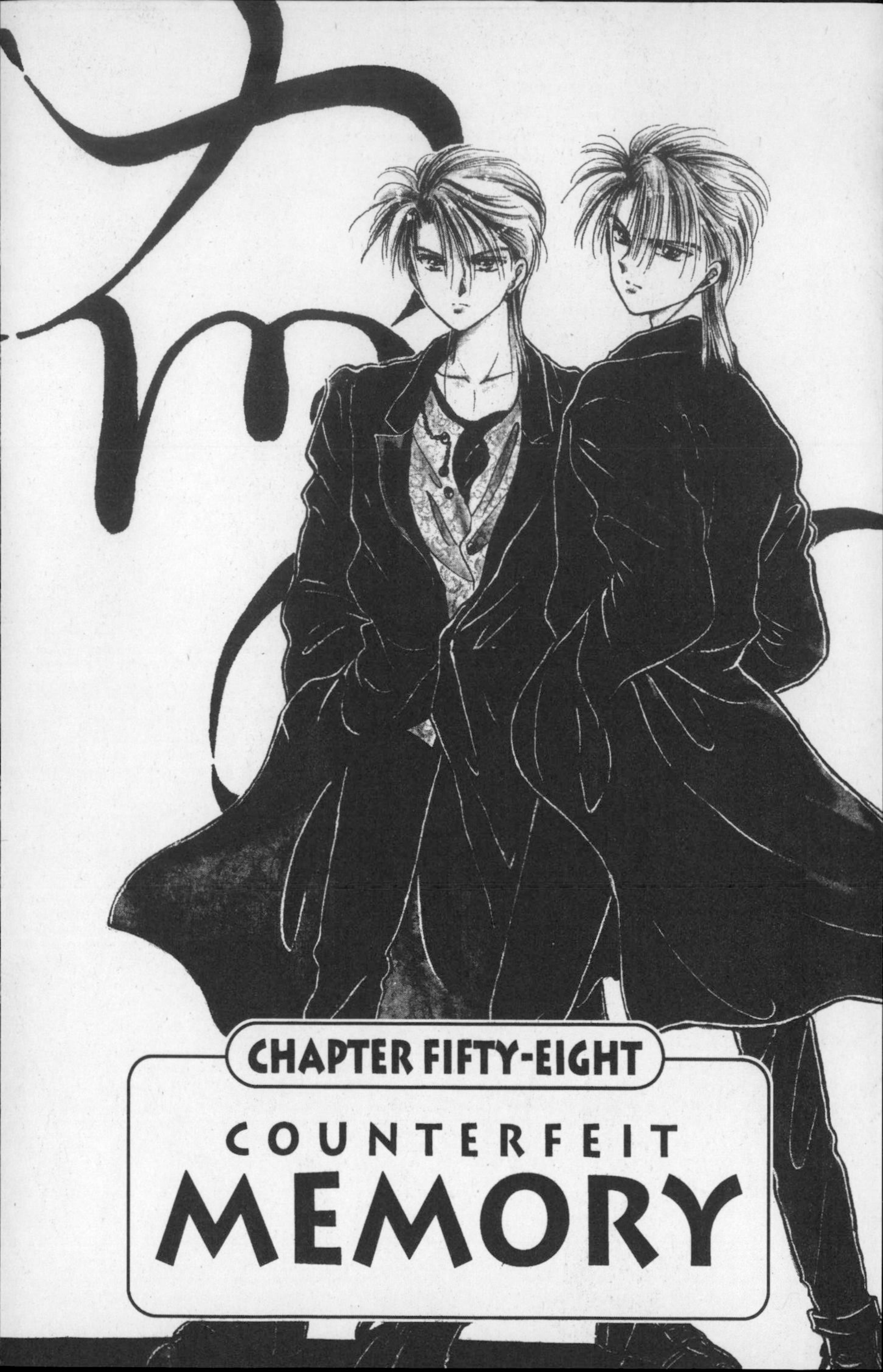

CHAPTER FIFTY-EIGHT

COUNTERFEIT MEMORY

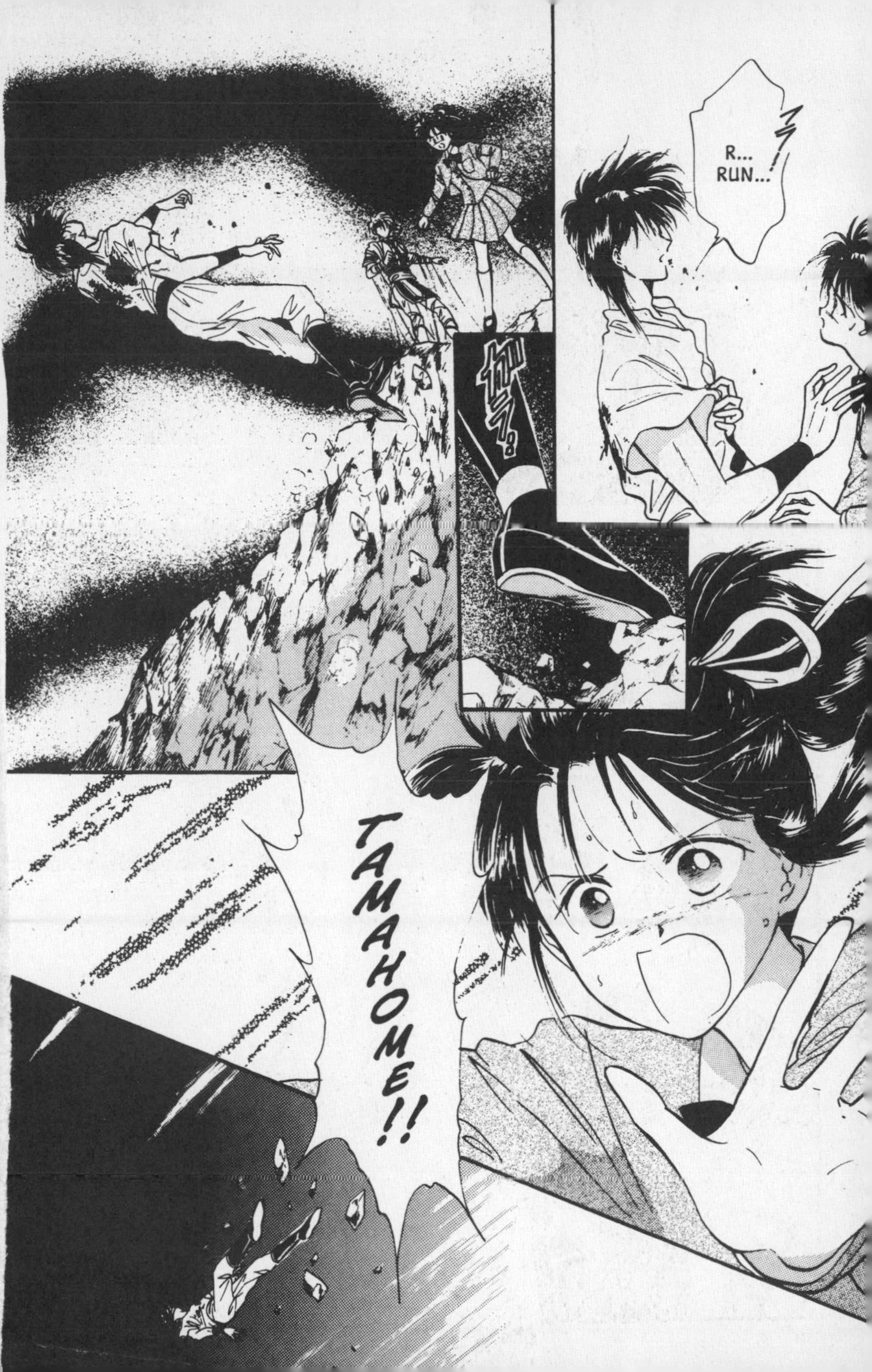
R... RUN...
TAMAHOME!!

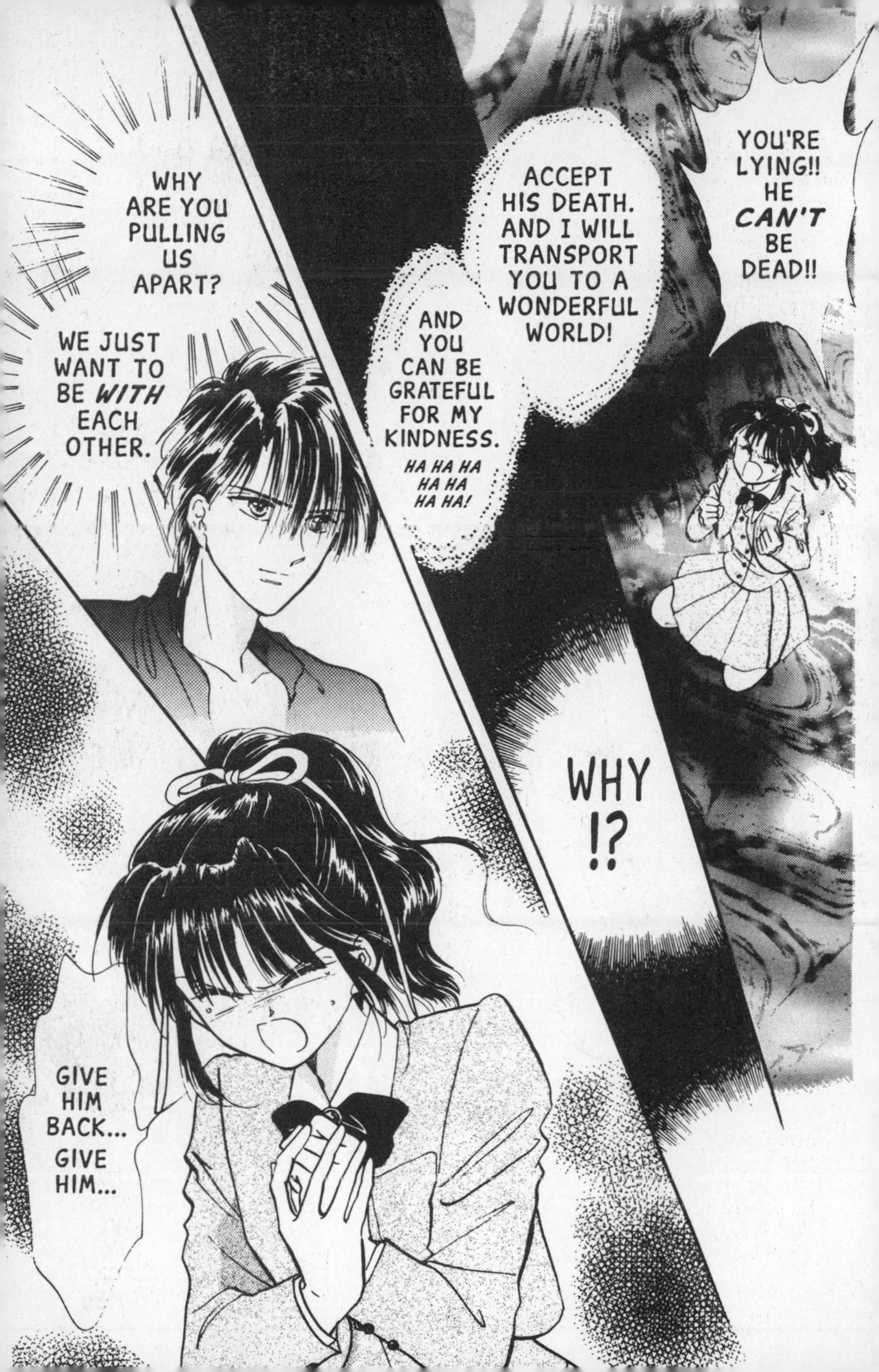
YOU'RE LYING!! HE CAN'T BE DEAD!!
ACCEPT HIS DEATH. AND I WILL TRANSPORT YOU TO A WONDERFUL WORLD!
AND YOU CAN BE GRATEFUL FOR MY KINDNESS.
HA HA HA HA HA HA HA!
WHY !?
WHY ARE YOU PULLING US APART?
WE JUST WANT TO BE WITH EACH OTHER.
GIVE HIM BACK... GIVE HIM...

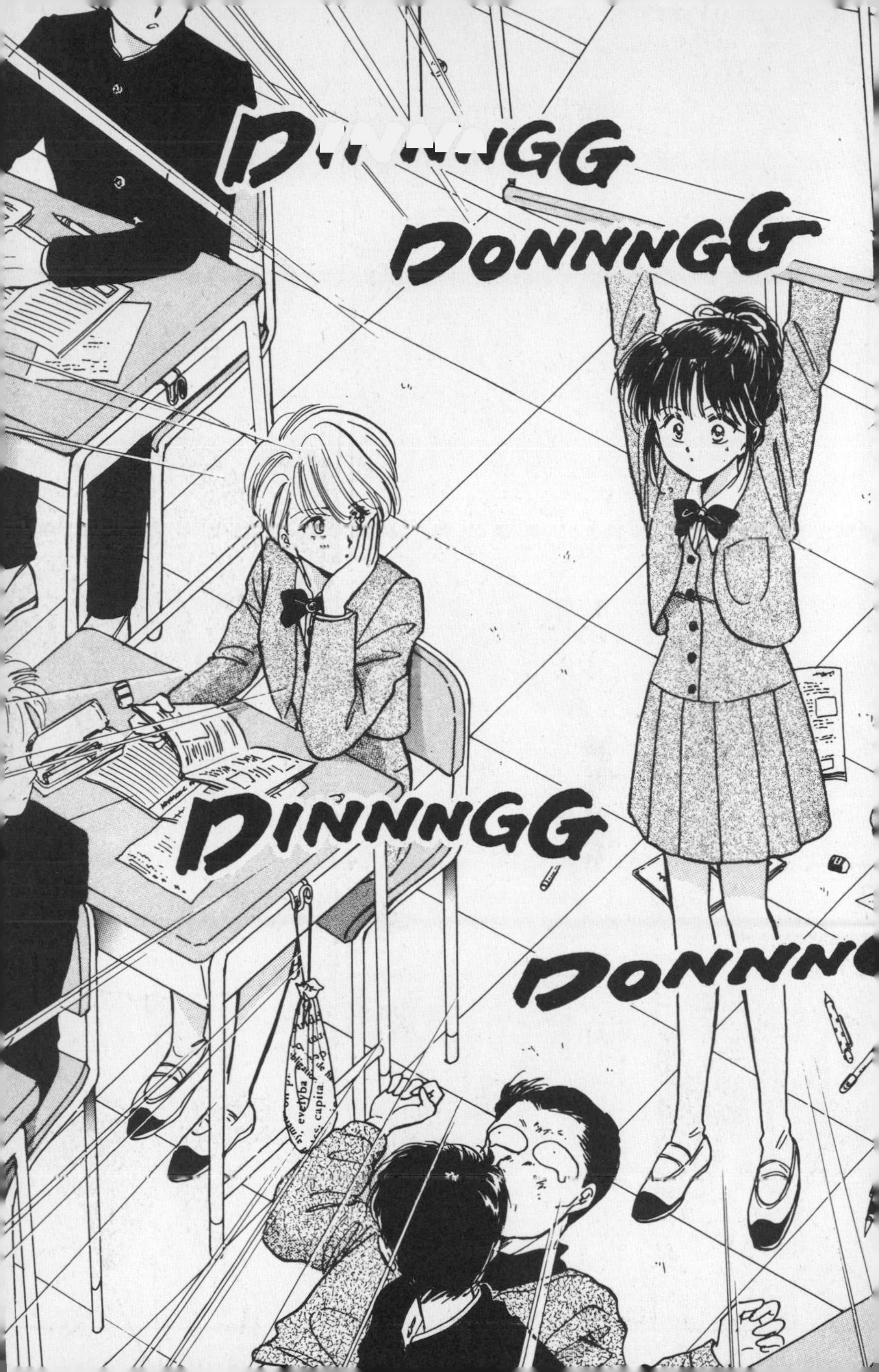
D NGG
DONNNGG
DINNNGG
DONNN

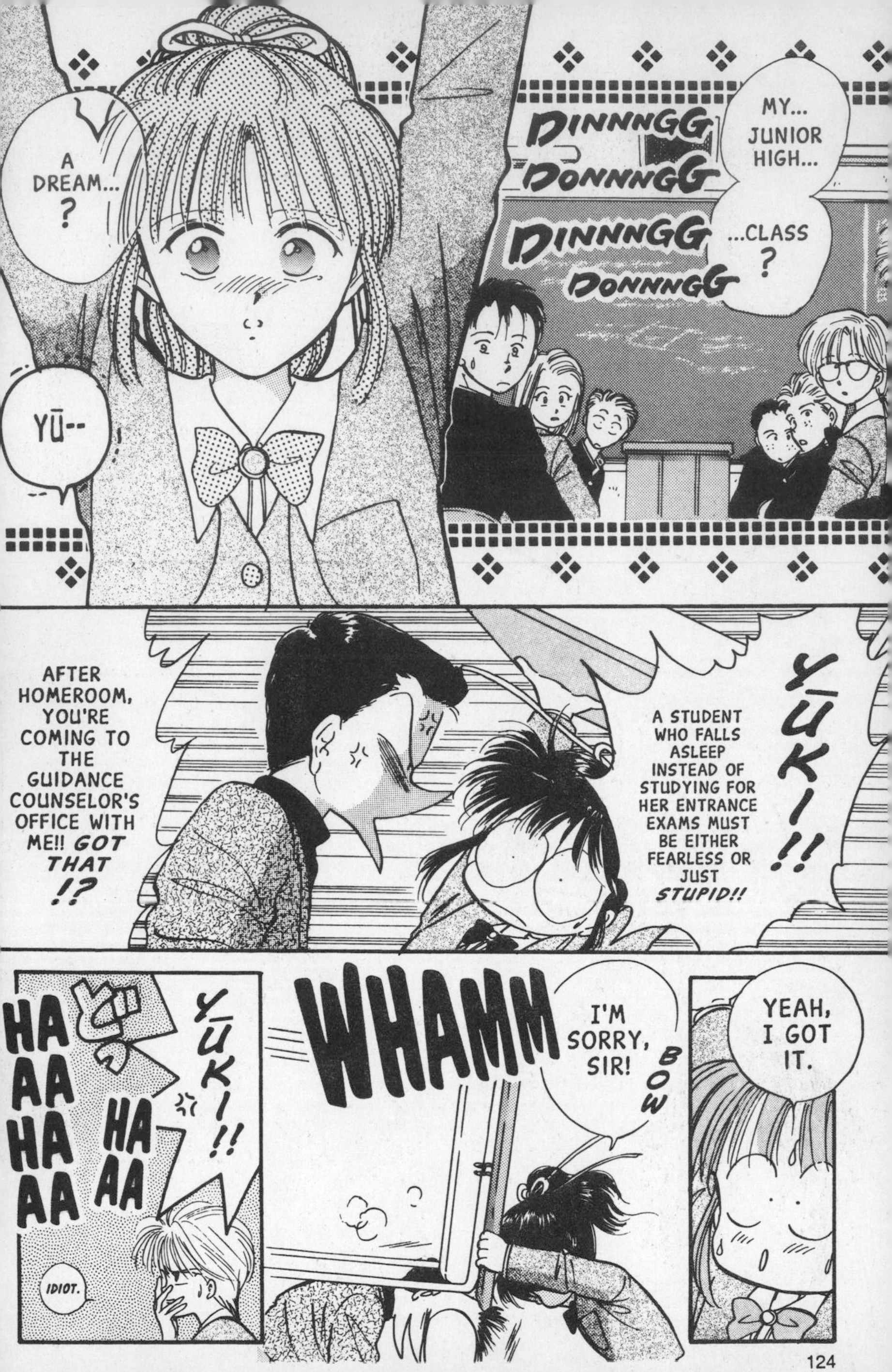
DINNNGG
DONNNGG
DINNNGG
DONNNGG
MY... JUNIOR HIGH... ...CLASS ?
A DREAM... ?
YŪ--
YŪKI!!
A STUDENT WHO FALLS ASLEEP INSTEAD OF STUDYING FOR HER ENTRANCE EXAMS MUST BE EITHER FEARLESS OR JUST STUPID!!
AFTER HOMEROOM, YOU'RE COMING TO THE GUIDANCE COUNSELOR'S OFFICE WITH ME!! GOT THAT !?
YEAH, I GOT IT.
WHAMM
I'M SORRY, SIR!
BOW
YŪKI!!
HA AA HA HA AA
HA AA
IDIOT.

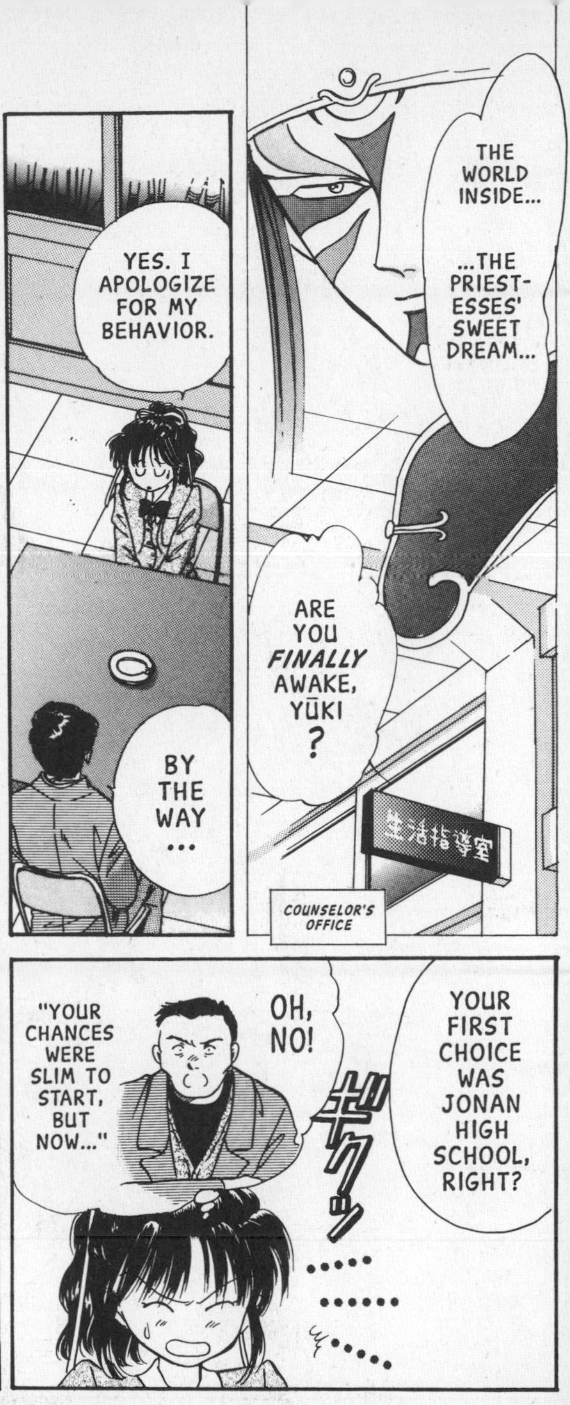
THE WORLD INSIDE...
...THE PRIESTESSES' SWEET DREAM...
ARE YOU *FINALLY* AWAKE, YŪKI ?
生活指導室
COUNSELOR'S OFFICE
YES. I APOLOGIZE FOR MY BEHAVIOR.
BY THE WAY...
YOUR FIRST CHOICE WAS JONAN HIGH SCHOOL, RIGHT?
ギクッ
OH, NO!
"YOUR CHANCES WERE SLIM TO START, BUT NOW..."
.....
......

Now to change the subject. Here, something I read in your recent fan mail. It says that "Fushigi Yūgi" graphic novels and merchandise showed up on TV in Hanakin Dataland. I didn't know about it at all and didn't watch the series. My editors didn't know about it either! Meanwhile, my '94 calendar showed up all the time in the TV drama Tanin no Fukō wa Mitsu no Aji ("The Delicious Woes of Others") which made me happy! It was a while ago.
By the way, the second CD book will be released on August 3. This time, it is amazing, if I do say so myself. First of all, there are so many voice actors. 14 actors. 14!! There are the leads Noriko Hidaka (Miaka), Toshihiko Seki (Tamahome), Wakana Yamazaki (Yui), Yasunori Matsumoto (Hotohori), Minami Takayama (Nuriko), Rin Mizuhara (Tai Yi-Jun)!! Then on top of that, Kazuki Yao (Tasuki), Kappei Yamaguchi (Chichiri), Megumi Origasa (Chiriko), Jurota Osugi (Mitsukake), Tetsuya Iwanaga (Amiboshi), and Ryutaro Okiayu (Nakago) were in it. Eiji Yanagisawa and Toru Furusawa gave a fierce (so fierce it terrified me) performance as the men attacking Yui. I was so impressed I had to write them all down!! My right hand's trembling. What a terrific cast!! *Tremble, tremble!* They're all on the same recording! What a great deal. I actually visited a recording session at the studio... but given my origins as an anime fan, I completely lost control, went haywire, lost my mind, went nuts, etc.

OH, BOY! OH, BOY!
OH, BOY! OH, BOY!

EH?

...LOOK WHAT IT *DID* TO YOU!

MAYBE IT'S TIME I QUIT THE SOCCER CLUB...

O-OH, I'M FINE. I GUESS I LOOK A LITTLE LIKE A GOAL POST.

WHAT DOES THAT MEAN?

YUI SAID IT WAS MY CHANCE.

YOU'RE TAKING EXAMS FOR JONAN HIGH SCHOOL, RIGHT?

...I'M TRYING FOR THE SAME SCHOOL.

YOU SEE, SINCE YOU'RE GOING THERE...

I AM, TOO.

WOW-EEE-EEE!

D-DOES THAT MEAN...

...WHAT?

133

HA HA... THIS TECHNIQUE IS OF A DIFFERENT ORDER THAN WHAT I USED ON THE CELESTIAL WARRIORS.

I HAVE SEALED AWAY, NOT ONLY HER MIND, BUT HER BODY AS WELL.

WHAT ARE YOU DOING TO HER!?

HAVE YOU FORGOTTEN HOW I CAN CREATE NUMEROUS ILLUSIONARY DOUBLES? THEY ARE, IN FACT, ME.

AND ONE OF ME WILL BE THE ONE TO TAKE HER VIRGINITY.

...WILL *NEVER* BE FOOLED BY YOUR *TRICKS*!!

M-- MIAKA...

MMBL MMBL

IT'S TRUE... I DISLIKE FORCING THE WILL OF WOMEN IN THIS WAY, BUT...

YUI'S GOING THERE... AND NOW, SO WILL AONO.

I REALLY WANTED TO GO TO YOTSUBADAI, BUT I'M A SHOO-IN FOR JONAN! SO, IT'S ALL GOOD.

YOU ALL COULD LEARN A THING OR TWO FROM YÜKI!

QUADRATIC EQUATIONS STUMPED ME IN CRAM SCHOOL, BUT I BREEZED RIGHT THROUGH THEM. EVEN THE *TEACHER* WAS NICE.

"I LIKE YOU."

MIAKA, YOU'RE FLAVORING YOUR STEW WITH DROOL.

HEH HEH HEH

BEH HEH HEH

"AONO, THE GUY I'VE ALWAYS LIKED, SAID TODAY THAT HE LIKED ME!!"

WHAT A GREAT DAY TO PUT IN MY DIARY!

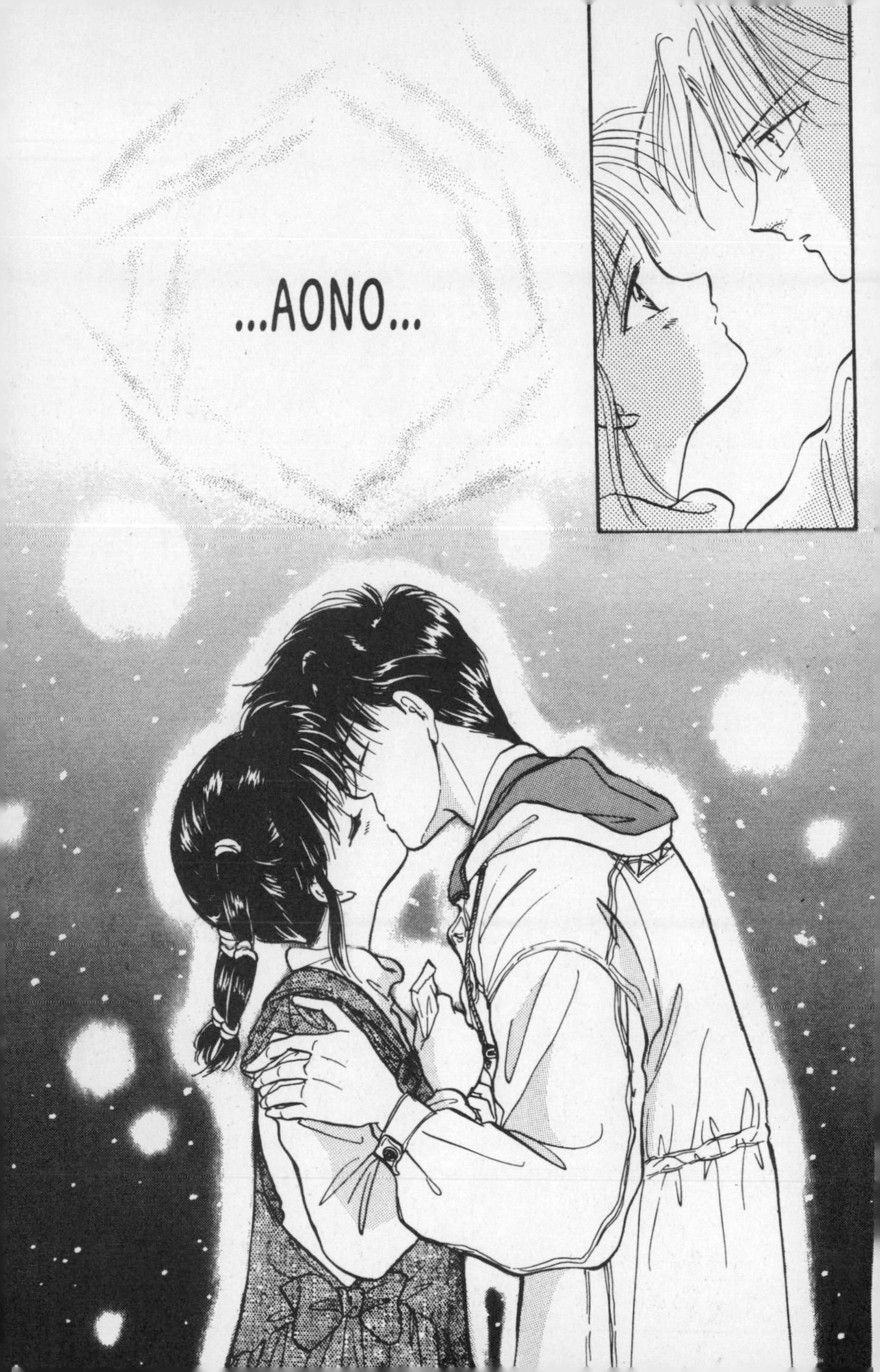
...AONO...

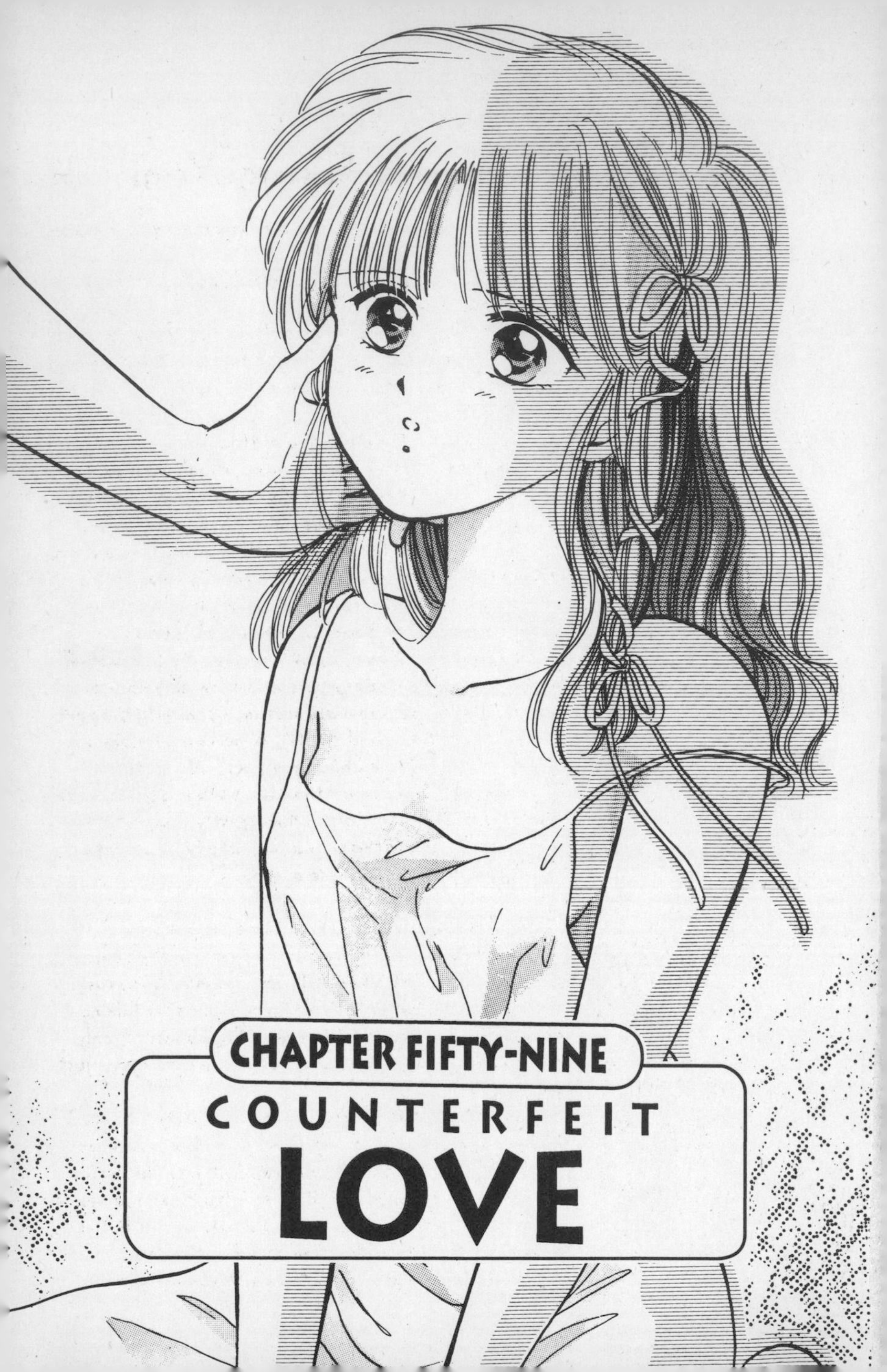
CHAPTER FIFTY-NINE
COUNTERFEIT
LOVE

SPECIAL STRIP
What's So Fushigi about Fushigi Yūgi, Special Edition

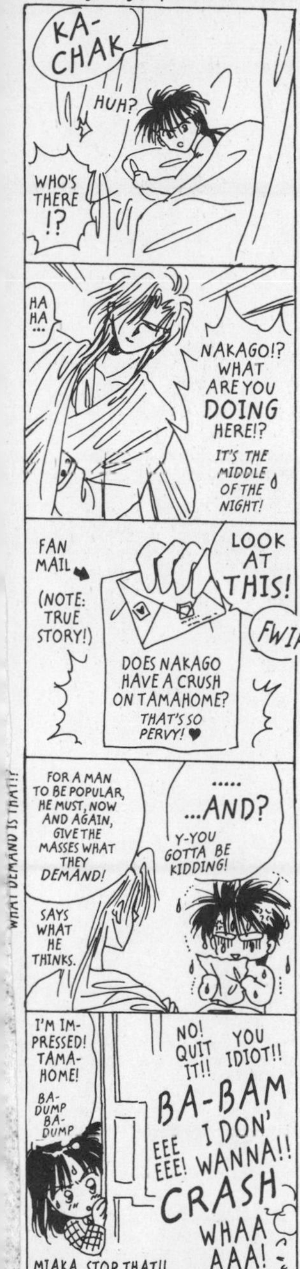
KA-CHAK
HUH?
WHO'S THERE !?
HA HA ...
NAKAGO!? WHAT ARE YOU DOING HERE!?
IT'S THE MIDDLE OF THE NIGHT!
LOOK AT THIS!
FWIP
FAN MAIL
(NOTE: TRUE STORY!)
DOES NAKAGO HAVE A CRUSH ON TAMAHOME? THAT'S SO PERVY! ♥
....AND?
FOR A MAN TO BE POPULAR, HE MUST, NOW AND AGAIN, GIVE THE MASSES WHAT THEY DEMAND!
Y-YOU GOTTA BE KIDDING!
SAYS WHAT HE THINKS.
WHAT DEMAND IS THAT!?
YOU IDIOT!!
NO! QUIT IT!!
I'M IMPRESSED! TAMA-HOME!
BA-BAM
I DON' WANNA!!
EEE EEE!
BA-DUMP BA-DUMP
CRASH
WHAA AAA!
MIAKA, STOP THAT!!

There must be dojinshi like this! ☺
I heard there was one for Tasuki and Nuriko. I'd like to see it!

What's So Fushigi About Fushigi Yūgi #2

Hey, the name keeps on changing!

Q1: I know Miaka has spare clothes, but what is Yui doing about her clothes?
A: Yui has very nimble fingers. I'm sure she can sew her own underwear using silk-like fabrics! She probably has her uniform washed every night.

Q2: Is Tomo gay? I mean the outfit...
A: Yep. (To be blunt.) Tomo is homosexual. Furthermore, he's in love with Nakago! ☺ His criticisms of Nakago may be an expression of love. "Why," you ask. He just ended up this way. Those of you who know Chinese opera might've realized that I had the opera in mind for his character. The feathers are also from it. In fact, they might be even more gaudy in the actual opera.
After I first drew Tomo, I saw "Farewell My Concubine," and there was that scene where the female impersonator lead is in love with the male protagonist during the performance of "Front and Back." Which might make you think, "so it's a movie about gay guys." No, not at all!! The drama's much deeper than that. What a great movie! *Really!* Then there was also "M Butterfly" (about a man who doesn't realize the woman he falls for is in fact a man), and then this Chinese opera...

Personally, a gay theme is no different from a straight theme for me. Those factors were simply in the atmosphere when I came up with Tomo. But ever since Fushigi began, assistant after assistant would not stop talking about it! ☺ With characters like this, I guess it's only natural. *What does ya thinks, Olive Oyl?* I guess everyone just got into it.
And so Tomo got his look and personality. By the way, I had the same kind of question with regard to Nakago (refer to left comic). Although he isn't gay, he wouldn't let gender stand in his way if he is attracted to someone. It seems natural if you think of it as attraction between people rather than attraction between the sexes.
That's what I thought after seeing "Farewell My Concubine."

🐟 Enemy 🐟

And because of that... I was so nervous I started sweating! (My entire body was drenched!) My voice broke. Blood rushed to my head. I almost fainted. I just totally clammed up... and couldn't even talk to them!! *Dammit!!* 😣
It was so sad and pathetic. I really missed my chance!
I couldn't even look at them.♭ Why am I so shy!? Argh!! If I could only be more social!! B-but, no!! Readers who know anime and voice actors must know what I'm talking about!! I mean voice actors are like super stars!!!
I would recall the voice of the character from the anime that I watched all through high school, and I'd realize, "S-so this person did..." There was no way I could start up a conversation.✏️ But finally a reporter from Animate arranged for a short interview with myself along with Mr. Seki, Mr. Matsumoto, Ms. Hidaka, and Ms. Yamazaki... "Wow, we're actually breathing the same air in the same room!" Am I a sickie or WHAT!? 😊 I actually sat next to Ms. Hidaka! She actually shook my hand. She actually shook my hand!! Pant, pant, pant. *She seemed so cheerful and kind.*
She and Ms. Yamazaki told me they had bought my graphic novels, and I almost burst out crying. Sniff, sniff... But I was so shy, I couldn't watch and had my back to them. I'm such an idiot! (During the entire time they were recording!) That's right! I hear that if you send in the survey form that comes with the CD, you'll get an autographed sign card with the signatures of all 12 voice actors and Yū Watase! Really!? They must be copies... One of them might be real! (I have one displayed in my room!🎵) *I'm acting like a junior-high-school girl!!*

H-HE...

...KISSED ME!

UM MM...

YOU DON'T DESERVE BOYFRIEND BLISS!!

MIAKA, YOU'RE *BAD!* SOME EXAM STUDENT YOU ARE!

...MIAKA!

?

152

ANYBODY STUDYING FOR THE ENTRANCE EXAMS, GRAB A DICTIONARY AND MEMORIZE.

TIME FOR JAPANESE-LIT STUDY HALL.

∻AHEM∻ ALL KIDDING ASIDE, I'M GLAD YOU BOTH FEEL THE SAME WAY.

Y-YEAH... THANKS, YUI.

3-4

IS THIS BECAUSE MR. TAKAGI'S LATE FOR CLASSES *AGAIN?* HE'S GOT TO GET IT TOGETHER!

I'M COOL. I GOT MY WORK-BOOK.

MY LUCKY DAY! ♪ GIVE ME THE KANJI DICTION-ARY!

FLIP FLIP FLIP FLIP

SO SERIOUS....

OH! HERE'S ONE. "LOOK UP PAGE 581!"

YEAH, AND THAT PAGE ALWAYS HAS SOME DIRTY WORD!

HEY! SOMEONE'S ALWAYS WRITING NOTES IN THESE SCHOOL DICTIONARIES TO LOOK ON A CERTAIN PAGE!

HA HA HA HA!

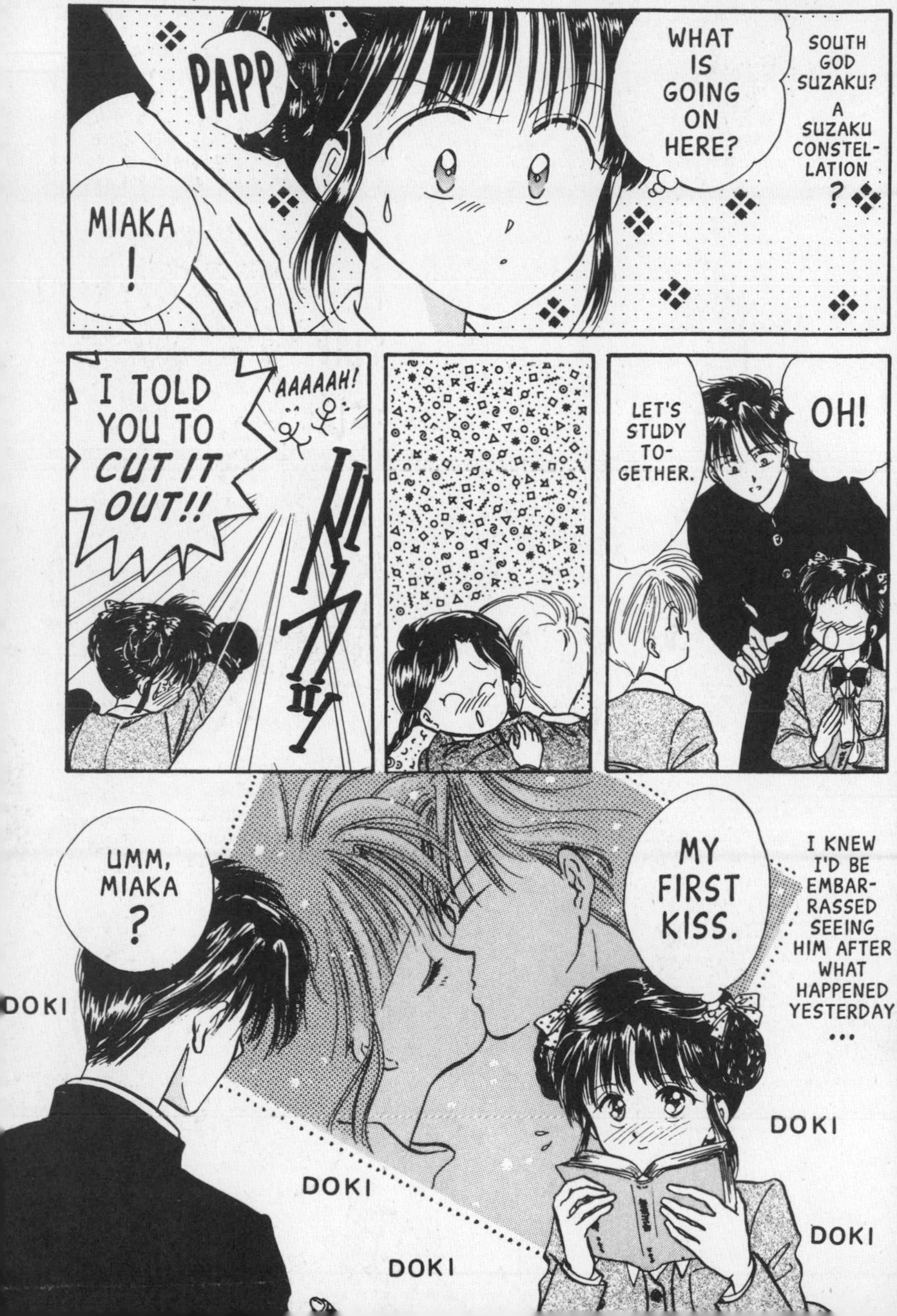
SOUTH GOD SUZAKU? A SUZAKU CONSTEL-LATION ?
WHAT IS GOING ON HERE?
PAPP
MIAKA !
OH!
LET'S STUDY TO-GETHER.
AAAAAH!
I TOLD YOU TO CUT IT OUT!!
I KNEW I'D BE EMBAR-RASSED SEEING HIM AFTER WHAT HAPPENED YESTERDAY ...
MY FIRST KISS.
DOKI
DOKI
UMM, MIAKA ?
DOKI
DOKI
DOKI

HUH?

IT'S OKAY, ISN'T IT?

TOMORROW IS SUNDAY... WHY DON'T YOU COME OVER TO MY HOUSE?

N-NO, TOMO!! THERE'S *DANGER* IN WHAT YOU SUGGEST!

AFTER YESTER-DAY, WHAT DO YOU EXPECT WITH THAT INVITATION?

"STUDY"!?

I MEAN, WE'RE TRYING TO PASS EXAMS FOR THE SAME SCHOOL. WE SHOULD STUDY TOGETHER.

WHAT WERE YOU THINKING?

I WASN'T THINKING ANYTHING... MUMBLE, MUMBLE.

MIAKA, YOUR HUGE GRIN DOESN'T FIT WITH YOUR FACE.

...MIAKA...
?

CALM DOWN. YOU'RE IN MY HOUSE. YOU WERE IN THE THROWS OF ILLUSION. I BROKE IT WITH ACUPRESSURE.

NO MORE MISERY, RIGHT.

WH-WHERE AM I !?

!?

DAMMIT! HE TRICKED ME!!

YOU MEAN, THAT WAS ILLUSION?

GOOD, YOU'RE ALL RIGHT NOW.

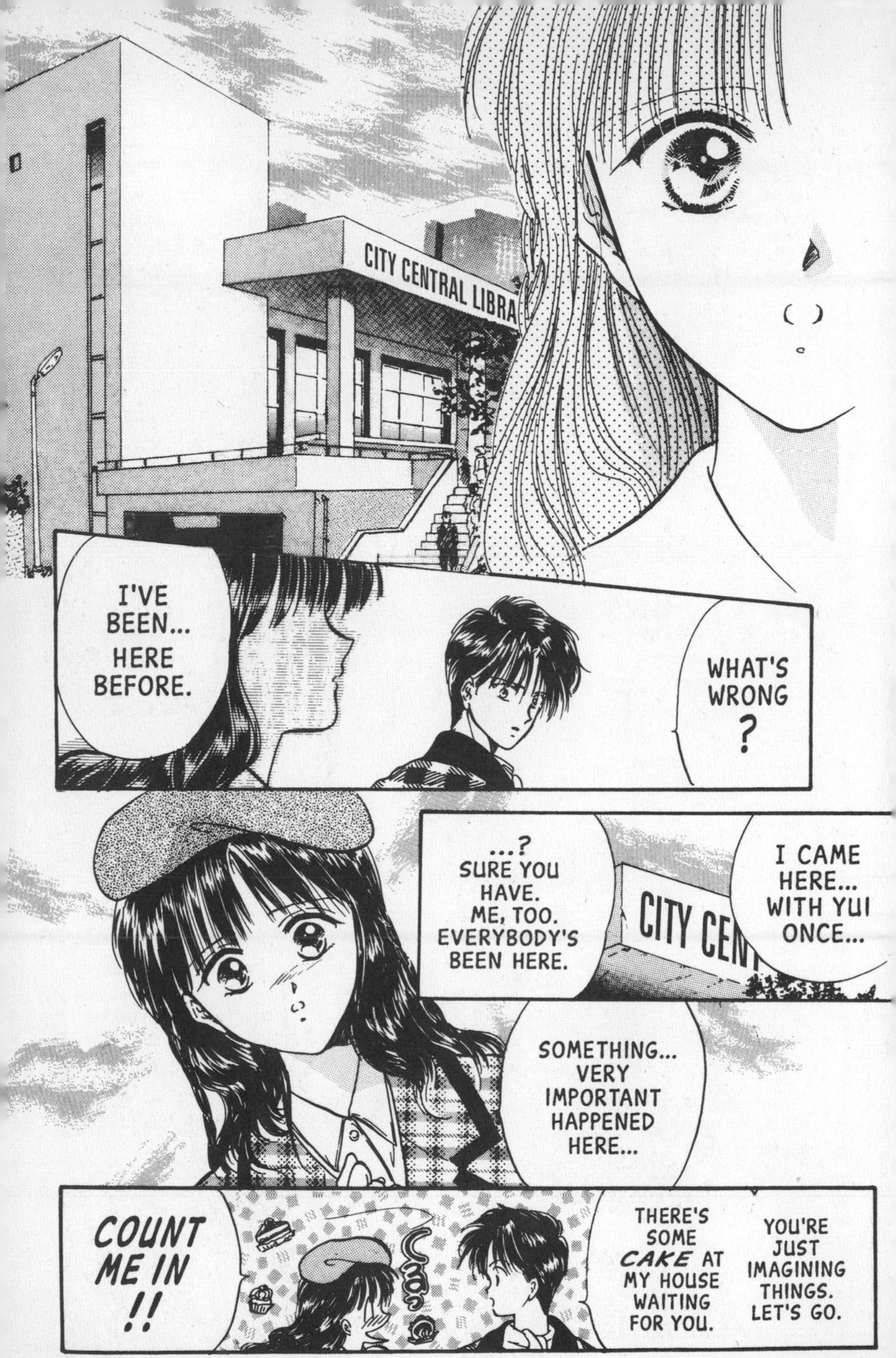
CITY CENTRAL LIBRA
WHAT'S WRONG ?
I'VE BEEN... HERE BEFORE.
I CAME HERE... WITH YUI ONCE...
CITY CENT
...? SURE YOU HAVE. ME, TOO. EVERYBODY'S BEEN HERE.
SOMETHING... VERY IMPORTANT HAPPENED HERE...
YOU'RE JUST IMAGINING THINGS. LET'S GO.
THERE'S SOME *CAKE* AT MY HOUSE WAITING FOR YOU.
COUNT ME IN !!

WHY DOES IT BOTHER ME SO MUCH? WHAT HAPPENED THERE?

YOU CAN SEE THE LIBRARY FROM HERE.

HEY!

HMM.

THAT "DEMON" CHARACTER, SUZAKU, THE LIBRARY...

HEY, TOMO! LET'S GO TO THE LIBRARY LATER. I WANT TO LOOK SOMETHING UP.

AH...

OH, YEAH, THE LIBRARY.

I HAVE TO REMEMBER! WHAT HAPPENED THERE?

HEY! LOOK AT THIS, YUI!

PEOPLE AREN'T ALLOWED IN THE RESTRICTED PRIVATE LIBRARY.

"READ TO THE STORY'S END; THE SPELL SHALL GRANT YOUR WISH."

"SUCKED INTO A BOOK?" YOU'RE REMEMBERING SOME DREAM. THINGS LIKE THAT DON'T HAPPEN!

WE GOT SUCKED INTO THE BOOK SOMEHOW... WHAT WAS ITS NAME...?

WE FOUND AN OLD BOOK IN THE RESTRICTED PRIVATE LIBRARY!

TOMO! I WENT TO THE LIBRARY WITH YUI!

BUT I REMEMBER THE WORLD OF THE BOOK. IT WAS A PLACE LIKE ANCIENT CHINA.

A DREAM... SO IT WAS... A DREAM.

FORGET ABOUT IT.

!

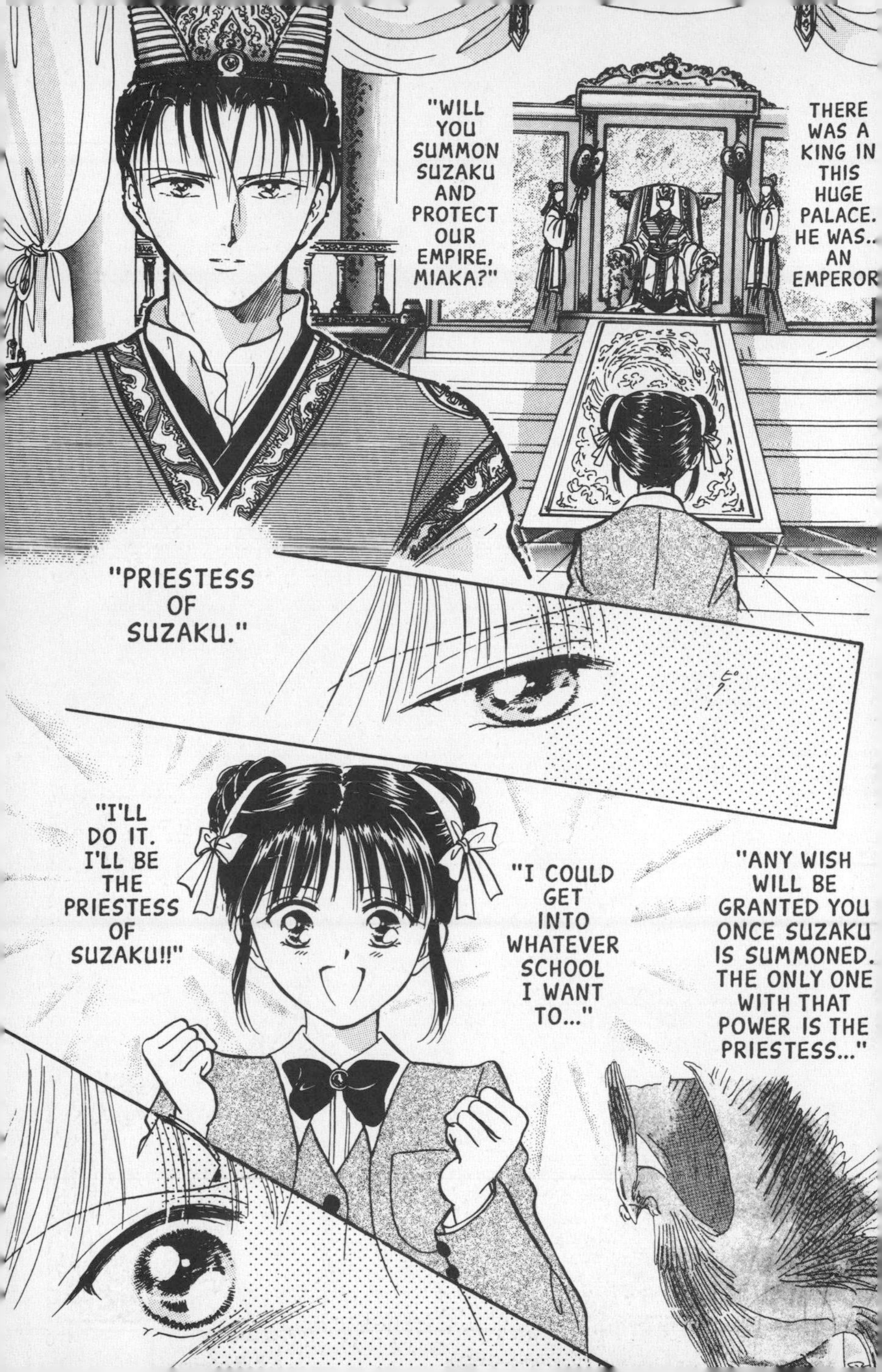
THERE WAS A KING IN THIS HUGE PALACE. HE WAS.. AN EMPEROR
"WILL YOU SUMMON SUZAKU AND PROTECT OUR EMPIRE, MIAKA?"
"PRIESTESS OF SUZAKU."
"ANY WISH WILL BE GRANTED YOU ONCE SUZAKU IS SUMMONED. THE ONLY ONE WITH THAT POWER IS THE PRIESTESS..."
"I COULD GET INTO WHATEVER SCHOOL I WANT TO..."
"I'LL DO IT. I'LL BE THE PRIESTESS OF SUZAKU!!"

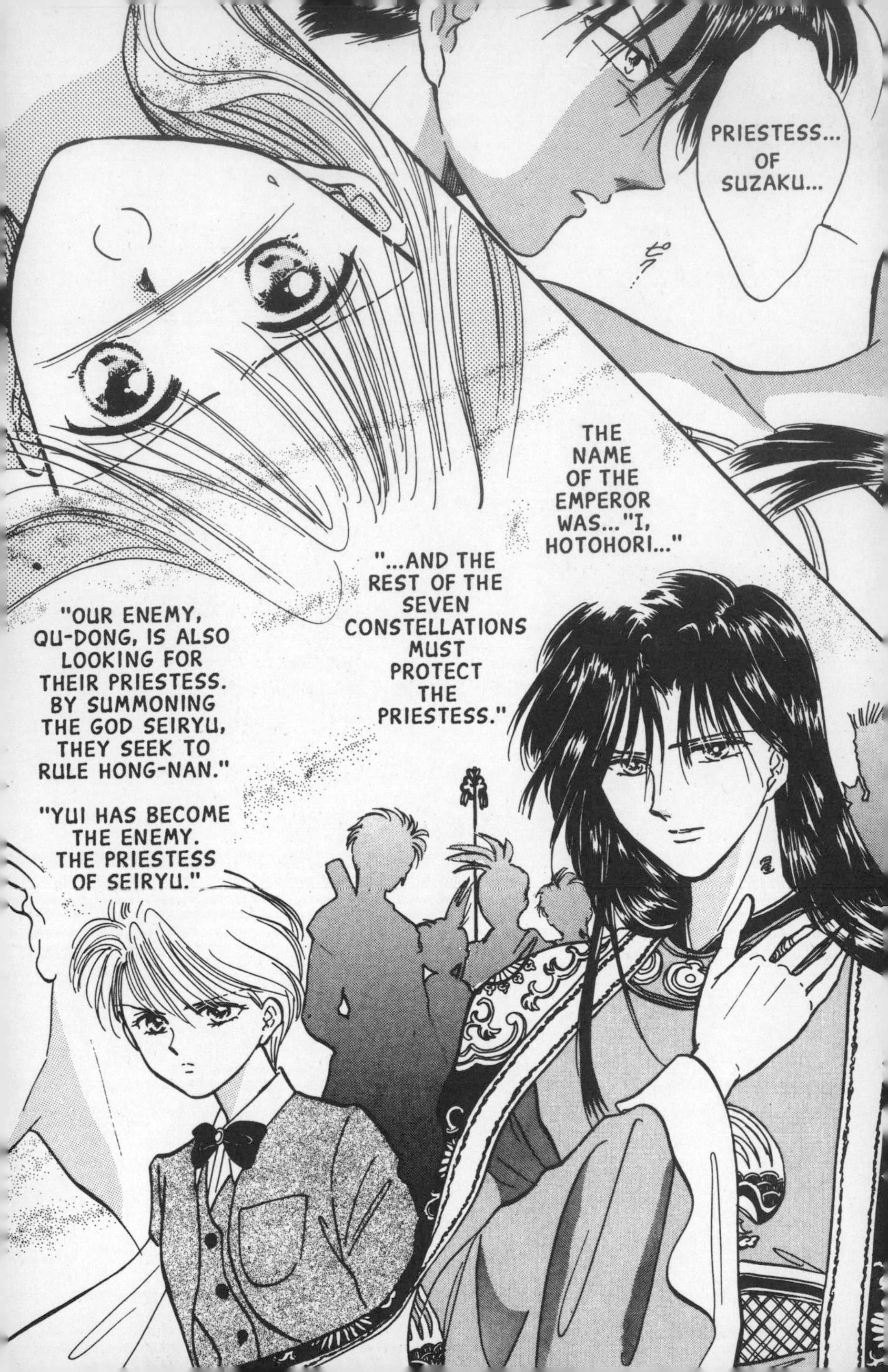
PRIESTESS... OF SUZAKU...
THE NAME OF THE EMPEROR WAS... "I, HOTOHORI..."
"...AND THE REST OF THE SEVEN CONSTELLATIONS MUST PROTECT THE PRIESTESS."
"OUR ENEMY, QU-DONG, IS ALSO LOOKING FOR THEIR PRIESTESS. BY SUMMONING THE GOD SEIRYU, THEY SEEK TO RULE HONG-NAN."
"YUI HAS BECOME THE ENEMY. THE PRIESTESS OF SEIRYU."

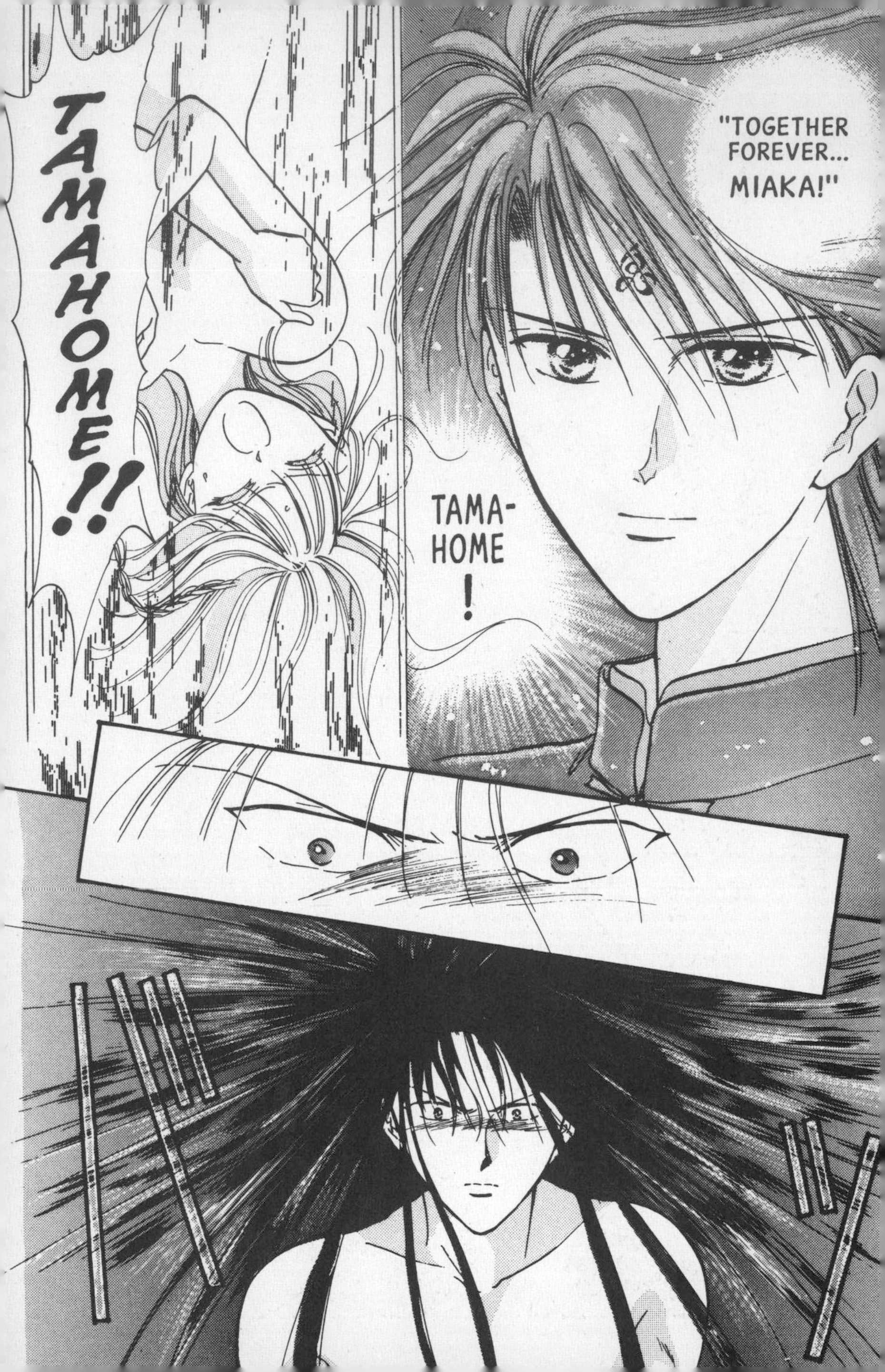
"TOGETHER FOREVER... MIAKA!"
TAMA-HOME!
TAMAHOME!!

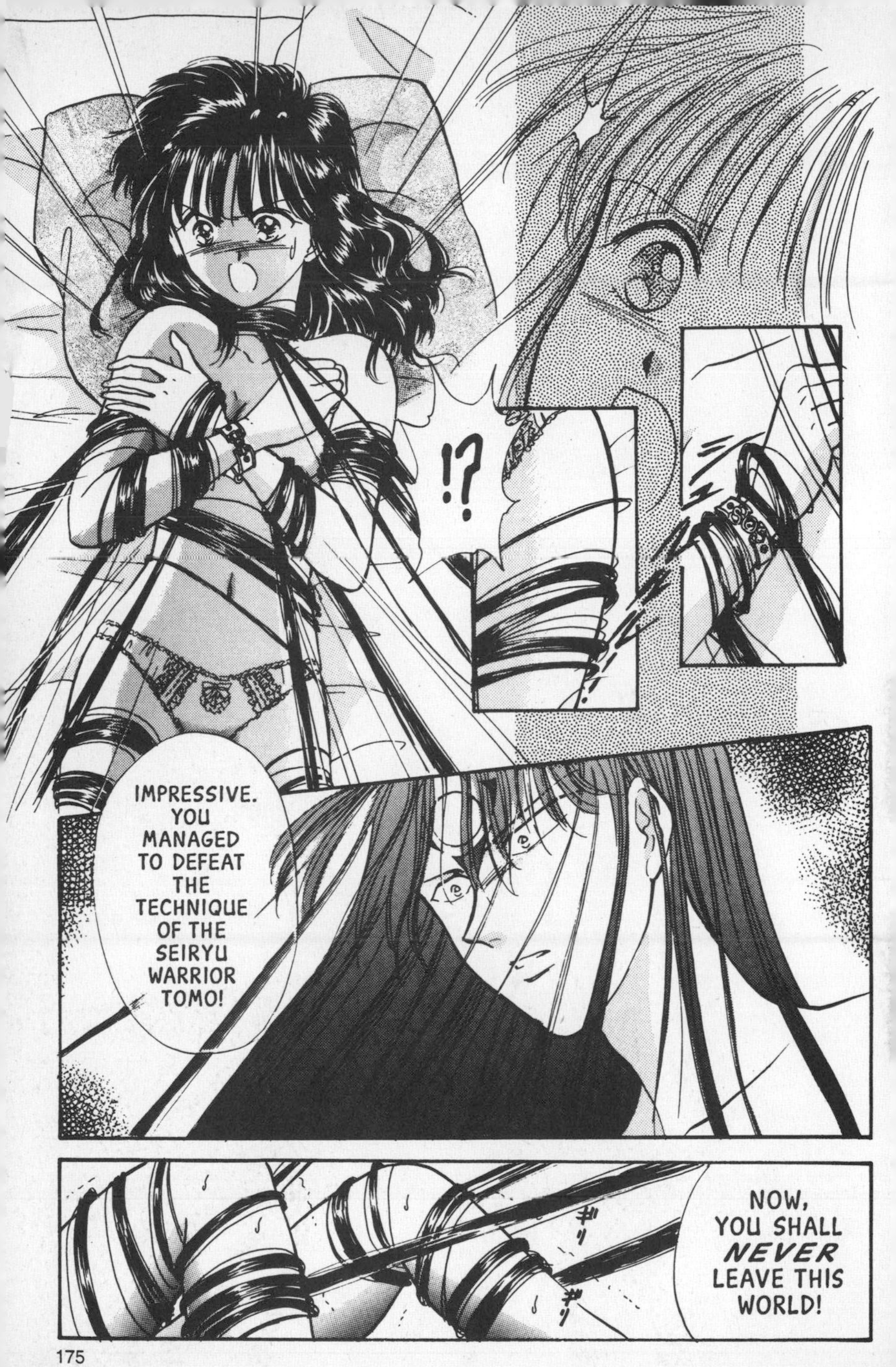
!?
IMPRESSIVE. YOU MANAGED TO DEFEAT THE TECHNIQUE OF THE SEIRYU WARRIOR TOMO!
NOW, YOU SHALL NEVER LEAVE THIS WORLD!
ギリ
ギリ

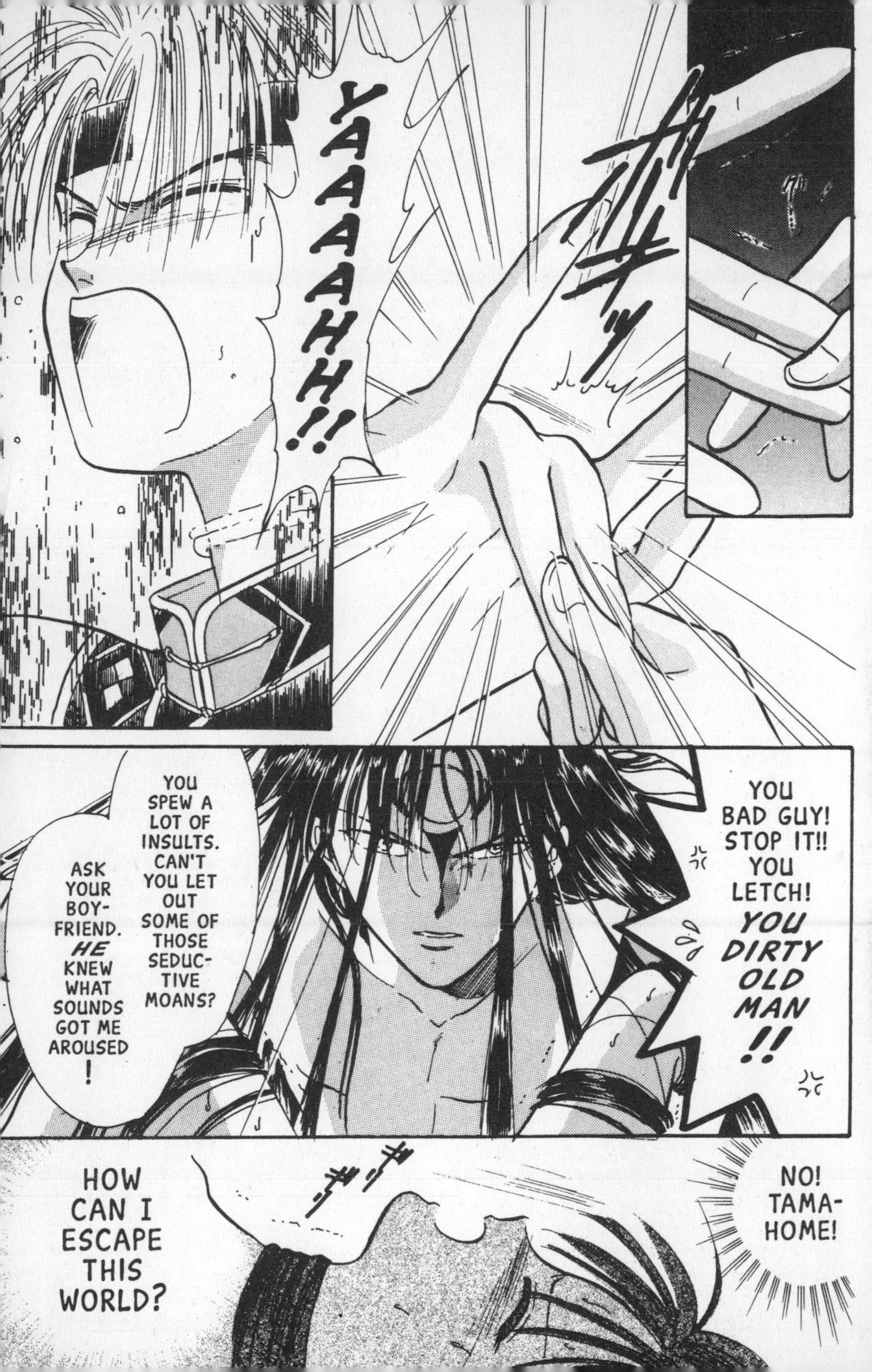
YAAAAAHH!!
YOU BAD GUY! STOP IT!! YOU LETCH! *YOU DIRTY OLD MAN!!*
YOU SPEW A LOT OF INSULTS. CAN'T YOU LET OUT SOME OF THOSE SEDUCTIVE MOANS?
ASK YOUR BOYFRIEND. *HE* KNEW WHAT SOUNDS GOT ME AROUSED!
NO! TAMAHOME!
HOW CAN I ESCAPE THIS WORLD?

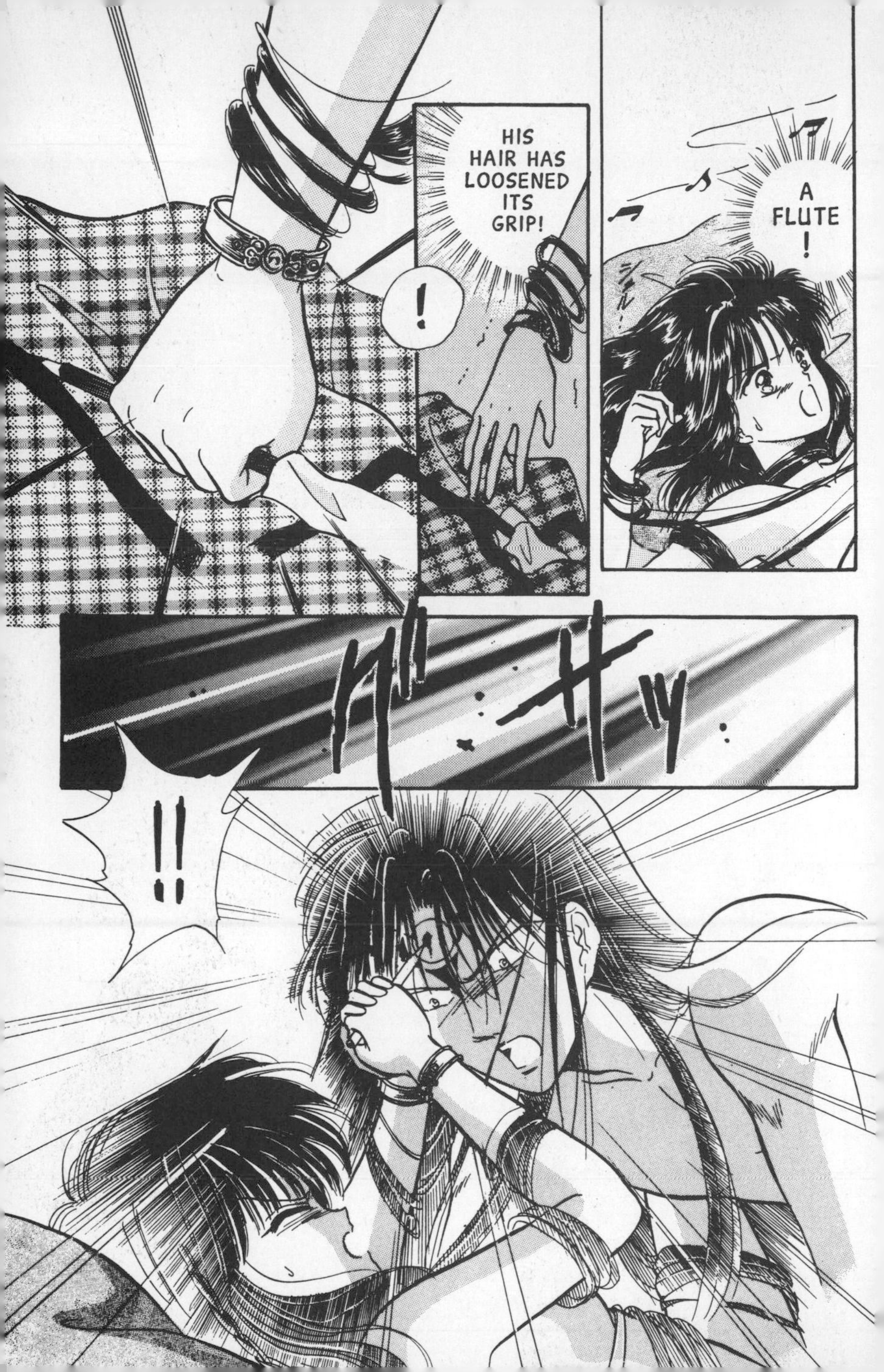
A FLUTE!
HIS HAIR HAS LOOSENED ITS GRIP!
!
!!

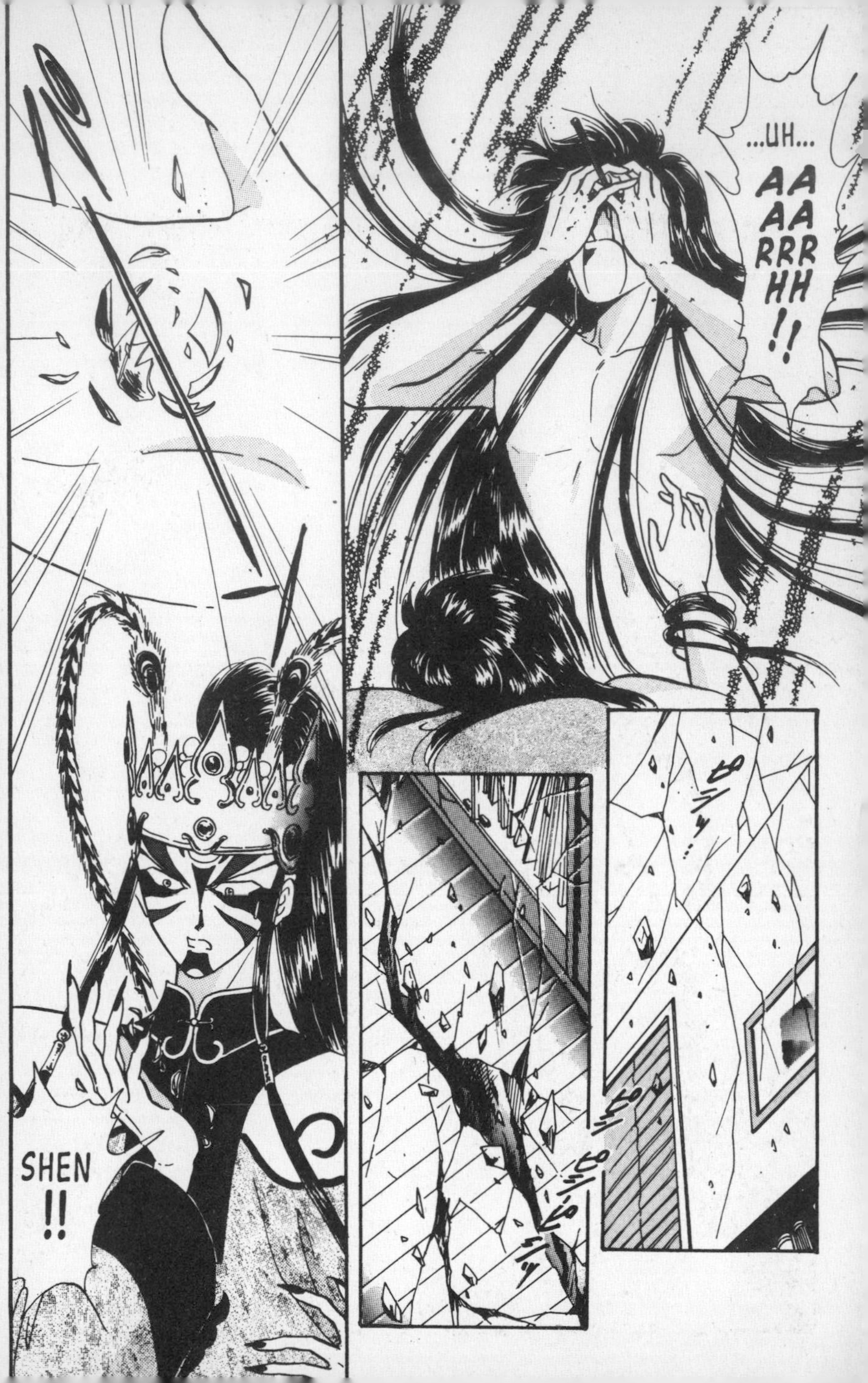
...UH...
AAAARRRHH!!
SHEN!!

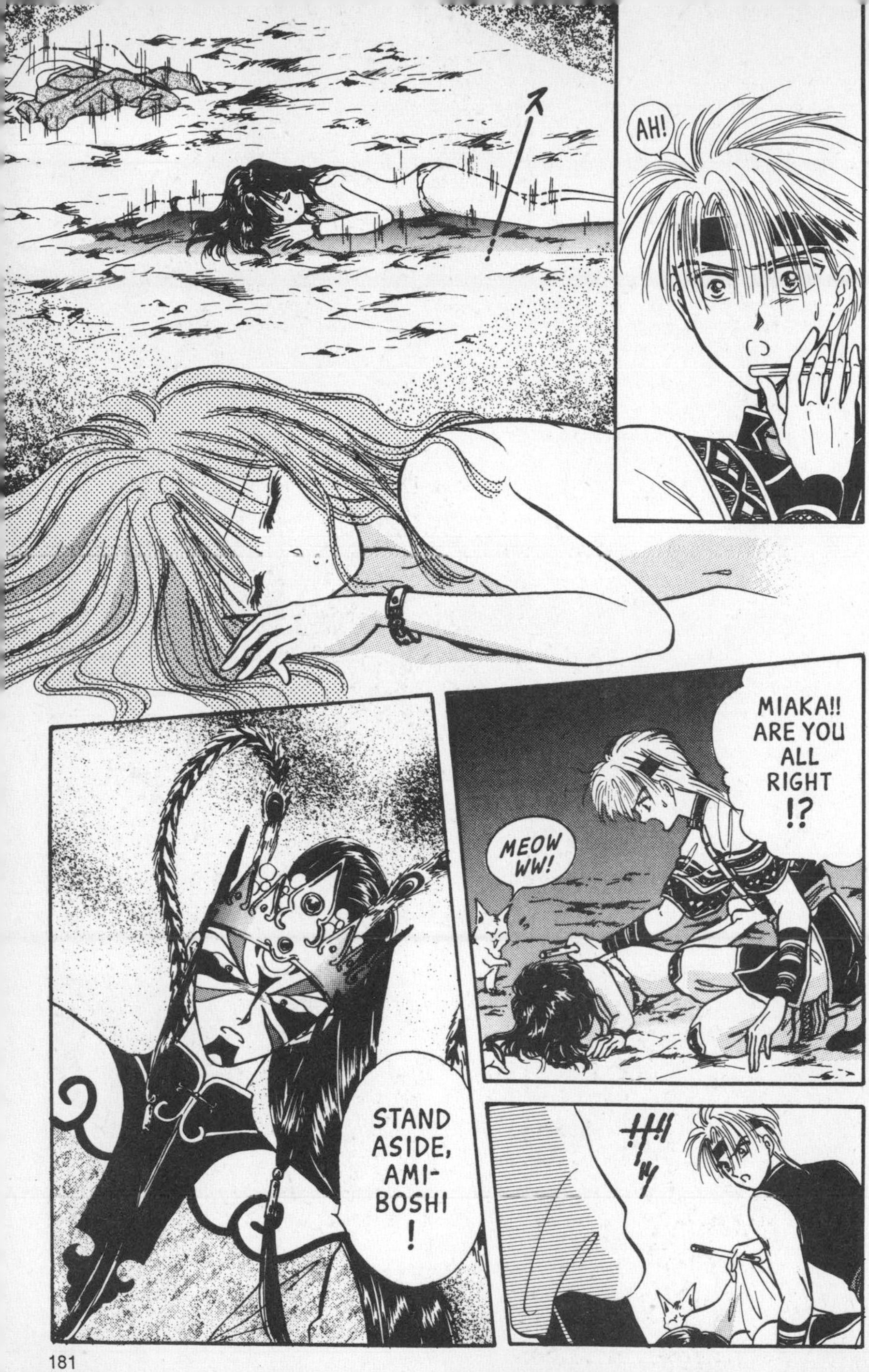

AH!
MIAKA!! ARE YOU ALL RIGHT !?
MEOW WW!
STAND ASIDE, AMI-BOSHI !

182

TO BE CONTINUED
IN VOLUME 11: VETERAN

ABOUT THE AUTHOR

Yû Watase was born on March 5 in a town near Osaka,
Japan, and she was raised there before moving to Tokyo to
follow her dream of creating manga. In the decade since
her debut short story, *PAJAMA DE OJAMA* ("An Intrusion in
Pajamas"), she has produced more than 50 compiled vol-
umes of short stories and continuing series. Her latest
series, *ZETTAI KARESHI* ("He'll Be My Boyfriend"), is currently
running in the anthology magazine *SHŌJO COMIC*. Watase's
long-running horror/romance story *CERES: CELESTIAL LEGEND*
and her most recent completed series, *ALICE 19TH*, are now
available in North America published by VIZ. She loves
science fiction, fantasy and comedy.

The Fushigi Yûgi Guide to Sound Effects

Most of the sound effects in FUSHIGI YÛGI are the way Yû Watase created them, in their original Japanese.

We created this glossary for a page-by-page, panel-by-panel explanation of the action and background noises. By using this guide, you may even learn some Japanese.

The glossary lists page and panel number. For example, page 1, panel 3, would be listed as 1.3.

26.1 FX: SHA [moving curtains]
26.5 FX: KYU [tightening]

28.3 FX: ZAZAAAAA [scarfing down food]
28.3 FX: KARAN [dropping chopsticks]
28.4 FX: MOSHA MOSHA [munch munch]
28.6 FX: KATAN [klak]

30.2 FX: POTA [drip]
30.3 FX: HA [Gasp]
30.4 FX: PORO PORO PORO [crying]

31.3 FX: GATAN [chair clunking]

32.1 FX: HYOI [lifting]
32.2 FX: MUSHI [ignoring her]
32.3 FX: SUTA SUTA SUTA [quick stomping]
32.4 FX: JITABATA [struggling]

33.3 FX: WAI WAI WAI [crowd noise]
33.4 FX: SUPO [slipping on]

37.2 FX: KURU [a sudden turn]

40.1 FX: PATAN [door closing]

41.7 FX: POKO POKO [pouring]

43.1 FX: GURARI [swaying]
43.3 FX: KARAN… [klak…]
43.3 FX: DOSA… [thud…]

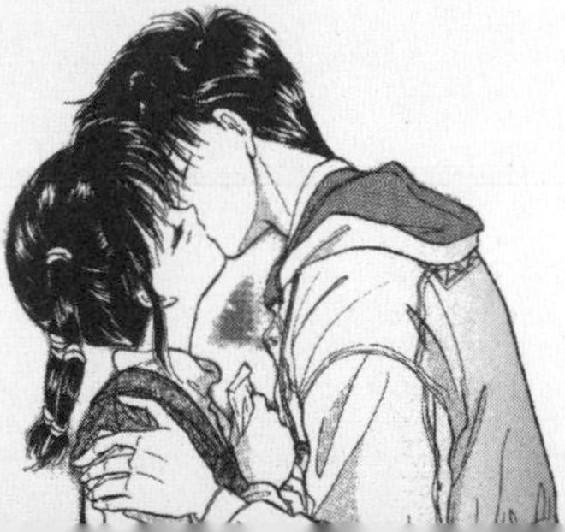

CHAPTER FIFTY-FIVE: ILLUSIONARY WARMTH

5.2 FX: DOKUN [heart beats]
5.3 FX: DOKUN [heart beats]

9.2 FX: DOKUN [heart beats]
9.3 FX: GASA... [shifting her weight]
9.4 FX: DOKUN [heart beats]
9.4 FX: DOKUN [heart beats]
9.4 FX: SU… [rushing air]

10.3 FX: BYU [flying blade]
10.4 FX: GYAAAAA [a loud scream]

11.1 FX: DOSA [falling to the ground]
11.2 FX: BA [grabbing]

12.1 FX: ZURU… [slipping]
12.3 FX: ZAN [a hard hit]
12.4 FX: SHURURU [whirling]

13.1 FX: GYU [clenching]
13.2 FX: KORO [turning]

14.4 FX: ZAKU ZAKU [steps in sand]

15.1 FX: ZAKU [steps in sand]
15.3 FX: ZURU [going to one knee]
15.5 FX: BAN [striking rock]

18.2 FX: HA [surprise]

20.1 FX: BATA [footsteps]

24.2 FX: GAAA [a mystic sound]
24.3 FX: BASHI [crackling]

25.2 FX: PIKU [surprise]
25.4 FX: SU [moving curtains]

46.2 FX: GYU [squeeze]
46.3 FX: PUCHI PUCHI [unbuttoning]
46.4 FX: BASA BASA [clothes dropping]
46.5 FX: GISHI… [bed noise]

48.1 FX: YORO [wobbling]
48.5 FX: FURA… [falling]

49.3 FX: GYU [hugging]
49.5 FX: HA HA HA!

50.3 FX: BIKUN [a surprised jerk back]
50.4 FX: BIKU [a surprised jerk back]

51.3 FX: SUUU… [a slow appearance]
51.4 FX: HYU [flashing by]
51.4 FX: BIKU [a surprised jerk back]

52.1 FX: FU ["breath" passing]

53.3 FX: TORO [slow movement]
53.4 FX: HA [a small gasp]

54.1 FX: ZURU… [slipping]
54.2 FX: DOKUN DOKUN DOKUN DOKUN [rapid heartbeat]
54.3 FX: DOKUN DOKUN [rapid heartbeat]

CHAPTER FIFTY-SIX: DAWN FOR THE HEART

57.1 FX: DOKI DOKI DOKI [heart thumping]
FX: DOKI DOKI DOKI [heart thumping]

58.4 FX: HA [surprise]
FX: DOKI DOKI DOKI [heart thumping]
58.5 FX: DOKI DOKI DOKI [heart thumping]

59.2 FX: ZEKUN [tensing up]
59.4 FX: HA… [Oops]
59.5 FX: GISHI [bed movement]

61.4 FX: GURA… [swaying]

62.3 FX: BASA BASA [clothes falling]

63.2 FX: PIKU [sudden surprise]

64.2 FX: HA [gasp]

66.5 FX: PASA [light object falling]

68.2 FX: HA [a gasp]
68.4 FX: SU [quick movement]

72.1 FX: DOKUN DOKUN [heart thumping]
72.2 FX: KIRA [shining]
72.3 FX: BIKU [surprise]

73.3 FX: PAN [crashing]

79.5 FX: BA [sudden movement]

82.4 FX: KYUU [squeeze]

83.3 FX: HA [surprise]
83.4 FX: SU [sudden appearance]

84.3 FX: KYU [tying]

CHAPTER FIFTY-SEVEN: OMINOUS EYES

88.2 FX: KUWAAA [burning]
88.2 FX: KYAAAAA [a scream]

90.3 FX: KA [horse appearing]

91.2 FX: BIKU [surprise]
91.2 FX: KIIIN [piercing noise]
91.3 FX: BA [explosion]

92.2 FX: BIKU [surprise]

94.2 FX: GARA… [pebble falling]

95.3 FX: BOKO BOKO [ground breaking]
95.4 FX: ZAAA [whipping through]

98.1 FX: GIRI GIRI [sliding]
98.4 FX: SHURU [feather movement]
98.5 FX: BIKUN [sudden twitch]

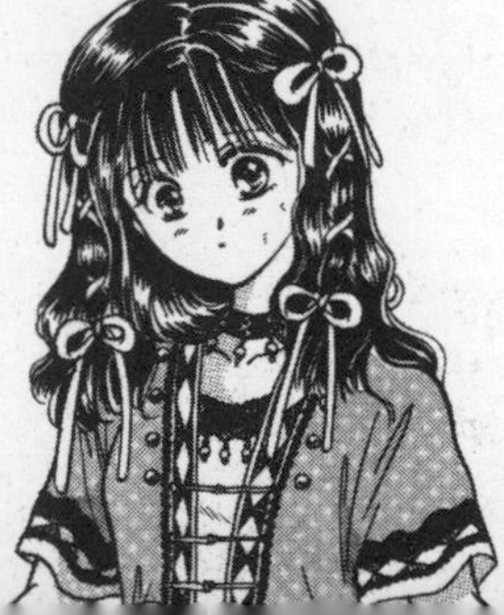

120.1 FX: HA [realization]
120.2 FX: ZAAAA… [swirling]

122.3 FX: PITA [freezing]

124.5 FX: DO [burst]

125.5 FX: DOKI… [heart beat]

126.2 FX: FUWA [floating]
126.3 FX: HYUUUU [wind blowing]

127.3 FX: GIKU [alarm]

128.3 FX: JIIIN [overflowing emotion]

129.1 FX: PISHAN [gleeming]
129.5 FX: DOKA [strike]

130.1 FX: KORO KORO [rolling]
130.2 FX: GAN GAN [throbbing]
130.4 FX: HA [surprise]

131.2 FX: DOKI [heart beat]
131.5 FX: DOKI DOKI DOKI [heart beating]
131.5 FX: DOKI DOKI DOKI [heart beating]

132.5 FX: DOKI DOKI DOKI DOKI [heart beating]

135.3 FX: ZAKU ZAKU [footsteps]
135.4 FX: HYUU [wind]

138.3 FX: GASA GASA [flipping pages]
138.4 FX: DOSA DOSA [falling objects]
138.4 FX: BASA [opening]

139.1 FX: GIKU [alarm]
139.3 FX: DOKUN DOKUN [heart beating]
139.4 FX: DOKUN DOKUN DOKUN [heart beating]
139.4 FX: DOKUN DOKUN DOKUN[heart beating]

140.1 FX: DOSA [object falling]
140.2 FX: DOKUN DOKUN [heart beating]
140.2 FX: DOKUN DOKUN [heart beating]
140.3 FX: DOKUN [heart beating]
140.4 FX: KARA [door opening]

141.3 FX: PA [light changing]
141.4 FX: KII [door opening]
141.6 FX: ZUZAZAZAA [sliding]

99.2 FX: GIRI [sliding]

102.2 FX: DOKUN DOKUN DOKUN [heart thumping]
102.3 FX: DOKUN DOKUN DOKUN [heart thumping]

104.1 FX: DOKUN DOKUN [heart thumping]
104.1 FX: DOKUN DOKUN [heart thumping]

106.3 FX: BIKU [shock]
106.4 FX: HYU [flash]

107.1 FX: PAN [explosion]
107.2 FX: FU [relief]

109.2 FX: SHU [flash]
109.3 FX: FU [sudden movement]

110.1 FX: DOKA [strike]
110.4 FX: SUTO [landing]
110.4 FX: BASA [falling]

111.2 FX: HA HA HA [rapid breathing]

113.1 FX: HYUUU [wind]

114.3 FX: BA [whipping]
114.5 FX: DO… [piercing]

CHAPTER FIFTY-EIGHT: COUNTERFEIT MEMORY

115.1 FX: ZU [removing]
115.4 FX: GEHO [cough]

118.1 FX: FURA [falling back]
118.2 FX: GARA [rocks falling]

119.4 FX: NYA [smirk]
119.5 FX: KAAA [flash]

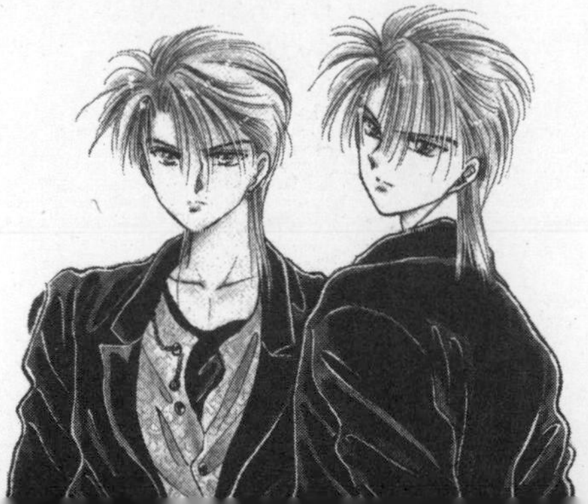

168.1 FX: DOKUN DOKUN DOKUN [heart thumping]
168.1 FX: DOKUN DOKUN DOKUN! [heart thumping]

169.2 FX: FUU FUUU [pencil falling]
169.4 FX: KA [flash]

171.2 FX: PIKU [a twitch]

172.1 FX: PIKU… [alarm]

174.4 FX: BA [shooting out]

175.6 FX: GIRI GIRI [tightening]

176.1 FX: GI GI [tightening]
176.4 FX: GI GI [pulling]
176.5 FX: GU GU [tugging]

177.2 FX: BOKI [cracking]
177.5 FX: GIRI GIRI [tightening]

178.1 FX: PIIIIII [a musical note]
178.2 FX: HA [realization]

179.1 FX: SHURU… [loosening]
179.4 FX: GUSA [stab]

180.2 FX: PISHI [cracking]
180.3 FX: PISHI PISHI PISHI [crumbling]
180.4 FX: PAN [breaking]

181.2 FX: SUUU [fade in]
181.4 FX: ZA [footstep]

182.1 FX: SA [quick movement]

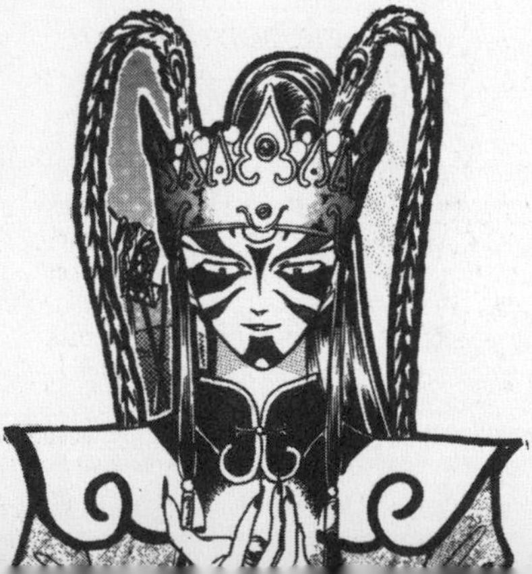

143.1 FX: ZUKIN [pain]
143.2 FX: BUN BUN [shaking off]

144.3 FX: DOKI DOKI DOKI [heart beating]

CHAPTER FIFTY-NINE: COUNTERFEIT LOVE

151.3 FX: DOKA DOKA [hitting]
151.3 FX: GURI GURI [noogies]

152.1 FX: NIKO [smile]
152.2 FX: NIKO [smile]
152.3 FX: NIKO [smile]

153.2 FX: GARA [door opening]
153.3 FX: SAWA SAWA [crowd sounds]

154.2 FX: DOKIN [surprise]

155.4 FX: DOKA [punch]
155.5 FX: DOKI DOKI [heartbeats]

156.2 FX: DOKKUN [heavy heartbeat]
156.2 FX: Koron [clattering]

157.1 FX: NYA [leering smile]

159.4 FX: POKI [crack]
159.5 FX: TON [thump]

160.3 FX: GABA [rising]

162.1 FX: DOKI DOKI DOKI [heart beating]
162.1 FX: DOKI DOKI DOKI [heart beating]
162.4 FX: DOKA DOKA [punching]
162.4 FX: JIRO JIRO [staring]

163.5 FX: KURU [turning]

164.2 FX: TON TON [footsteps]
164.4 FX: KIII [door creaking]
164.5 FX: GACHAN [locking]

165.1 FX: BASA… [clothes falling]

167.1 FX: DOKUN [a heavy heartbeat]
167.1 FX: DOKUN DOKUN DOKUN DOKUN [heartbeats]
167.3 FX: DOKU DOKUN… [heart thumping]
167.6 FX: KASHAN! [shutters closing]

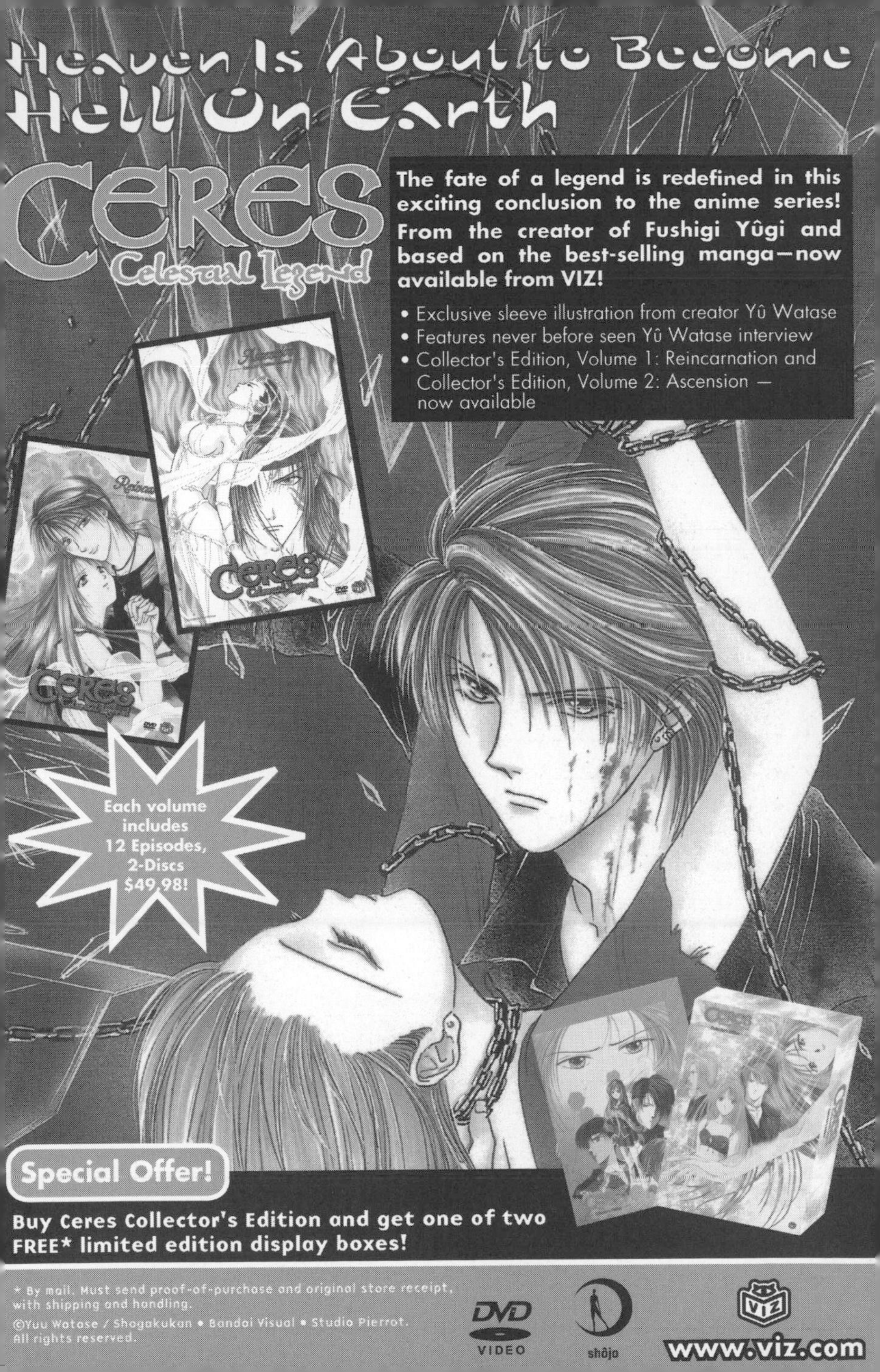
Heaven Is About to Become
Hell On Earth
Ceres
Celestial Legend
The fate of a legend is redefined in this exciting conclusion to the anime series! From the creator of Fushigi Yûgi and based on the best-selling manga—now available from VIZ!
• Exclusive sleeve illustration from creator Yû Watase
• Features never before seen Yû Watase interview
• Collector's Edition, Volume 1: Reincarnation and Collector's Edition, Volume 2: Ascension — now available
Each volume includes 12 Episodes, 2-Discs $49.98!
Special Offer!
Buy Ceres Collector's Edition and get one of two FREE* limited edition display boxes!
* By mail. Must send proof-of-purchase and original store receipt, with shipping and handling.
©Yuu Watase / Shogakukan • Bandai Visual • Studio Pierrot. All rights reserved.
DVD VIDEO
shôjo
VIZ
www.viz.com

EDITOR'S RECOMMENDATIONS

Shôjo in the Fast Lane

Let's face it—only ten graphic novels in over five years of editing is a pretty poor pace.

For the most recent additions to our readership, let me explain why things have been going so slowly up until now...

For the past five and a half years, and for the foreseeable future, *Fushigi Yûgi* is published in a magazine, *Animerica Extra*. Because there is an extremely limited amount of space in the magazine (at first it was only 128 pages for up to seven different manga series), all we could fit into the magazine was about thirty pages of Miaka's adventures per month (that works out to about one chapter per month). That means that a graphic novel will only come out, at most, once every six months. Why did we do it that way? Economics. When Fushigi Yûgi debuted, thousands more people bought the magazine than bought the graphic novels.

Then, in 2002, the world of manga changed, and fans who only grumbled at the long wait started into open revolt (okay, that's a tiny exaggeration), and the new fans felt that the shorter waits were a standard part of manga publishing. It wasn't then, but it is now.

So we're churning out books as fast as we can—putting double the amount of *Fushigi Yûgi* into the magazine and thereby halving the waiting period. Making sure you have more of Watase goodness in your hands on a more regular basis, but not compromising one whit on quality! (I think a whit is comparable to a furlong, but much shorter than a league. You have to deal with these things in fantasy manga.)

So enjoy this manga, and soon, very soon, the next one will be in your hands too!

Bill Flanagan
Editor of *Fushigi Yûgi*

Did you like *Fushigi Yûgi*? Here's what VIZ recommends you try next:

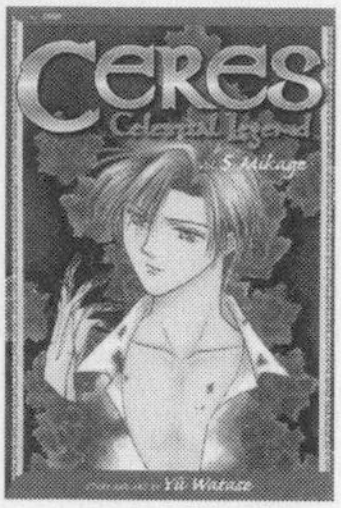
Ceres
Celestial Legend
S. Mikage
Yû Watase

© 1997 Yuu Watase/
Shogakukan, Inc.

CERES: CELESTIAL LEGEND is an engaging story of love, betrayal and revenge by *Fushigi Yûgi*'s creator Yû Watase. Aya's world is turned upside when her family tries to kill her on her sixteenth birthday because of her family's deep, dark secret.

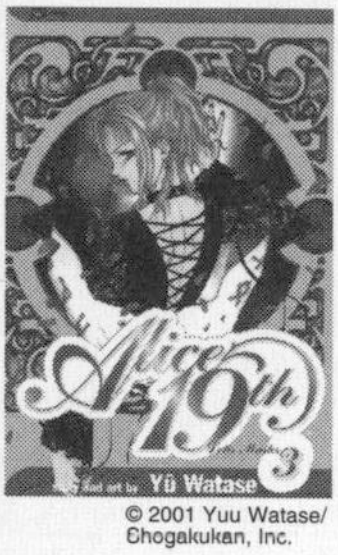
Alice 19th
3
Yû Watase

© 2001 Yuu Watase/
Shogakukan, Inc.

ALICE 19TH is the latest completed series by the author of the very book you hold in your hands, Yû Watase! Alice is the forgotten younger sister of one of the most popular girls in school and at home. And when Alice falls in love with the handsome Kyô Wakayama, it's only natural that Alice's sister, Mayura, would be his most likely girlfriend. Then a magical white rabbit enters Alice's life to tell her that she can be a master of the world-changing Lotis Words—a power that can alter the world into a dream, or a nightmare!

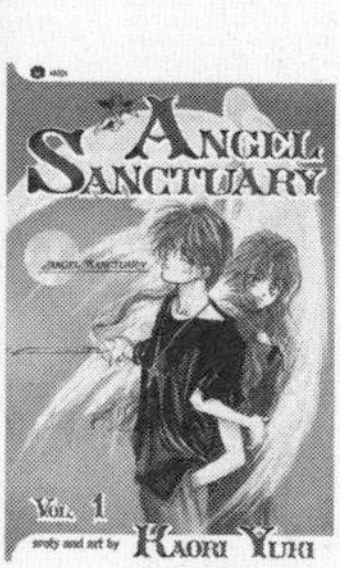
Angel Sanctuary
Vol. 1
story and art by Kaori Yuki

© Kaori Yuki 1994/
HAKUSENSHA, Inc.

ANGEL SANCTUARY breaks every taboo subject you have been taught not to talk about. Sadistic angels, determined demons, supernatural powers, and at the center of the crisis is Setsuna Mudo, a mixed-up high-school boy who is trying his best to suppress a growing love for the girl of his dreams, his own sister Sara. Kaori Yuki's epic vision, gorgeous art, and down-to-earth main characters come together in a fantasy that would make Milton and Dante blush! Don't miss it!